Journey From Somerset, England To Ohio

A Journey From Somerset, England To Ohio

For the
Hawkins and Haine Families
1700-2010

Sue Hawkins Bell

Copyright © 2011 by Sue Hawkins Bell.

Library of Congress Control Number: 2011903115
ISBN:
    Hardcover   978-1-4568-7601-2
    Softcover   978-1-4568-7600-5
    Ebook   978-1-4568-7602-9

All rights reserved. No part of this book may be reproduced or transmitted in any form or by any means, electronic or mechanical, including photocopying, recording, or by any information storage and retrieval system, without permission in writing from the copyright owner.

This book was printed in the United States of America.

To order additional copies of this book, contact:
Xlibris Corporation
1-888-795-4274
www.Xlibris.com
Orders@Xlibris.com
91069

CONTENTS

Acknowledgments xv

SECTION ONE: As I Remember It

Chapter 1
          My Ancestors: As I Remember It. 3
          The Hawkins Family Bible 4
          Westbrook Farm Evercreech, Somerset 5
          An Immigrant Ship 7

Chapter 2   Treasure in the Attic 9
          Batcombe Farm in Somerset 10
          William Goddard Went West 11
          Returning Home to England 15
          Cheddar-Cheese Making 16
          A Visit with Frances Goddard Dowding 17
          The Depression in England 18

SECTION TWO

Chapter 3   Starting Life in Ohio 23
          William Dredge Hawkins and
             Mary Ann Goddard Hawkins 24
          William and Mary Haine 25
          House Guests: The Coles 27
          The Hawkins's and Haine's Farms 28
          Thomas Goddard Hawkins at Twenty-Eight Years 28

	Tuberculosis	31
	My Great-Grandparents	32
Chapter 4	The War Escalated	34
	Brothers Are Now Soldiers	36
	-1863-	37
	Commutation	37
	Underground Railroad	38
	Thomas Hawkins's Account Ledger	39
Chapter 5	Frances Haine Hawkins: Marriage License	41
	Married Life	43
	Clover Hill (photo)	44
	Haine Reunion—July 4, 1907	46
	Hawkins Homestead	46

SECTION THREE

Chapter 6	Memories of William and Mary Hawkins	51
	Memories of Haine Grandparents By Pliny Hawkins	53
	Mary Haine at Clover Hill	54
	A Western Pioneer	57
	The Great Depression	61
	Vivian Lansworth Hawkins	62
	Letter from Vivian	64
Chapter 7	Diaries Uncovered in California	65
	Diary of Frances Haine (Age Twenty)	65
	Second Family Gathering (1978)	68
	Reunion in 1979	68
	First International Reunion 2000	69

Chapter 8	The Next Generation	71
	Emma Hawkins's Adventure West	71
	Transcontinental Railroad	77
	Great-Aunt Bertie	77
	Jesse Hawkins a Good Grandfather	80
	Ernest Hawkins	83
Chapter 9	Marriage of Sarah Goddard Hawkins to William Haine	84
	Dosia's New Stepmother	85
	"Sunshine Corner"	88
	Haine Family Reunion (1907)	89

SECTION FOUR

Chapter 10	The Younger Generation:	93
	Riding the Rails West	93
	Pickets, Airplanes, and Machine Guns	96
	Letters Written to Martha	97
	Brother Charles Hawkins Marries	102
	Sons: Thomas Hawkins and Robert Hawkins	103
	Lloyd and Martha Hawkins at Clover Hill	104
	Cousin Charles Hawkins: Pliny's Grandson	105
Chapter 11	Hawkins—Haine International Reunion 2005	106
	Photos of Family at Reunion	108

SECTION FIVE: The Somerset Generations

Chapter 12	Traveling Back in Time	113
	Transportation	113
	Foods and Preserving	114

Tithe Barns 115
Education...117
Childbirth..117

SECTION SIX

Chapter 13 The Village of Pilton and Evercreech............................121
Siblings of William Dredge Hawkins...................................121
Somerset Home of Hawkins, Haine, and Goddard's........123
Young Frances Goddard Dowding.......................................125
Afternoon Tea 125

Chapter 14 Time Marches on in Evercreech 127
Church and Clock...128

Chapter 15 Pilton's: John the Baptist Church 131
Monument Inscription in Pilton 132

Chapter 16 Peter Hawkins (1772–1846) and
Nancy (Ann) Dredge...135
History of Parish Records...137
Somerset..138
George Hawkins Fourth Great-Grandfather 138

Chapter 17 Somerset-Gloucester Generations..................................140
George Hawkins: Son of Peter (1687) 140
Children of John Hawkins 141
The Siblings of Peter Hawkins...142
"John the Baptist" Anglican Church in Pilton 143

Chapter 18 Joining of the Hawkins and Huntley Families...............144
Bishop's Transcript of Their Son John
Hawkins Born (1722). 144

Burial Transcript of Wykes Huntley 147
"Christenings Transcript for
   Frances Huntley (Hawkins) 148

SECTION SEVEN

Chapter 19 A Visit to Boxwell Court 151
            Paintings Early Huntleys 154
            Ancient History of the Huntley Name 157
            Architectural and Historical Tidbits 158
            Early Huntley's 159

SECTION EIGHT

Chapter 20 Hawkins Cousins in Somerset (2008) 163
            Australian Cousin Michael Haine 164
            Fellow Researchers 165

Chapter 21 John Wesley Founder of the Methodist Church 169
            Faith in the Family 170
            A Final Word 171
            Map of Somerset's Villages 172
            Hawkins-Huntley Linage Chart 174
            Ten Generations of Hawkins and Haine Families
               Noted on Descendant Charts 176

Bibliography 213
Index 217

DEDICATION

This book is dedicated to three special women, who married into the Hawkins and Haine Family. They have inspired us to remember and preserve the valuable history that has become our family.

Martha Schout Hawkins, my mother, was always helpful in encouraging my family research. She shared her memories of the Hawkins and Haine families. She grew up in the same church as the Hawkins family in Warren, Ohio.

1914-2007
92 years of age

Hazel (Carlson) Cox was always a gracious hostess, welcoming all who came to visit Clover Hill for nearly seventy years. Hazel treasured the history and the antiquities of Clover Hill. She donated copies of photographs to the North Bloomfield Historical Society, in the Township Hall, that she had of the family, property, school, and village.

1913-2008
94 years of age

Vivian (Lansworth) Hawkins had the insight to recognize the value of the lost diaries found in California. Vivian found and dedicated her time deciphering and typing the otherwise lost historical information of the Haine and Hawkins families. She shared the diaries with all who might be interested.

1902-1997
95 years of age

The photograph on the front cover
was taken at the
Abbey Gardens
Wells Cathedral
Wells, Somerset, England

The photograph on the back cover
was taken at
Clover Hill,
the ancestral home of the Haine Family,
North Bloomfield, Ohio.

ACKNOWLEDGMENTS

I would like to express my thanks to the following:

- Warren-Trumbull County, Ohio, Genealogy Library
- Somerset, England, Public Record Office
- LDS Family History Library, Salt Lake City, Utah

Appreciation to the following family researchers who have made the search possible:

- Carrie Jean Cox, Bloomfield, Ohio
- Beryl Hawkins, Somerset, England
- Dr. Charles H. Hawkins Ellensburg, Washington
- Hanna Nicholas, London, England
- David Walsh, London, England
- Richard Welsh, Cheltenham, Gloucester

A sincere thank-you to Dr. Carol Hawkins for her assistance in editing and support.

Grateful appreciation goes to my husband, Roger Bell, for all his computer assistance and technical support.

SECTION ONE

As I Remember It

CHAPTER 1

My Ancestors

LIFE IN THE West Country of England in the early 1800s had its hardships and struggles. Sailing to America brought a final separation for brothers, sisters, and friends. Emigrating was a difficult decision to make, especially if one had to leave an aging parent; but their faith, love, and kinship made life worthwhile.

In 1835, the Haine family purchased land in North Bloomfield, Ohio. Their daughter Frances was born there. As she was writing her diary at age twenty, Frances could never imagine that her words would be read 150 years later. Her writing described country life in Ohio, her impending marriage, and the sorrow of the Civil War. Her home, Clover Hill, is still alive, connecting the past to the present.

Living in Ohio in the 1970s and finding the old family Bible after the death of my grandparents was the start of my curiosity about our family. On the center pages of the Bible, I saw births and marriages listed, along with the name of William Dredge Hawkins and places like Somersetshire, England. Where was Chesterblade Hill, Evercreech, Somersetshire, England? I wondered.

The beautiful handwriting in the center of the Bible listed family birth dates, marriages, and death dates. The ink had faded, and the names were becoming difficult to read. When I was visiting Brownwood Cemetery in Bloomfield where my Hawkins grandparents were buried, I found other Hawkins relatives' names along with Haine names, matching the family names that were in the Bible. My father, Lloyd Hawkins, had never talked about his grandparents or great-grandparents, but I realized later that his grandfather would have been fifty years of age when Lloyd's father was born and had died before Lloyd was born.

The Hawkins Family Bible

The first listing in the Bible was the birth of William Dredge Hawkins, born the seventh of August in 1804. He married Mary Ann Goddard Hawkins, born on the second of November 1804. They were both from Somerset (shire), England. The Bible listed William's birthplace as Chesterblade Hill, Evercreech, Somersetshire, England; and Mary Ann Goddard, his wife, was born at Pugh's Bottom, Batcombe, in Somersetshire, England.

The following page in the Bible, listed *marriages* and noted William Hawkins and Mary Ann Goddard were married the tenth of November 1831 at St. Mary's Church in Batcombe. The two villages, Evercreech and Batcombe, were three miles apart. Also under the heading for *births* were listed their four children.

1. *Thomas Goddard Hawkins* was born on 5 November 1832 at Westbrook Farm, Evercreech, Somerset.
2. *Sarah Goddard Hawkins* was born 26 July 1834, Westbrook Farm, Evercreech, Somerset.
3. *Mary Ann Hawkins* was born at Westbrook Farm, 4 March 1839, Evercreech, Somerset.
4. *Martha Hawkins* was born 17 April 1842, at Street-on-Fosse, Somerset. (It is ten miles east of Evercreech.) This move from Westbrook Farm could have been because they were getting ready to immigrate to America.

The Bible listed the death of their youngest daughter, Martha Hawkins, who died on the twentieth of October 1844 in Montreal, Lower Canada.

Westbrook Farm
(Photo by Sheila Williams Savage, 2008)

Westbrook Farm in Evercreech where the Hawkins family lived during the 1800s.

The Voyage

This death date of little Martha at age two and a half gave a very important clue to the path of their voyage. They sailed from England, but Martha died in Montreal, Quebec. This documented that they arrived in North America traveling to the United States through the Canadian route.

The port from which the Hawkins's sailed was probably Bristol. Previously, others from Somerset boarded sailing ships from Bristol, Somerset, or Liverpool, England. After setting sail, they would have headed for Newfoundland, Canada, and then south into the Saint Lawrence River. The location of Montreal, Quebec, where their young daughter died, is located along the St. Lawrence River, where many immigrant ships arrived.

Typical immigrant ship with the passenger quarters.

* * * * * * * * * * *

    This being an example of a sailing ship in the 1800s, they were at the mercy of the wind and sails. Steam-driven vessels were becoming available by the 1840s. Fuel, either coal or wood, would be necessary to produce steam power. The SS *Great Britain* was built in Bristol, Somerset, and was launched in July 1845. It sailed from Liverpool to New York in fourteen days and twenty-one hours. A propeller-driven ship was all the latest, and later, it carried thousands of immigrants to Australia. It held the capacity of 1100 tons of coal, but four masts were again added for use when wind was available.

An Immigrant Ship

The voyage from England to Quebec usually took six to seven weeks, and landfall was about two hundred miles east of Montreal. Sailing to Canada took longer, but was less expensive than going to the United States' ports of New York City, Boston, or Philadelphia. On the return voyage, the sailing ships from Canada could be used for transporting timber, a valuable commodity back in England.

After arriving in Canada, ships were frequently towed up the St. Lawrence River to Montreal by a wood-fired steam tugboat. Then the passengers had to transfer to barges to ascend the St. Lawrence before catching a steamer on Lake Ontario.

Most ships crossing the ocean had very cramped living conditions. They had a six-foot square berth for three adults or six children. The cooking aboard was usually done by the passengers.

Steerage accommodations

No diaries or letters were found of the details of the Hawkins's voyage. Since Mary Ann had been a dairymaid prior to being married, she may not have known how to write. On their marriage certificate, William wrote his name, but Mary only put an *X*.

Martha's death was a real loss to the family. After this tragedy, the family was delayed while William Dredge Hawkins began working on the docks in Montreal to earn money to continue travel on to Ohio. It is known that the cost of sailing from England to Canada was about five pounds for each person. The shorter passage to a port in the United States would have been twice that or ten pounds each. It was less costly to go the Canadian route.

After working and earning sufficient money in Montreal, William, Mary Ann, and their three surviving children continued their journey. It is assumed that they had to portage on land around Niagara Falls from Lake Ontario to Lake Erie. Travel on Lake Erie was usually on a steam-driven boat and went from Buffalo, New York, to the Grand River at Fairport, Ohio. Steamboat use was gaining in popularity on the Great Lakes at that time.

The Grand River meanders through Geauga and Ashtabula Counties before reaching Trumbull County. Many times, the inland portion of the trip would take longer than the voyage across the ocean. The Grand River, which was used for navigation at that time, would have taken them south to Bloomfield Township in Trumbull County where many others from Somerset, England, had settled.

William and Mary Ann's eldest son, Thomas Goddard Hawkins, noted in his diary that they arrived in Bloomfield the tenth of June 1845, fourteen months after they left England. Soon after their arrival, William and his son Thomas both filed the immigration papers at the courthouse in Warren, Ohio, the county seat for Trumbull County in 1845.

There was an account of an earlier voyage documented in a diary written by William Goddard, Mary Ann's brother, and found in Batcombe, Somerset. William Goddard and his youngest sister, Elizabeth, traveled to America prior in 1831 to see if they might decide to immigrate, but later that year, they both returned to Somerset.

* * * * * * * * * * *

Our ancestors, I am sure, had many stories to tell. Beyond all the names and dates, there were unspoken stories of adventure, love, faith, and frustration. There is no better tribute to those who have lived before us than to tell their stories and share them with those who will come after us.

CHAPTER 2

Treasure in the Attic

LOWER EASTCOMBE FARM

IN 1831, WILLIAM Goddard, my great-great-great-uncle, kept a diary of his journey to America. The diary was not discovered until 1976, over 140 years later, by his great-niece, Frances Goddard Dowding.

In 1976, Michael McGarvie of the *Somerset Guardian/Standard* wrote a newspaper article dated Friday, July 30, 1976, about the recently discovered diary. Frances presented the full-page article to me in 1980 when I first visited Somerset. She had previously sent the article to the post office in North Bloomfield, Ohio, in 1976, but unfortunately, there was no "Hawkins Family" currently residing in North Bloomfield; and the post office returned the letter to Frances.

The diary was found in the attic of Frances's Lower Eastcombe Farmhouse in Batcombe, Somerset, the home where Thomas Goddard, her great uncle, had lived. The date on the south gable of her home read 1619. (Lower Eastcombe Farm is located on the map in the upper right hand corner of the map.) In 1843, it was occupied by Elizabeth Goddard

Fitz and her husband Stephen Fitz. Elizabeth was the sister of William Goddard.

Pugh's Bottom Farm, next door to Lower Eastcombe Farm, shared a gristmill with other farms on the brook. Pugh's Bottom Farm was the birthplace of Mary Ann Goddard who was born in 1804. Her parents were Thomas Goddard and Dorothy Ryall. Mary Ann was one of their seven children. In the 1841 census lists, Thomas Goddard Hawkins, age eight, was living here with his grandmother and his aunt and uncle. Perhaps the reason for Thomas living there was that his family was preparing to leave for America.

Pugh's Bottom Farm in Batcombe, Somerset, birthplace of Mary Ann Goddard.

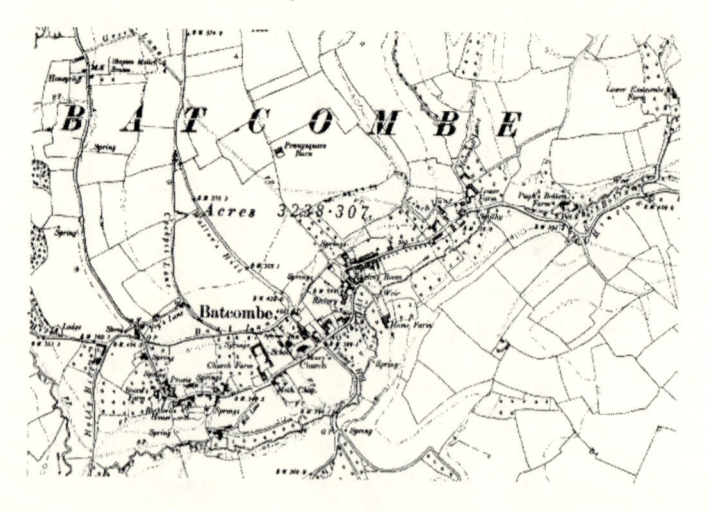

SUE HAWKINS BELL

William Goddard Went West
The Somerset County—Newspaper Article (1976)

In the diary written in February 1831, William stated that "with England's economic position, his country and his family were having a difficult time." He was disgruntled and wrote that while "carefully labouring under the sense of injustice of the squirearchy." William, at thirty years of age, and his sister Elizabeth, only seventeen years of age, decided to "leave Batcombe and undertake the long and perilous voyage to America." The decision was made easier by the fact that they would join with other neighbors also making the trip.

The newspaper reported that "William Goddard packed carefully and he recorded in his diary exactly what he was taking. It is revealing of the respectability of his upbringing, that he found it necessary to take two table clothes as well as three pairs of gloves, a silk handkerchief and 16 other handkerchiefs.

"Apart from doing their own catering on the voyage, passengers had to provide their own bedding. Goddard took a 'pilla,' besides two 'pilo casese,' sheets and blankets. He had a man's weakness for shirts of which he took 13, two of flannel. Other items in his wardrobe were six coats, two pairs of trousers, eight pairs of stockings and eight assorted hats and caps. He also took 'gaters,' rather than garters." *Garter* is a Celtic word to describe the elastic band either worn on the leg to hold up one's socks or worn on the arms to hold up one's sleeves. "His supply of food, as well as shirts, was ample, so much so, that on arrival he still had potatoes, plenty of flower [*sic*] and beans half left."

The voyage started from Bristol, on the West Coast, just south of Wales, on the (ship) *Casino*. Two other ships, including the *Suffolk* and the *Superb*, accompanied them. The master was Captain Gilsbury, "a fine gentleman and was very good and civil and attentive to the sick passengers."

Once on board, there was a long and frustrating three-week delay apparently due to bad weather. This caused much alarm to the passengers because they were using their food provisions before they even started. By March 5, 1831, the *Superb*, which had set sail on February 28, was still no farther than the *Casino*. {It was further in the British newspaper.}

The newspaper reporter stated the following:

I now hand the narrative over to Goddard, a much better storyteller. I have left the original spelling stand, but added some punctuation.

March 6: We have had a universal sickness on board by all the passengers, but myself and a few others. We had such a lark, the Excise Officer and Mr. West and myself running with buckets to and fro, two or three spewing at a time. Some of the poor things were dreadfully ill, but it did not last an hour, they were soon well and were very hungry.

March 12: There is a great deal of uneasyness on board with the poor passengers eating up there provisions and making no progression on their voyage. The Captain and first mate were very kind to Elizabeth and myself. He gave us two very fine [mackintoshes?]. Today the weather is ruf and ship is rolling in a dreadful manner . . . about 6:00 in the evening, the Suffolk and our ship ran fowl of each other and to hear the sailors hallow, it was really dreadful. But no harm was done and some of the other vessels were near each other. Elizabeth and some others were very sick. I went to sleep and left the sailors hard at work.

March 13: 7 o'clock in the morning, the wind, freezing hands and feet, blaning (blowing) from the west and the sea running mountains high. (Chilbains, inflammation of the hands and feet caused by exposure to cold and moisture.)

March 16: This morning a man came on board to claim his wife, a Lady in the cabin, her name was Mrs. Smith, a fine woman, not 20 years old, she had a child and the man took it away with him, a sweet little creature and what a scen, at parting, to see him taken away from his mother. I could not help crien.

March 17: A great many of our passengers still on shore . . . 11 o'clock, it was all hands ahoy. The pilot came aboard and swore that the ship would be put under way, for the captain and they began to draw up the anchor. (After waiting now for eighteen days to leave, it seems that March weather is a much less desirable time for sailing.)

March 25: Early this morning the four top sails went to pieces and the Gibbons carried away. We are going 10 nats an hawr. The people very sick, especially the females . . . the ship rolling about tremendously.

March 26: Eight miles an hour. Passed a vessel this afternoon. She hoisted American colors and the Captain hoisted up his.

March 31: Much neglected writing this . . . though very bad health having such a dreadful headache. Never ate anything for 4 or 5 days, it was dreadfully cold, lying sick but [?] all the time.

April 5: Just passed the banks of Newfoundland. The Captain took out 3 sheep and killed one yesterday and the other tonight. We are all anxious to land and I am in hopes to dine there.

April 7: We saw a great many birds today of two or three sorts, some of them were about the size of a black bird and flew about like partridges when half grown. The others were sea gulls. We have now two ships in sight and our Captain is putting on all the sail that he can in order to come up with them, but he cannot gain on them . . . the Captain told a lady in the cabin that we were 790 miles from New York, but they tell such different stories that we cannot believe what they say about it. Sunday morning: A fine [*sic*] breas spinning [breeze] up at 3 o'clock and came on to a hurricane and by it we were all most in danger. It carried away her topmast and we made but little way all day.

April 14: Today we saw such lots of proposes beast things like pigs.

April 15: Today by the Captain's calculation at 12 o'clock, 317 miles from New York.

April 17: Everybody is looking out for land, but the weather is very foggy and cannot see far and about 9 o'clock they took down all the sails for fear of running aground.

April 18: We rose early and anxious to see land . . . I think it was one of the most buttyful sceanes [beautiful scenes] I ever saw!

April 19: We made New York about 11 o'clock. We had a delightful journey coming down the river between the Jerseys and Long Island. We were much delighted, and were towed down by a steam boat and landed. We are anxious to get on shore to have some fresh provisions.

The voyage had taken twenty-seven days, and Goddard was well pleased with the ship and recommended it to others. With the excitement of the arrival and sightseeing, the diary breaks off until June 3.

It notes that he "traveled to Belmont Co., Ohio, Mount Pleasant and Marietta. He traveled through 4 states: Ohio, *Verginina, Pensilveina and Mary Land* [Virginia, Pennsylvania, and Maryland]. Went to the coach office and inquired about the *'fair'* to Philadelphia which was twenty dollars." He arrived in Baltimore and describes "the country as *romantick* and *hiley* [romantic and hilly]. I think that this place has the finest *gearls* [girls], I ever saw." The diary notes that he and his sister Elizabeth went their separate ways and must have planned to meet on a certain date and place.

"July 1st: This being our first day in Philadelphia, everything and every body was strange to me. We took 'privet logins' (private lodgings), at a boarding house at two dollars and a half a week.

July 2nd: There is great preparation going on for the 4th of July Independence Day with great spirit. Went into the country, the land is light and sandy with corn and Rye, and produce of cukumbers (cucumbers) and asparagus is growing, with the finest gardens you ever saw.

July 4, Monday: This is the day the Americans keep as a feast and day of independence. We took a walk threw (through) the city this morning to the water works, about three miles, where the water that supplies the whole city is lifted up 100 ft. out of the Scuylkill River, this is worth seeing.

July 6, Wednesday morning: We sailed in the steem (steam) boat for New York for 3 dollars. We came down the Delaware (River) about 36 miles, then about 14 miles on the canal boats and then 30 miles by coach and arrived in New York about 6 o'clock.

July 11: Began to get uneasy, not hearing from Mr. George nor Millard and have been going to the post office several times a day . . .

July 12: A Sailor came into my room this morning and informed me that there was a gentleman below that wanted to see me. Between sleeping and waking I bundled down stairs and there stood Mr. George and Millard. Shook hands and almost ki . . . . each other."

On this joyous note the diary breaks off, but we may infer that William Goddard returned to New York. No further notes were written of their return voyage home to Somerset.

Returning Home to England

William and Elizabeth Goddard finally met up with their fellow travelers in New York City when they were scheduled to leave for Somerset. At any rate, they were both home by November 10, 1831, where they attended the wedding of their sister Mary Ann Goddard to William Dredge Hawkins at St. Mary's Church in Batcombe.

On the literacy of William and Mary Hawkins, it is noted on their marriage certificate from the tenth of November 1831 in Batcombe, Somerset, that William Hawkins signed his signature and Mary Ann only placed an *X*, noting that she probably did not read or write.

William Dredge Hawkins was the "Butcher of Evercreech." Yet in the business directory, it states that William was a "wheelwright" and also listed as a carpenter. In addition, he is also described as a "wagon-maker."

Another sister, Dorothy Goddard, had married James Hawkins, William's brother, also a butcher. William Goddard's report must have been sufficiently enthusiastic as both couples eventually immigrated to Ohio.

William Goddard remained a bachelor, and Elizabeth married and remained in Somerset. William Goddard never seems to have lost his interest in America and, in 1851, again toyed with the idea of going out to Ohio. Thomas Goddard received an enthusiastic reply to a letter that he wrote to his brother-in-law, William Dredge Hawkins, in Bloomfield, Ohio.

In a letter a year later, the son of William Dredge Hawkins, Thomas Goddard Hawkins, and daughter Mary Ann reported that they were "milking 24 cows, killing two for beef, and keeping three for producing calves. They had two bulls, five steers, two heifers, and 26 calves." They had "a very good yoke of oxen, three horses, a doe rabbit, 30 sheep, 26 lambs, pigs, fowl and geese." They were "selling wool for 26 cents and butter for 12 cents. Free schooling was available until the age of 21, with geography and 'all other useful studies." A "woman teacher would teach school in the summer and a man would teach in the winter."

In excerpts from a letter sent from William D. Hawkins to family back in Somerset, he states, "Hunting was good for rabbits, partridge, quail, squirrels, turkeys, and deer. Apples were plentiful for pies and cider." They also urged William's sister-in-law, Sarah Goddard, to immigrate and bring someone named Mary because she could get a very good job as a maid. The final stretch of the route that he recommended was "by boat from Buffalo, to Fairport, Ohio and by plank road for 34 miles to Bloomfield."

Steam-driven ships available on lakes and rivers.

Ships were powered by sail, and the steam-powered ships were gaining in popularity by 1830. These ships were more commonly used to navigate the rivers and inlets. (Robert Fulton's steam ship was first sailing on the Hudson River in 1807.)

Cheddar-Cheese Making

This area of Somerset was known for their cheese making. Cheese was a way of preserving the milk from the local dairy farms and being able to take it to market. Ohio also became a center for cheese making.

The oldest English cheese on record comes from Cheddar, Somersetshire, it being the best cheese in England. The largest cheddar cheese ever was a gigantic one-thousand-pound wheel of cheddar made from the milk of 750 cows by the neighbors and family of East and West Pennard, in Somerset, in the Cheddar district. The wheel was to be a wedding gift to be sent to Queen Victoria in 1840. The cheese, of record breaking size, was nine feet in diameter and twenty inches in depth. The Queen graciously accepted the present, but the farmers asked that it be exhibited first. Having it transported to London was a challenge, but as time went by, the Queen declined to have it returned after it was on exhibit.

Farmhouse cheddar is made between May and October with milk from the same herd of grass-fed cows. The texture is close and buttery with a full and nutty flavor. The flavor improves with age and time and depends on the skill of the cheesemaker.

The local tale is that a milkmaid kept a bucket full of milk in the Cheddar Caves. She forgot to collect it and, at a later stage, found the milk had transformed to something else that tasted good. The incident prompted the villagers to try out the possibility of developing the product. An official account book of King Henry II in 1170 mentions the purchase of ten thousand pounds of cheddar cheese, so it can be dated back to the twelfth century.

In Batcombe, most farmhouses had cheese rooms usually on the first floor that had to have a sturdy floor. A cheese of about fifty pounds would be produced from the milk of twenty-five cows each day. Easy access to the space was necessary for unloading and also to enable the cheese to be turned frequently during the ripening period, which could last from one to eighteen months.

In addition to cheddar-cheese production in Somerset, there was also the harvesting of apples and cider making. Cheese, apples, and cider—the products of Somerset—were just as popular in Ohio as they were in Somerset.

A Visit with Frances Goddard Dowding

After giving me the newspaper article about William Goddard, eighty-four-year-old Frances Goddard Dowding, a retired schoolteacher, shared other information. Though she was only four at the time, she could remember the sadness her family felt when Queen Victoria died in 1900. Frances also shared that she was an only child, and her father was sixty-six years of age when she was born and her mother was forty-two. Her father lived into his eighties. Her memory was a gold mine of information and proved to be a very memorable visit. I recall sleeping in the bedroom at the top of the tight spiral staircase in a home that was more than 350 years old.

Frances Goddard Dowding at age eighty-four
and Sue Hawkins Bell in 1980 at Glastonbury Abbey.

The Depression in England

Between 1837 and 1844, England was going through the worst economic depression to hit their country. An estimated one million people were starving because of the lack of employment.

During the nineteenth century, the prediction of overpopulation seemed to come true. With the disappearance of the bubonic plague and the use of the smallpox vaccine during the seventeenth and eighteenth century, the birthrates began to exceed death rates in the young, giving way to population growth. This prompted the wealthy to look for a way of reducing the population through emigration to Upper Canada (Ontario). This was accomplished by giving ten pounds per person for the cost of the voyage. It wasn't uncommon for many to have crossed the United States border for Ohio and other opportunities once in Canada.

An emigration scheme was set into place, where about 1,800 of the working class people from the south of England left for Upper Canada (Ontario) between 1832 and 1837. The scheme was part of a larger initiative in Britain during the 1830s in which churches, charitable organizations, and private individuals were active in promoting emigration as a solution to unemployment.

The harbor and docks in Liverpool, England, grew larger in the 1840s, with better and safer ships and more reliable sailing schedules. This led to Liverpool becoming the center for emigration for thousands in England, Ireland, and others across Europe.

Memories

Never let them fade from your memory
All the days of your life
But make them known to your children.
And to your grandchildren.

—Deut. 4:9 N.B.V.

*   *   *   *   *   *   *   *   *   *   *

We are the sum of all the family before us.
—Unknown

SECTION TWO

CHAPTER 3

Starting Life in Ohio

AT THIS TIME in Somerset and in all of England, the oldest son would have inherited the home and all the property upon the death of his father. This law had been in effect since the middle ages. This would make Thomas Hawkins, William Dredge Hawkins's oldest brother, the eldest in his generation of twelve siblings. Thomas was born in 1798, and their father Peter Hawkins died at age fifty in 1822, leaving twelve children, the youngest being about two years of age. The Hawkins family rented the dairy farm named Westbrook Farm in Evercreech from Mr. Maidment.

My great-great-grandfather, William Dredge Hawkins, born on the seventh of August in 1804, was the fourth child of Peter and Nancy Dredge Hawkins and would soon have to seek other employment. William and Mary Ann Goddard were married in 1831, followed by the birth of their children Thomas Goddard Hawkins in 1832, Sarah Goddard Hawkins in 1834, and Mary Ann Hawkins in 1839; and by 1842, they were expecting their forth child.

William D. Hawkins had corresponded with others in Ohio, who had previously left Somerset. It is assumed that the Hawkins and the Haine families were acquaintances, as William's oldest brother, Thomas Hawkins, had married William Haine's first cousin, Sarah Haine, in 1823. Tombstones for Thomas and Sarah (Haine) Hawkins continue to stand against the outside stonewall of St. Peter's Anglican Church in Evercreech. It clearly states their birth and death dates and that they were from "Westbrook Farm."

William Dredge Hawkins and Mary Ann Goddard Hawkins.
Born 1804 Chesterblade Hill in Evercreech, Somerset;
Mary Ann born on 1804 in Batcombe, Somerset.
(Photo taken circa 1870)

St. Peters Anglican Church in Evercreech and church where the
Hawkins children were baptized.
(Postcard received in 1978)

The William D. Hawkins family left England on the eighth of April 1844, whereas William and Mary Haine had left in 1835, nine years prior.

* * * * * * * * * * *

*Those who do not look upon themselves
As a link, connecting the past with the future,
Do not perform their duty to the world.*
Daniel Webster
The Crossroads of Our Nation

William and Mary Haine
of Clover Hill Farm, Bloomfield, Ohio

William Haine and his wife, Mary Haine, his first cousin.
(Photos taken about 1870)

Great-great-grandfather William Haine, who was born on the eighth of February 1806, was from East Pennard, Somerset. He sailed as a single man from Somerset, landing on Prince Edward Island. The *Royal Gazette* newspaper noted on the twenty-sixth of May 1835 that he was a passenger traveling to Ohio on the *Mary Jane*. Others traveling with him were Stephen and John Symes (his brother-in-law) and John West. William Haine was visiting his youngest sister, Mercy Haine Coles, and her husband, George Coles, who were now living at Charlottetown, Prince Edward Island. Mercy was sixteen years of age when she married George Coles. George and Mercy set sail to start their life in Canada. George's family had once lived in Somerset.

In 1835, William left Prince Edward Island, Canada, and sailed, stopping at Nova Scotia, then on to Maine, Boston, and New York City. A canal, later called the Erie Canal, was used to cross the state of New York, ending in Buffalo, New York, on Lake Erie. William then traveled on to North Bloomfield in Ohio in hopes of purchasing land. He found 150 acres that appeared fertile, with good drainage, and a creek in the ravine. He cleared an adequate portion of land before returning to Somerset to marry his betrothed, Miss Mary Haine, his first cousin, on April 11, 1836, at Lovington Church in Somerset. They immigrated shortly after to North Bloomfield, Trumbull County, Ohio. He and Mary had packed four wooden chests with belongings. The chests were clearly marked using nails, spelling *"HAINE"* on the top of each chest. (These chests belong to different family members today.)

William Haine purchased the land in Bloomfield from Ephrim Brown, a wealthy gentleman from New England. William was responsible for obtaining the land and having it surveyed. After clearing the land, he built their log cabin. William and Mary lived in the log cabin for fourteen years, and it was there where seven of their eleven children were born. The Haines had the largest gristmill in the township, and it was built along with a millrace near the creek. The gristmill, which provided an income for the family, was created by damming up the Haine Creek, which later formed a pond. Ice was harvested in the winter from the pond.

House Guests: The Coles

In the fall of 1848, William and Mary Haine were hosts to William's sister *Mercy Coles* and her husband, *George Coles* of Prince Edward Island, Canada. Shortly after their marriage in 1833 in Somerset, they returned to Prince Edward Island, Canada, to live. Later, Mercy was to bear him twelve children.

George was not born of the local elite and received very little formal education. On Prince Edward Island, he managed a farm, rented homes in Charlottetown, and was a merchant, manufacturer, brewer, distiller, and politician.

Politically, Coles, and the rest of the established elite, had a conflict of interest as he was politically opposed to the British government that owned two-thirds of the land in Prince Edward Island. At this time, the money or profits would be returned to absentee landlords in Britain.

George envisioned the idea of *land reform* where residents could purchase and own land. He also envisioned the idea of *free education* for children on Prince Edward Island. His *Free Education Act of 1852* was inspired by his 1848 visit to Massachusetts and Ohio.

George Coles became known as the Father of Responsible Government in Canada. By 1851, he became the island's first and greatest premier of the province and the "Father of the Confederation."

George Coles   Mercy Haine Coles

Letters were shared back and forth from Somerset, Prince Edward Island and Bloomfield, Ohio. The Somerset families were eager for news from their American cousins. These letters and photos were kept and shared with others in Bloomfield.

The Hawkins's and Haine's Farms

In the year 1847, William Hawkins purchased one hundred acres of land for $250 and used it to grow timothy hay for the cattle. In the year 1850, the Hawkins family rented a dairy farm for $200/year; and seven years later, they purchased it. Using the back half of the house, they shared the house on the property with the owner Henry W. Sanson, who lived in the front half. At this time, the Hawkins farm was around the corner from Clover Hill, the Haine farm.

Many families in Ohio kept in touch by mail with those from Somerset. Family names of others mentioned in the letters sent to Bloomfield were Symes, Dunkerton, Goddard, Welshman, and Creed. Richard Dunkerton had fourteen children, of which four moved to Iowa. One account from Cary Look shared with those in Somerset that "he would not go through it again for five hundred pounds" (referring to the voyage). The name of *Look*, pronounced *Luke*, was a family name of Mary Haine.

William Haine lived next door to the Hawkins's and operated a sawmill and a gristmill that provided his income. About 1870, a cheese factory and a grocery store were added to supply income for his sons.

Thomas Goddard Hawkins at Twenty-Eight Years

In 1860, January 1, Thomas's diary starts, "Attended Watch Meeting at Bristol, Ohio in company of Professor Henning, my sisters and several other Christian friends. The mercury was below zero as we glided on the fleecy snow, listening to the jingle of the many sleigh-bells. Soon we were in the house of God for the purpose of dedicating ourselves anew."

On February 3, he noted, "Sisters have gone home and I am here alone [he was obviously at the Western Reserve Seminary], joined several friends discussing the subject of slavery with interest. In the evening sisters returned with good news from home."

Other daily entries entered were the following:

March 9, Friday: "Packed up and came home—it snowed nearly all the way. I was glad to enjoy the Association of Kind Parents. We never expect to leave them alone again."

March 10, Saturday: "Commenced to work for father: did chores and went to town with the eggs. Then on Monday it snowed nearly all day. Fed the cattle twice on East Farm and settled with father."

April 8: "It is sixteen years ago today we left our native home for America." (The year that he left would have been 1844.)

April 20: "Sister and I went to Orwell—got my tooth filled." He continued that the peach trees were all in bloom and then apples two weeks later. Then sowing oats and planting the corn.

May 26: "Have been to Farmington in company with Mrs. Haine—had a very pleasant ride indeed."

May 26: "Sheared our sheep in company with Mr. Fry, 63 sheep in all."

May 10, Sunday: "It is 15 years today we came to Bloomfield our providential home." (The year 1860 minus fifteen years—arrived in 1845.)

July 4: "While milking, could hear the cannons roar from almost every quarter. Went a-berrying and picked twenty quarts. Cannons were probably being fired in Warren and perhaps West Farmington."

August 8: "Enjoyed a pleasant ride with aunt, cousin and sister Sarah to Fowler. Stopped at Mecca and saw them pumping oil from the interior of the earth. They had 150 wells in operation."

August 20: When "taking visiting family to the train station in Warren, he received a gift of Webster's pocket dictionary and he procured the Biography and Speeches of A. Lincoln and read 25 pages on the way home."

September 19: "On the way home had a pleasant chat with Frances and Sarah. Finished reading Lincoln, whom I hope will be successful in obtaining the office to which he has been nominated."

November 8, 1860: "I voted for Uncle Abe Lincoln today."

December 25: "Thought how differently Christmas used to pass when with relatives in my native land."

December 29: "Settled with Father. He gave me his note for $922."

January 22, 1861: "Enjoyed a pleasant interview at Mr. Haine's and John Haine gave us information about the oil discoveries in Penn., Ohio, Michigan and Canada. Also of the movements in South Carolina, this is causing great excitement throughout our country." (Apparently the firing on Fort Sumter.)

In the back cover of his diary, he noted the wedding dates of his sisters. In 1862, August 11, Sarah Goddard Hawkins married William J. Haine, and on November 23, Mary Ann Hawkins married James Goddard Hawkins, her first cousin.

Account book kept by
Thomas Goddard Hawkins.
1860-1874

Bloomfield Township of Trumbull County, Ohio.
Haine property is along Haine Creek;
Hawkins property was just south.
(County Atlas, 1874)

Tuberculosis

The Hawkins and Haine families were now neighbors. The children grew closer and became best friends, doing daily chores, sharing rides to church, and singing in the evening, then later marrying. The Hawkins family had three children, and the Haine family had eleven. The Haine family lost two daughters: Mercy Jane Haine, who drowned in 1849 in the millpond at age three while clutching her kitten. Ellen Haine, at age seventeen, contracted TB in 1866. TB was the leading cause of death in the nineteenth century. Also, William and Mary Ann Hawkins lost their daughter Sarah Goddard Hawkins on 1868 at age thirty-four to TB. Sarah was the wife of William J. Haine. Much later, William and Mary Haine's daughter Emma Haine Beatty and her husband Dr. B.F. Beatty both died of TB in California in 1901. There was no treatment other than rest and fresh air for tuberculosis at this time. (It was not until antibiotics were developed in the 1940s that there was a hopeful outcome.)

My Great-Grandparents

Thomas G. Hawkins had been helping his father daily with the farm work by clearing the land, doing the chores, building a barn for the horses, and maintaining the fences. His father, William Dredge Hawkins, kept an account of the hours that Thomas put forth, and his father "paid him as able."

Thomas Goddard Hawkins and Frances Haine Hawkins

Frances Haine and Thomas Goddard Hawkins both attended the Western Reserve Seminary. In May of 1862, she began teaching in a one-room school in nearby Bristolville. In her diary, she notes "that it is by no means a small thing to be entrusted with the education of the rising generation. The souls of these little ones are infinitely precious . . . and yet—how little do I realize their value."

July 31, 1862: "The children were quite restless today, as it was so warm. We had school in the woods, as the children seem to enjoy that."

August 8, 1862: "My school closed today. I had my usual morning exercises at the close of which I gave each a card, also three prizes consisting of two pencils and a money purse. The children seemed very pleased with their presents. Each one of the girls made me a star block [a quilt block], which I prize very much. In the afternoon we had a picnic. I was sorry to part with my scholars, as some of them were *so good*. It seems as if I had not done enough for them." Frances was a sincere and dedicated teacher.

In her diary of Sunday, August 3, 1862, she notes from the morning sermon, "If it be possible, live peaceable with all men . . . Yet there are times when it is right to take up arms. It is not right for us to let the South tyrannize over us and make slaves of us. We should feel it a privilege to defend our government which is the *best* in the world. If anything is worth fighting for, surely this is. He [the Pastor] then tried to arouse the young men to a sense of duty. The call is for 600,000. It does seem hard to see our young men going to die and suffer for our country. I want our country to be saved but still I dislike for any of my friends to go—which shows how selfish I am. But I do hope this is the last call."

CHAPTER 4

The War Escalated

Frances's diary continues:

AUGUST 11, 1892: "The boys start for Camp Cleveland today. Eighteen are going from Bloomfield. We were very much surprised to hear William say that he intended to be married in the evening. I went to Warren with the boys. Just when we got to the center of Bloomfield, Rev. Potters joined us and the others gave them *three cheers*. The rest of the company did not arrive [at the train station] until 8 o'clock. We went to Camp's Hotel [in Warren], where William and Sarah were married by Rev. Potter. It did not seem like much of a wedding to me. It was so sad to think that William was going to War the next morning.

"There was a great war meeting that evening and the drums were beating and the cannons were firing at the time they were married. The horrors of war took away all the pleasure of the occasion. Sarah was dressed in a very neat silk dress which she had bought for the occasion and had a very pretty collar and shoes. We spent the rest of the evening very pleasantly. We girls, six of us, had a large bedroom [at the hotel] with three beds in it. Allie Hay, Sarah Cook, Mary Day, Mary Hawkins, [sister] Lottie and I. It was so warm that we could not sleep, so we played and sang and had a good time. I did not get to sleep until about two o'clock, as it was so warm."

August 12, Tuesday: "There was quite a crowd out to see the boys start. I shook hands with the boys after they were in the cars [train] and bade then good-bye for a short time for they have the promise of furlough. Still I could not help thinking that it was the last time I would see them on earth. After doing some trading [shopping] we started for home. Thomas and I came together and had a very pleasant time."

August 22: "Sister Sarah [her new sister-in-law] came home from Cleveland today. I went over to see her. She saw the boys all mustered into service and start for Kentucky. She said that they left in good spirits. They had their uniforms and blankets but not their arms. George wrote a few lines home and sent them with Sarah."

August 29: "We received another letter from George. He was well and sent along their pictures, wearing their uniforms and with all their arms, which made them look quite warlike." They continued to receive letters from George and William again.

Frances Haine's brothers William and George Haine

September 16: "Very pleasant, Thomas and I started for the State Fair. Had a very pleasant ride to Warren and stayed all night at the Camp Hotel... waited at the depot to wait for the [train] cars to go to Columbus."

(With a page missing from the diary, it is unknown how long they were gone to the State Fair.)

October 21: "We received the intelligence that John Cook was *killed*; William Creighton wounded and brother Will was *wounded* slightly. And that William Creighton has died since the battle."

October 26: "We received a letter from George. He has been ill with lung fever and staying at a good home and they are caring for him. He gives a hard account of the rebels that are stealing, and destroying everything they can. I hope that George may soon be able to get home.

Staircase to Frances's bedroom at Clover Hill.

"It was late at night when I was awakened to the sound of voices from downstairs. I listened but I did not know the voice. *It was brother George.* It seemed like having the dead brought to life to see him again.

"He had been taken prisoner [in Kentucky] and paroled and as soon as he could get a chance he started for home. George had come home with his canteen, blanket and knapsack. His gun was taken away when he was taken prisoner and he was sent to Camp Chase in Columbus [Ohio]. He said there were over 1,000 prisoners there . . . Our family rejoiced and thanked God for his goodness for bringing our loved one home again."

Brothers Are Now Soldiers

The diary notes that no matter how many letters Frances received from her brothers during the Civil War, she was never completely reassured. Brothers William and George joined the OVI 105, Ohio Volunteer Infantry, and were transferred from Columbus, Ohio, to Kentucky at Perryville where a battle was to take place.

November 16, Sunday: "Went over to Mr. Hawkins, Anna showed me her wedding dress and bonnet. Her dress was made of blue silk trimmed with black lace and blue ribbon. Her bonnet was made of the same kind of silk as her dress with a white plume and a bunch of ribbon on the outside. She had a brown jacket trimmed with blue. It is all very neat."

November 23: "James and Anna were married in church this morning by Rev. Potter. This is the first couple I ever saw married in church. I like the plan very well. It was after the sermon."

"The year of 1862 [December 31, 1862], had brought many sorrows to our community," as Frances continues, "I am thankful that both of my brothers are still spared while so many have been cut down . . . and laid low in a Soldier's grave. Truly God has been good to us as a family."

* * * * * * * * * * *

-1863-

January 20, 1863: "Thomas and I went to Warren. It was good sleighing. I bought a wedding dress and bonnet, went up to the Printing Office and ordered fifty wedding cards and also bought a wedding ring. We were quite pleased with all that we had bought."

January 29, 1863, Thursday: "Today is my 21st Birthday and Sarah Cook came to visit as we are both 21 today. After playing games we went down to the mill to get weighed. Sarah was 130 pounds and I was 110."

On March 1, 1863, Frances and Thomas were married.

(Apparently, life became very complicated for Frances as she did not write again for the next fifteen years.)

* * * * * * * * * * *

Commutation

At thirty-one years of age, Thomas notes in his account book that he frequently sent money, usually $.25 to $.50 at a time, for soldiers' aid. Also several large payments in increments of $75 to $100, totaling $300 for "commutation" were noted in his account book. The Enrollment Act (for the draft) passed on the first of March in 1863 was for all men twenty to forty-five years of age. Commutation ruling accepted that one could legally find a substitute to serve in one's place *or* pay $300. This money was then used to support the war effort. The *draft* was not popular, and there were uprisings in some areas of the North. This did soften the effects of the draft for the pacifists. The draft was successful at increasing the enrollment of volunteers.

The draft was biased toward those who could not afford the $300 fee. Before learning more about the rules of the draft, I thought that Thomas was exempt due to the fact that he had two elderly parents and was the only male child to work the farm, but this was not the reason.

Underground Railroad

Trumbull County, Ohio, was a strong abolition area. When Ohio became a state in 1803, it was an "antislavery-state." The abolitionists took an active role in opposing slavery by supporting the Underground Railroad that was illegal by federal law in 1850. In spite of this, one line ran through Bloomfield Township toward Lake Erie. Runaway slaves that would escape from the South were assisted secretly toward freedom and safety. The route was north across the Ohio River, then along tributaries toward Canada to areas where they would be safe. The Emancipation Proclamation, issued on the first of January 1863, freed slaves. Abolitionists continued to pursue freedom for all slaves. Slavery officially ended in all states in 1865. At Clover Hill, oral history told of slaves being hid at times behind the gristmill in the ravine on the Haine farm, but no notations were made in any of the diaries.

Thomas Goddard Hawkins

While Thomas had been helping his father with the chores and farm work, he continued his education at Western Reserve Seminary, a school for higher learning, in West Farmington. The school was located about fifteen miles west of his home in Bloomfield.

His journal noted that he was five foot eight inches tall at age twenty-four. He and Frances spent time together while they were both going to school. Thomas was ten years older than Frances. At times, in the diaries, I thought that it might mention their growing friendship, but at first, he would say, "I drove F. home from a get-together," or he would say, "I went to visit Mr. Haine's" or "We had a very nice interview," later followed with statements of enjoying each other's company very much. Thomas was thirty-one years of age when he married Frances.

His account book reflected that money was given to support the war effort and the church. His diary showed that he was very devout and studious about religion. He routinely attended church, Bible classes, and hymn singing. He was a member and supporter of the Methodist Episcopal Church in Bloomfield and, later, in West Farmington. Later, he became a trustee of the Western Reserve Seminary for twenty years, two years of which he was President.

Thomas Hawkins's Account Ledger
Started in 1860 to 1875

From 1860, Thomas kept a financial book accounting for the money spent at school. It told a story in time with the buying of a marriage license $1.10, a wedding ring for $2.25, clothes $13.50, announcements $1.80, hotel $.78, bureau $16.50, shawl $5.00, $.78 for diaper material, $5.00 for the doctor when Emma was born, $.20 for nipples, $.38 for medicine, $.35 for bottle and bitters.

With the effects of the Civil War, Thomas's ledger noted the purchase of a book titled *Life of Lincoln* for $.25. He paid bounty payments of $25, $25, $75, and $100 in support of the war effort. Plus, a donation was given for a town bell, to call people for emergency meetings at $.50, and seven different donations to soldiers' aid. He also noted that he voted for "Uncle Abe Lincoln."

After marrying Frances Haine on the first of March 1863, the newlyweds lived with his parents, William and Mary Ann Hawkins. In their first year of marriage, Emma was born on February 13, 1864, and in the second year, little George joined the family, followed by Pliny in 1869. In October 1868.

could only be imagined that sharing quarters, cooking, and doing laundry with two small children all underfoot had to be stressful. Frances insisted that she and Thomas find another place of their own. In time, they moved and rented the former Peck Farm, eight miles away in East Farmington. The Trumbull County Atlas 1878 showed that Thomas later owned that piece of property.

Thomas's account book also noted that he purchased a sewing machine for $51.50 and $170.00 for a parlor organ and stool, along with a spring wagon for $170.00.

His character and tastes could be described as "religious, a good singer, fond of debate on religious topics, honest and thrifty." This was a description of Thomas made by Grace, his daughter-in-law, Pliny's wife.

* * * * * * * * * * *

Thomas Goddard Hawkins's Account Ledger

CHAPTER 5

Marriage License for Frances and Thomas Hawkins

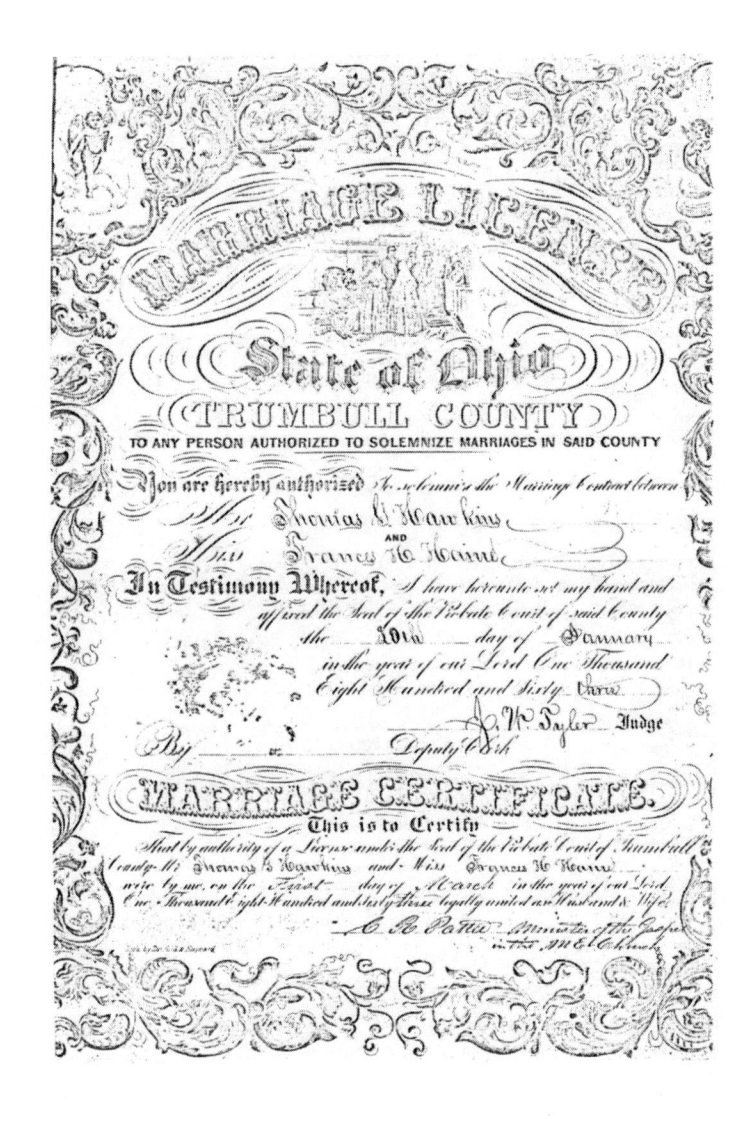

~41~

Sister Mary Ann marries

Thomas's sister Mary Ann married James Goddard Hawkins four months prior to their wedding on the 23rd of November 1862. James was the son of Dorothy Goddard Hawkins of Batcombe and his father James Hawkins of Evercreech. They also planned to immigrate to Ohio when James's father unexpectedly died when young James was sixteen years of age. James at sixteen years sailed with his first cousin Thomas Biggin, his wife and three children. They sailed from Liverpool, England to New York City in 1856. James upon his arrival came to live with his Uncle William Dredge Hawkins for at least four years.

James and Mary Ann "Anna", after marring moved to the state of New York, as he was studying to become a Methodist minister. Their first child was born in North Bloomfield, OH, the second child, Delaware Grove, PA, then Cooperstown, PA and Ellsworth, Ohio. The youngest daughter died in Mantua, OH.

It is imagined that they had many hardships. Their first child, Florilla was born (and she later married and had a family), the second child died at birth, the third child had no children, the forth died at age 49 having a mental disability and the youngest son upon completing his education died at 23 years of age of typhoid.

Marrying ones first cousin was not uncommon in the 1800's and by the 1900's the practice was less popular and it was later outlawed in some western states. James and Anna would have been 'double cousins".

Photo of nephew James Goddard Hawkins
Mary Ann (Anna) Hawkins, and their daughter,
Mary Florilla Hawkins, born 1865.

Married Life

After Frances and Thomas were married the 1st of March 1863, they lived with his parents. Their first year of marriage, Emma was born and the second year little Georgie joined the family, followed by Pliny in 1869.

In October 1868, Frances, while visiting Thomas's sister, "Anna" Hawkins over in Cooperstown, Pennsylvania had misfortunate. Little Georgie at three years of age, had died unexpectedly. It was said that it was because he had eaten too many grapes. Obviously, it happened suddenly, and they were all distraught. Perhaps his death was due to dehydration. Georgie was brought home in a coffin. This was Frances and Thomas's second child.

Life became very close at the Hawkins Farm. Frances was very unhappy. I am assuming that her mother-in-law was very critical of her. It could only be imagined that sharing quarters, cooking and laundry with two small children, all under foot had to be stressful. Frances insisted that Thomas find another place of their own. In time they moved and rented the former Peck Farm, eight miles away in East Farmington, while in the Trumbull County Atlas 1878, showed that he later owned that piece of property.

Thomas's character and tastes could be described as he was "religious, a good singer, fond of debate on religious topics, honest and thrifty". (This was a description made by his daughter-in-law, Pliny's wife).

Clover Hill at North Bloomfield

Clover Hill built in 1850.
(Photo 1906)

Pliny Hawkins; Grace, his wife; and Milner, their six-year-old son, while visiting from Montana and about to take a trip around the world.

Photo taken by Grace Milner Hawkins.

Those present are Frances Hawkins (sitting), standing from the left are George Walker, Mildred and Jesse Hawkins, Lottie Wolcott, Pliny Hawkins, Ward Wolcott, Charlotte's husband holding baby Frances Wolcott, and Bertie Walker on the far right. The two boys are Milner Hawkins and Clyde Wolcott.

Clover Hill built on 1850.

Clover Hill
Haine Homestead, "Clover Hill" has been family owned for
160 years.
Photo taken at the reunion in 2005.
David Walsh from London, on right, is the author of *Haine Book* (2000).

Haine Reunion
July 4, 1907

This photo was taken on Adams Street in Warren, Ohio, home of Dosia Haine and her parents William and Cornelia Haine and family. The reunion was held on July 4, 1907. *Seated from left to right are sons and daughters of William and Mary Haine.* William Joseph Haine, Sarah Haine, George E. Haine, Frances Harriet Haine Hawkins, Charlotte Haine Lyman, John Haine, Clara Haine Cox, Charles Haine. (The only sibling missing was Emma Haine Beatty, who was residing in California prior to her death in 1901.)

Others present are spouses, their children, and grandchildren. The baby, sitting on Frances Hawkins's lap, is baby Frances Wolcott, her granddaughter, born on April 1906.

The Hawkins Home

The addition to the front right was recently added in the 1970s to accommodate the current Amish family. The Hawkins home was sold in 1923 after the death of Susanna Hawkins-Douglas-Hill, the granddaughter of William D. Hawkins. In the photo, Hanna Nicholas from London is on the left and Carrie Jean Cox, owner of Clover Hill, is on the right. They are fifth cousins through Mary Haine.

Hawkins Homestead from 1850
with addition added in about 1970.

SECTION THREE

CHAPTER 6

Memories of William and Mary Hawkins
By Their Grandson, Pliny Hawkins, from about 1930

"GRANDFATHER AND GRANDMOTHER lived alone in this house when I first knew them [1879]. William Linton was head farmer with Mr. Williams as assistant. Grandfather milked his six cows and others milked the other twelve. Grandmother had Fanny Hobdy assisting with the housework indoors.

"I was born in the northeast bedroom. Mother and Father [Thomas and Frances] lived here for about six years, when they were first married. Emma, George and I were born here. George died at three years of age of bowel trouble." (Elsewhere, it was noted that Little Georgie ate too many grapes, and possibly, dehydration was the cause of death.)

"Grandfather always slept in the room marked 'G.' A pitchfork was hidden behind the bedroom door to be used as a weapon in the event of burglars. The pitchfork was his favorite protection when he was among the cows also. The cattle were not familiar with the children and made a great mooing if we came around.

"All about the garden and house were cherry trees [red and black] in the orchard north of the house. Our annual holiday was near July 4th, when the cherries were ripe. Aunt Anna always wished to eat them, but Grandma insisted that my father had set [planted] the trees, he had a right to all he could pick in a day.

"In the autumn, we had another grand holiday picking apples. The apples usually came from the North Farm, a half-mile north. Greening's, Jelly flower, Rambos—a whole spring wagon load, all we could gather, were ours for the picking. Grandmother made fine boiled dumplings. This with the beef steak and potatoes was the usual dinner.

"The North farm also had the schoolhouse, the mill pond and hundreds of fine chestnut trees, with a few large cherry trees. The home farm was mostly cleared, but butternut, hickory, cherry and elm trees lined the roadside. This made a shady avenue past George Creighton's place, to William Haine's farm [Grandpa's] to the north.

"The home orchard had sweet apples, Seek-no-furthers, Baldwin, and many wild apple trees that made excellent cider [six barrels], for the ten o'clock lunch of bread and cheese. The hollow in this orchard was too wet for trees, but was full of mint and bluegrass. Towards the front of the house was a large white grapevine and on the south side were Concord [grapes] and on the cheese room we had Belle-grapes.

(Memories written by Pliny Hawkins at age sixty-one in 1930)

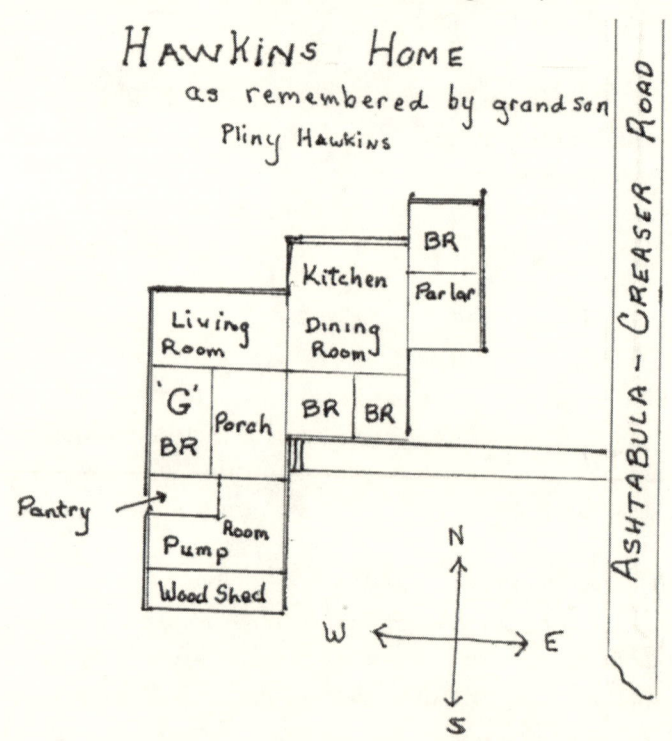

"Grandfather always rose at five [AM] and retired at nine very regularly. He sang well at family prayers till he was ninety—and was for many years leader of the M.E. Church [Methodist Episcopal], singing and class meeting. At noon or immediately after dinner he had a nap. Grandfather was very cheerful and optimistic, pleasant to live with, but not a good business manager." He lived in the same home for forty-five years, 1850 to 1895, as they were married for fifty-seven years.

"Grandmother never took time for a nap. She was economical and was much pained at Grandpa's easy ways. Just a little inclined to be close and to scold. She was not very kind to Mother [Frances Haine Hawkins]. Mother's years here were the most-unhappy of her life. This led father to rent the Peck Farm in East Farmington, when I was one year old." The Peck farm was seven miles south of Clover Hill. (The deed, dated the twenty-first of June 1873, reflected the purchase of the farm.)

"Grandfather Hawkins was the soul of honor in business not only an honest man, but one of the highest integrity. They came to Canada [Montreal] in 1844. Grandpa worked in the shipyards. The voyage at sea was six weeks, starting with Thomas, Sarah, Ann, and Martha, the baby. [Martha died at age two on the voyage.] Sarah married William Haine [the Haine's oldest son], and Sarah later died of tuberculosis at 33 years of age. Sarah and William had one child, "Dosia" [short for Theodosia]. Ann married James Hawkins [a first cousin]. They had four children—Flora, Susie, Willie and Jamie. All have died accept Susie, who lives on the Old [Hawkins] Farm. Jamie died in an accident at age 21 years and did not marry. [Willie on his death certificate noted a mental disability.] Susie [married twice, with no children] and Flora married George Fuller and had two sons and three daughters."

They were the last to remain on the Hawkins Farm until the farm was sold in 1923 as noted on the deed.

Memories of Haine Grandparents
By Pliny Hawkins

"Grandfather Haine's farm was called Clover Hill over-looking the Grand River Valley to the west. Haine Creek flowed behind the farm. The Grand River flowed for 25 miles north to Lake Erie."

Pliny also remembered that "Grandma Haine always sent him and his siblings' toys for Christmas and his mother would always give them useful things."

Clover Hill Farm consisted first of a log-cabin home, and then in 1850, a four-bedroom home was built where William and Mary Haine and the family lived. Buildings were added at different times—the gristmill, a sawmill, a dairy/cattle barn, the cheese factory, a corncrib, horse barn, and a general store next door. The first level was a general store, and upstairs was the home of Uncle George Haine and others later. The farm was located on 150 acres where crops were grown, grains milled, cheese made, butter sold, lumber was milled, and vegetables were grown.

Clover Hill was located facing the road with a ravine behind, sloping down toward Haine Creek. The gristmill sat on the creek with a millrace, plus the cheese factory, which was active until 1920.

William Haine	Mary Haine
Born on 8 February 1806	Born on 14 March 1815
Son of John Haine and Mary Creed	Daughter of Joseph Haine and Sarah Look
Married 11 April 1836	Death date: 31 July 1890
Death date: 14 September 1895	

John and Joseph Haine were brothers and were sons of William Haine (born 1743) and Elizabeth (Betty) Young.

Mary Haine at Clover Hill

Mary loved to read and enjoyed reading to her children. She attended a private girls' school near where she was born in Croscombe Parish, Somerset. Mary Haine had three diaries that survived from the years 1874, 1875, and 1877. In 1874, she shared her daily routine that would exhaust any woman of today.

She notes that friends and family from near and far visited frequently; they shared meals and often stayed the night. Visitors and nine family members led to crowded accommodations. The family attended the Methodist Church in Bloomfield Center each Sunday morning and evening, along with Bible study and prayer meetings most Thursday evenings. There were temperance meetings, literary meetings, and "quire" (choir) on some Friday evenings.

Mary Haine's Secretary

Mary's routine each week consisted of working together with the girls: Sarah, Charlotte, Emma, and Clara. They did the laundry, starting with boiling the water on Monday, with ironing on Tuesday. Emma churned butter weekly, plus housework, cleaning the pantry, the parlor, the east bedroom, and the upper west bedroom. Making bread, baking, and cookies were usually done by Mary. Some of the other duties assigned were boiling, cleaning, and canning molasses. "We picked tomatoes for ketchup and preserves, picked apples for cider, cut corn, washed and peeled pears and peaches for canning. We made pickles, peach butter, peeled apples to dry, picked elderberries and made grape jelly and preserves."

Mary noted that a chicken was killed for Thanksgiving, and she chopped mincemeat for pies, baked bread, and made cookies for Christmas. Other duties consisted of "making yeast, melting beeswax, dipping candles, making soap and today I washed the 'counterpane' [a prize white quilt]. Sewing was shared . . . a calico dress for Emma, pants for Charlie, and a shirt for John. I bought 12 yards of Japanese stripe for a dress skirt for myself."

The men were kept busy with other duties. Sons John, Charles, George, and husband William had the ongoing job of drawing wood. In the winter, ice needed to be cut, and sap for syrup needed to be collected from the sugar maple trees. The men dressed the millstones for the gristmill. A barn was needed for the horses, which required hewing the logs, obtaining the stones for the foundation from Windsor, and shingles were to be purchased in Orwell. The day of the barn raising called for food and many baked goods to be served to the men.

"On Sunday, May 31st, 1874, while at church, a thunderstorm hit and lightening struck the southwest corner of the parlor (of Clover Hill). It splintered the wood and the plaster came down, but no one was hurt." The following week, John purchased paper for the parlor, and the ceiling was repaired.

In June 1874, a Strawberry Ice Cream Festival was held at the Township Hall. The collection was $106 that day.

The men also sowed the oats, ploughed the garden, spread the manure, and sowed the radishes and vegetable oysters, which is a flowering vegetable and a medicinal plant. (It has a diuretic effect and effective for liver and gall bladder problems.) Other chores consisted of having a neighbor shear the sheep and butcher a cow. The family picked cherries in July, and potatoes were dug in October. At the end of a busy day, Mary noted, "I read about the life of Vanderbilt. I felt peaceful and happy."

In September, the family took a five-day trip to the Chicago Exposition, traveling by railroad to Cleveland and then by boat out of Cleveland to Chicago.

First Family College Graduate

Pliny, the eldest son of Thomas and Frances Hawkins, was born in 1869 and was the first grandson for the Haines and Hawkins. Pliny Haine Hawkins attended Western Reserve Seminary in West Farmington, in Trumbull County. This was the same "first-class" school (a distinction it had for over fifty years) that his parents and several aunts and uncles attended. In 1891, he graduated with a degree in science and a "commercial" degree.

Much later, he received an honorary degree in science after attending Valparaiso College in Indiana for two years. Later, he enrolled in the Law Department. To earn money for his education, he taught school. He graduated with a degree in law (BLL) and was admitted to the Ohio Bar Association. By 1893, he decided to head west. The Union and Central Pacific Railroad had begun service west toward Montana. When nearing Billings, a man called out, "Is there anyone who would like to teach school?" This was the start of his teaching career.

A Western Pioneer

Pliny was a teacher for a short time, then principal for six years, and then he became the school superintendent for Columbus and Absarokee, Montana. After three years, he hired a new teacher, Grace Alice Milner, a widow who was the same age. It was not long after that he fell in love with her. He stated in a letter that "she was the greatest event of my life." Pliny spent all of June 1900 working for the federal government, conducting the census in a Columbus, Montana, precinct. He counted 863 people in 190 households.

Pliny Haine Hawkins, Milner Haine Hawkins,
Grace Alice Milner Hawkins, Frances Milner Hawkins
(Photo taken in Montana 1910)

He and Grace were married that year of 1900 where her parents lived in Salt Lake City. They spent their honeymoon in Yellowstone Park and the mountains. Grace was an artist and also enjoyed photography, especially of mountain scenery. While on their trip, they toured London, Somerset, and Gloucester in England and also Wales. It is the area where both of their families had once lived.

Soon after the honeymoon, Frances had a very difficult pregnancy and barely survived. Their son, Milner Haine Hawkins, was born in 1901. In 1902, Pliny resigned as school superintendent and, with partners, founded Columbus (Montana) State Bank. He was a cashier and justice of the peace. The Northern Pacific Railroad was very close to their home in Columbus, as was the school, but their home had neither electricity nor running water.

Pliny attended Montana State University in Bozeman. He received an honorary master of science degree in botany, which later led to the writing and publishing a book in 1924 titled *Trees and Shrubs of Yellowstone National Park*.

(Photo taken at Clover Hill, 1906. Woman on the left is Mildred Hawkins, and Jesse is beside her. Next is Charlotte, his sister; Frances Haine Hawkins, sitting on the ground; Milner, six years of age; and Pliny behind her. Ward Wolcott is holding his daughter, Frances, along with son Clyde, and on the right, is Bertie Walker. George is standing on the far left.) Photo taken by Grace Milner Hawkins, Pliny's wife, prior to leaving on their trip around the world.

In 1906, Pliny and Grace, along with their son Milner, traveled back to Ohio for a family reunion and for an opportunity for Grace to meet Pliny's family. They went to Duluth, Minnesota, then sailed by steamer two to three days to Cleveland.

Many were surprised to learn that this was the start of their trip around the world. They were away from home between August 1906 and April 1907. The trip was Grace's idea, and they made the trip because of her interest in genealogy. She and Pliny both had family in England that they wanted to visit. It was a mystery where they found money for such a trip. Many wondered how he could possibly multiply a teacher's salary into sufficient wealth for a leisurely trip around the world without his striking oil or a vein of copper. Most of the family in Ohio was of sufficient means, but they could scarcely conceive of foreign travel, not to mention a tour around the world. The only conclusion was that Grace had received money from her first husband's estate.

The Haine family home in Somerset, in the town of East Pennard, was family owned since the 1600s and had recently burned in 1906. Pliny was disappointed to find that family and home were now all gone. Of course, it has been over seventy years since the family immigrated to Ohio. The Hawkins family was no longer in Evercreech, but Pliny did trace several relatives in Glastonbury, presumably Henry Hawkins's family and William D. Hawkins's brother. Pliny did find the Thomas Hawkins tombstone leaning against the outside wall of St. Peter's in Evercreech.

Pliny's younger brother Jesse, my grandfather, received a couple of postcards from India and another from Japan. Pliny sent nineteen letters to family members telling of their adventures, but asked for their return so they could document their trip.

Pliny was disappointed that he had not been able to contact more of his Hawkins and Haine family that remained in Somerset. He did recognize some of the homes from photos that had been sent to Ohio.

"While traveling about in Western England a verse kept running through my mind—' And the places which know us now, shall know us no more, even the memory of our family will soon be forgotten here . . . 'In Somerset, some faces and voices seemed so much like Grandfather's," (Hawkins and Haine).

Their daughter, Frances, was born on January 1, 1909, when both parents were thirty-nine years of age.

(Photo above was taken of Grace and Pliny, with Milner and Frances playing checkers on the bear skin rug at their home in Montana. Family photos are seen on the wall and fireplace mantle.)

During the winter, when the children were growing up, the family would play music almost every evening. Pliny played the piano skillfully "by ear," and Milner played the violin. They also owned a player piano with rolls of many of the classics. (Charles Haine Hawkins, his grandson, noted from an interview.)

Pliny, my great-uncle, took three or four trips to Yellowstone Park during the summer of 1924. He collected over two thousand botanical specimens for the Smithsonian National Museum at Washington D.C. He identified most of the specimens—dried, pressed, and shipped the plants to the herbarium at the University of Wisconsin. He was issued a complimentary permit each year to enter Yellowstone National Park. In 1933, Pliny received an honorary doctorate of science from the University of Montana for all his collections.

Pliny and Grace encouraged education for their two children. They gave the children five cents for brushing their teeth daily and another amount for good grades. Later, they gave the children $50 for not smoking before they were twenty-one years of age.

The Great Depression

By 1929, "the depression has already cost me half my capital and may take it all . . . I have no choice but to stay here rather than retire and dispose of some of the land," noted Pliny.

Milner, his son, returned to Wisconsin and obtained a degree in mining engineering, and his sister, Frances, graduated with a degree in physiotherapy. Her first choice was to be a physician, but she was persuaded to study physiotherapy. She married Joe Meek who worked to receive a law degree, but he never established a law practice.

Milner married Vivian Lansworth, and life became very difficult when Milner was diagnosed with a mental disorder. They had three boys. Vivian was a teacher, but problems continued as Vivian feared for her life. Pliny had to become the guardian of Milner and had him taken unwillingly several times to mental hospitals. Milner had an ongoing battle with paranoid schizophrenia, and later, it was felt that it was a bipolar disorder. (Medication was not in existence at this time and would not be developed until after the 1960s.)

Pliny realized that perhaps the problem was genetic, as Grace's eldest sister had spent most of her life in a state mental hospital. Pliny spent years financially supporting Milner, his children, and grandchildren. Pliny purchased a home for Vivian, his daughter-in-law and his three grandsons, Charles Haine Hawkins, Robert Pearson Hawkins and James Hawkins. Because Vivian feared for her safety, the location of the home was unknown to Milner. The house was in Portland, Oregon, near her family.

Milner was in a locked unit for sixteen months, and he accused his father of ruining his life. Pliny told his son in a letter, "It is natural to accuse the one nearest you and that he [Milner] was not to blame for his illness and I do not think that I [Pliny] am either."

Pliny developed pain in his hip joint, requiring a cane, then crutches. He redesigned his car with a hand-operated clutch so that he was able to drive. With more testing, doctors found that cancer was present in the marrow of the femur, and Pliny required morphine for the pain.

In Pliny's obituary on September 15, 1940, his occupation was listed as "Real Estate and Rancher/Own Business" but did not mention his being teacher, principal, lawyer, botanist, and banker as well. He was a frugal, thrifty man, who was always supportive of his family by teaching them to save and invest. Pliny and Grace retired to Palos Verdes Estates in Southern California to a home that they had built in 1935. The home had a panoramic view of Santa Monica Bay, Hollywood Hills, and the Pacific Ocean.

* * * * * * * * * * *

Vivian Lansworth Hawkins

A Strong Force and Inspiration

Vivian, Milner's wife who was born in 1902, remained in Portland, Oregon. There she raised their three sons, two of which acquired their doctorate, and continued teaching at the university level.

In January 1978, at seventy-six years of age, Vivian was visiting her sister-in-law Frances Hawkins Meek (Pliny's daughter) in her home in Tucson, Arizona. On this occasion, she happened to notice three bound black diaries in Frances's bookcase. She became fascinated. When exploring further, she realized that these diaries had been written by Thomas Hawkins in 1860, Frances Haine in 1862, and Mary Haine in 1874, 1875, and 1877. Frances Meek was willing to share the diaries with Vivian, who realized their value in our family's history.

Frances Hawkins Meek of course was Pliny's daughter and the granddaughter of Thomas and Frances Hawkins and the great-granddaughter of Mary and William Haine and William and Mary Ann Hawkins.

FRANCES WOLCOTT ROGERS, VIVIAN HAWKINS

Frances Wolcott Rogers, daughter of Charlotte Hawkins Wolcott, and on the right, Vivian Lansworth Hawkins in 1978 on a hayride at Clover Hill.

When Frances (Hawkins) Meek and Vivian were talking, Frances remembered "that the Haine Farm operation included a cheese factory and a gristmill. Frances clearly remembered that she was shown the millrace and was told that the gristmill served as a station on the underground railway for escaping slaves, before the civil war in Bloomfield." No other documentation could be found in the diaries, but of course, it was kept very quiet as those involved were at risk. Current maps of the underground in Ohio show the trail slaves made on their way to freedom in Canada, traveling from southern Ohio, north through Bloomfield to Ashtabula County.

Letter from Vivian

"I have tried to transcribe all three diaries in a way that preserves their character and flavor without copying the lengthy discussions about the weekly sermons they enjoyed so much. Family affection, support, pride of their home, neighborliness, and respect for learning, plus their love of music—all these traits are shown on these pages.

"It was necessary to hold a magnifying glass in my hand to read the faded ink much of the time. To complicate matters further, there are at least six Sarah's in Frances Haine's diary. Both her mother and her future mother-in-law were named Mary. Both her father and her fiancé's father were named William.

Vivian deciphered the handwriting and typed the journals, making them more readable, working for weeks on her project. She felt compelled to share this information with the family, which she had uncovered.

Throughout Mary Haine's diary, she used a code script reflecting thoughts, ideas, or problems that she didn't chose to share with others. We shall never know.

CHAPTER 7

Diaries Uncovered in California

IN 1978, MY mother received a large thick envelope in the mail with the return address from Vivian Hawkins, Portland, Oregon. What a mystery! The excitement mounted when we opened and read her letter. She introduced herself and explained how she found the three small leather diaries and typed their contents.

Vivian's letter and transcripts of the diaries were unbelievable. The first diary was written by Thomas Goddard Hawkins in 1860. Then, Frances Harriet Haine's diaries are dated 1860, 1861, and 1862; and Mary Haine's journal was written in the years of 1874, 1875, 1878, and 1879.

Diary of Frances Haine (Age Twenty)
(page 1)

January 1, 1862: "Very pleasant morning. I arose feeling very thankful that I have lived to see the beginning of the New Year. We are all at home this morning and as I sat at the table I wondered if we would all be together and be so pleasantly situated, one year from today. It is very uncertain. [The Civil War was looming with uncertainty and would soon take her two older brothers to war.]

"We spent the evening talking, singing, preparing puzzles and reciting poetry. Each one recited a short piece. We passed twice around the company in this way. Found it very pleasing entertainment.

"We went over to Mr. Hawkins' in the evening. We had a good time singing."

I shared the excitement of reading the diaries with friends and family. The word spread, and Janie Jenkins, a storywriter for the *Youngstown Vindicator* newspaper, called. She wanted to do a feature for the 1978, July 4 edition about the diaries. She printed nearly a full page that included the photos of Frances Haine and Thomas Goddard Hawkins, the Hawkins's and Haine's tombstones at Brownwood Cemetery, and a photo of my sister,

Millie Hawkins, and me. The writer, Janie Jenkins, was most interested in the notation in the diary written about July 4, 1862, with the cannons firing at the rally in Warren, sixteen miles away, encouraging young men to enlist in the Civil War. Frances's brothers, William and George, had both signed on.

The newspaper article soon was passed along to the relatives in North Bloomfield who lived at Clover Hill. Charles and Hazel Cox have lived on the farm since they were married in 1937 with the exception of several years during WWII. They had two grown daughters, Carrie Jean and Carol Ann.

We received a phone call from Carrie Jean, and we set a date for getting together for the first time. In Vivian's next letter, she shared plans to travel from Portland, Oregon, to visit her son in Morgantown, West Virginia. We set a date for September 1978 to meet at Clover Hill. In addition to Vivian, her son, Dr. Rob Hawkins; his wife, Kay; and their daughter, Anne, who was six years of age, joined Frances Wolcott Rogers from Cleveland, who was seventy-two years of age—a granddaughter of Frances Haine Hawkins. Lloyd and Martha Hawkins, Ernest and Pat Hawkins, Roger, I, Douglas, and Jennifer Bell attended. Of course, Charles, Hazel, Carol Ann, and Carrie Jean Cox were there. We met and shared stories, photos, and letters. Charles Cox drove the tractor with at least seventeen cousins aboard on the hay wagon to tour the farm. The Clover Hill property has remained continuously with the Haine family for five generations since 1835.

Carrie Jean Cox was "the archivist" at Clover Hill and had a gold mine of historic scrapbooks. The scrapbooks included letters from family in Somerset, England, obituaries, news clippings of anniversaries, plus the Haine family Bible, and photographs of deceased family members. Carrie Jean also had photos of the former cheese factory and other earlier buildings.

Clover Hill has remained nearly the same through the years. It is a one-and-a-half-story home, white in color with green shutters on either side of the front windows. The only changes were the addition of a bathroom and water available in the kitchen. The well and pump handle are still located outside the kitchen door.

The focal point in the living room is the tall curly maple secretary with her diary, pen, and ink. It stands alongside of Mary Haine's petite rocking chair. The dining room easily accommodates the expandable dining room table with chairs to seat twelve, along with two built-in corner cupboards full of family china. Above the dining room table is a hand-painted antique blue glass fixture.

Oval frames in walnut display photos of William and Mary Haine, taken at their fiftieth wedding anniversary in 1885. The pictures are along with Mary's gold-rimmed eyeglasses and William's gold-headed walking cane.

In the den, two small tintype Civil War photos hang of their sons, William and George, in uniform with riffles, and hanging beside the canteens that they carried during the war. Above the photographs is a framed "Haine Grist Mill" feed sack, plus the wooden peak that was saved from the early gristmill.

On our first visit, interested family strolled around behind their home, and Carrie Jean pointed into the ravine where the millstones that had been part of the gristmill now lay. It had been the largest mill in the township and was a good income producer. Carrie Jean also pointed out the Hawkins Farm that was located across the field. We then visited the Brownwood Cemetery located just west of the village square where all the Haine and Hawkins families have been buried.

Vivian Lansworth Hawkins, Vivian's granddaughter Anne Hawkins, son Dr. Robert Pearson Hawkins Brownwood Cemetery in North Bloomfield, Ohio.

Second Family Gathering (1978)

Each autumn we took it as a time to gather. Vivian Hawkins was again able to visit from Oregon to Morgantown, West Virginia, for two weeks and joined us for the weekend visiting Clover Hill. At least twenty cousins were able to attend. Our lunch included the food everyone brought to share. We walked down the road where the old Clover Hill School previously stood, passed the millpond, walked through the cornfields, and gazed at the dairy cows in the barn. Charles Cox collected colorful Indian corn and passed an ear to all. Along the unpaved road in front of Clover Hill, we heard the *clip-clop, clip-clop* of the Amish horse and buggy traffic going by.

This was just another of the many get-togethers that would happen in years to come. The following year, in 1980, Carrie Jean asked the Amish family, now living in the Hawkins home, if we could see the inside of their home. They kindly showed us the inside of the house and the addition recently added to accommodate their growing family of twelve children. It is heartwarming to know that both homes were in good repair and being used.

Reunion in 1979
At the home of Martha and Lloyd Hawkins

Seated Lt. to rt.: Anne Hawkins (Young), Angela Hawkins Fichter, Gladys Hawkins, Meredith Hawkins (Melnick), Sue Hawkins Bell, Ernest Hawkins, and Larry Lloyd Hawkins.

James Fichter (standing), George and Gloria Hansen, Vivian Hawkins, Carol (Oravecz) Hawkins, Michele Hawkins (Schwartz), Millie Hawkins, Hazel Cox and, Martha Hawkins.

Robbie Hawkins (King), Roger Bell, Larry Hawkins (Rob's son), Charles Cox, Patricia (Heiple) Hawkins, and Rev. Rob Fichter, standing. Photographer: Dr. Rob Hawkins.

First International Hawkins-Haine Reunion 2000

Photo taken at Punderson State Park.
(September 9, 2000)

Family from England, British Columbia, Washington, West Virginia, Iowa, Connecticut, Michigan, California, and Delaware.
The two babies in the front row, Sara Bell and Samantha Sassey, are part of the tenth generation of the family born in 1999.

Haine Reunion

Haine-Hawkins-Cox and Dunkerton Families

First row, left to right: Robert C. Hawkins, Glacier Hawkins Kingsford-Smith, Najma Bachelani-Bell, Jeffrey Bell (holding) Sara Bell, Adrienne King, Jonathan King, Linda Sassey (holding) Samantha Sassey, Frances Haine Dawson, and Phillip Cox.

Second row: Rev. Robert Fichter, Angela Hawkins Fichter, Martha Hawkins, Dr. Charles Hawkins, Roger Bell, Sue Hawkins Bell, David Walsh, Hazel Cox, Marian Cox, John Cox, and Morris Jones.

Third row: Jan Hawkins, Kay Hawkins, Millie "Mildred" Hawkins, Meredith Hawkins Melnick, Dr. Carol Hawkins, Roberta Hawkins King, Patricia 9Hawkins, Carol Rogers Beers, Jean Rogers Kwait, Carrie Jean Cox, Carol Ann Cox Sassey, Delores Dunkerton, Joseph Dunkerton, Ronald Miller, Marilyn (Williams Storey Dunkerton) Miller, and Shirley (Dunkerton) Jones.

Forth row: Thomas Hawkins, Dr. Robert Hawkins, Dr. Jeremy Schwartz, Michele (Hawkins) Schwartz, Larry Hawkins, Thomas King, Douglas Bell, Jennifer Bell-Shipman, Ruth Jones, and Willard Jones.

CHAPTER 8

The Next Generation

Photo taken 1892

Emma Hawkins's Adventure West

From Teacher to Tragedy

EMMA HAWKINS WAS the eldest child of Thomas and Frances and sister of Jesse Hawkins, my grandfather. She was born on the thirteenth of February 1864. At the age of twenty-six after teaching for five terms, she noted in her diary that she decided to travel to San Francisco. She was planning to finish her schooling and teach in San Francisco. Unfortunately, she found that her credits would not transfer. Consequently, she stayed in San Francisco with her aunt Emma (Haine)

Beatty, eleven years her senior, and Emma's husband, Uncle B. Frank Beatty, a physician.

Starting in August 15, 1890, her diary begins, "I closed my district school today after five terms." Then she visited cousins Dosia (Haine), Flora, and Susie (Hawkins). The following day, she tells about going to church. "Bertie went to college, Pliny and Ernest brought me to Bloomfield to go with Aunt Emma Haine [on the trip]. Staid all night at Grandpa Haine's and he took me to the station in the morning. Uncle Charley (Haine) came to Warren with us. Left Warren [on the train] in the afternoon and arrived in Chicago by noon."

August 21: "The countryside looked very much the same all through Indiana, except the oil regions. We left Chicago about six in the evening. We crossed the Mississippi soon after midnight. I could now see nicely by the aid of the electric lights. Arrived in Des Moines, Iowa at Aunt Lottie's [Charlotte Haine Lyman, Emma Haine's older sister], in time for breakfast, and found all well." Emma Hawkins describes the capitol building, with the dome, ten-foot walls, halls, and paintings. "After going in the elevator to the 3rd floor, we went up 237 steps to the top of the middle of the dome, and went outside where we had a splendid view of the city."

As they traveled on, they crossed the prairie all day and part of the next. She tells of "riding along the Great Salt Lake. The ground looks white with salt. The Sierra Nevada Mountains are beautiful and grand. They differ from the Rocky's in being covered with fine pine forests. Some of the time we could look out and see a beautiful little mountain lake below, while we were nearly even with the top on the mountains.

"On the opposite side, which were, but a short distance from us, part of which were snow capped, again we were following a beautiful little river as it dashed over the rocks, with the mountains towering above our heads. At the top of the Sierra Nevada's, a fine hotel called the Summit House, which is 7,049 feet high. It was very cool and you could gather snow within a few yards. We were detained three hours due to a landslide on the track on account of a cloud burst the previous night.

"Wadsworth is a pretty little village in the desert. This is where I first saw Indians. One squaw had a fine papoose about three months old. They were dressed in gay colors and their faces painted red. They seemed to have nothing to do but beg.

"Sat. night—we whorled down the Mts., crossed the Sacramento valley and landed in Oakland about 3 AM, where our train was run onto a boat. We waited in the cars until about six, when we crossed the bay. This is my first boat ride of importance. When landed in S.F. (San Francisco), we took the street car and landed at 942 Valencia about 7 AM and found Uncle Frank in bed, he had waited at the depot until about midnight for us."

The diary continues, "Sept 9th, Tuesday, was a great day, 40 years before, the state (of California) was admitted to the union and the procession and decorations were immense. It was estimated that 12,000 men were in marching order and the streets and windows and houses were a mass of people. The procession was composed of soldiers, pioneers, native sons, firemen, sailors, brewers and others, all in the finest costumes. 71 bands of music were interspersed. It took 3 hours for the procession to pass us. The banners and decorated wagons were beautiful.

"Aunt Emma took me to the Golden Gate Park. It is a beautiful place . . . the play ground for the children is fine, consisting of swings, boats, donkeys, goats and goat carts. A fine stone building furnished with tables and chairs in which to eat a lunch. Around the fine bandstand are seats to accommodate several thousand people. Near by, are fine statues, one of Garfield, the other of Lincoln. Also, we spotted a beautiful monument to the memory of Francis Scott Key."

The diary continues with her awe of the museums. "The birds are zoologically arranged and the largest and finest specimens, I ever saw, from all parts of the world. Some from Africa, Asia and S. America, all were gorgeous. The collection of animals, both land and marine is very good. Among the monstrosities was a dog with one eye in the middle of its head, a deer with its head on upside down, and 8 legged goat, a double pig, a 4 legged chicken and a pig with a monkeys head."

October 4, 1890: "In the afternoon Aunt Emma [Haine] Beatty, and I took the street car and went to Knob Hill, a part of the city where several of the richest men have their homes. They are so large that they look more like grand hotels than private dwellings. And so high are the hills on which they are built that you can look down on the main part of the city with a fine view of the Bay.

"From there we descended to the Chinese quarters and went into some of their stores. All the goods were Chinese and many of them very pretty. The dolls looked just like little Chinese children."

October 6, Tuesday: "Aunt Emma and I went to the Ocean, I, for the 1st time. It was just grand to watch the waves chase each other to the shore. The day was fine and there were hundreds of sea lions barking and sunning themselves on the high rocks a little way out from the Cliff house. The beach is not very good there. Found a few shells but most of them broken. Found a little water bird and Uncle Frank stuffed it for me. There were steps, cut into the rocks, so you can go to the top and have a fine view of the ocean. Near the beach were several stores, furnished with beautiful collections of sea shells, pebbles, fishes and mosses. Each Sunday was filled with church in the morning and evenings with invitations, frequently for lunch or dinner."

October 13, Monday: "Uncle Frank's birthday, is 42 today."

Monday, the twenty-first: "We started to Pescadero. We went on the train to Mayfield, 30 miles, and then G.W. Beatty; [Frank's brother] met us with a team [of horses] and riding in a buggy. The country going over the Coast Mountains, is beautiful, we could see the bay from several places. When we reached the top of the mountains we could see the reflection of the sun shining on the ocean. The redwood forests that we passed through were grand. Thousands of acres were on fire. We could see the fire as we came down the mountain in the evening. Emma talked about seeing vineyards and apple orchards."

November 27: "In the evening, went to Epworth M.E. [Methodist Church], I feel that I have innumerable blessings, for which to feel thankful to my Heavenly Father." Two days later, she heard an evangelist preach, "If the Lord be God, follow him."

December 25: "A beautiful day, Merill picked a bunch of roses from her yard for me—quite different from an Ohio Christmas. Uncle and Aunt gave me $5, a white apron, perfume and several other useful articles. Cousin Dosia sent money and mother a handkerchief."

New Year's Day, 1891: "By God's assisting grace, I will be a more earnest worker and follow him more closely than ever before. In Sunday school today, Miss Bancroft spoke on her theme 'Deaconess Work.'" The year progressed with classes, lectures, and sightseeing.

June 11, 1891: "Pliny's graduation, Aunt E. and I sent him a pin. I would have liked so much to have been there."

June 16, 1891: "Attended teachers' exam in Oakland, three days, failed in analysis."

July 3, 1891: "Went to the exam for the applicants of the Deaconess House. The Bishop said, 'If we are in this work, we had undertaken no easy task. Others would turn missionary, and think themselves as good or better than we . . .' I hope whatever the decision may be, that it will be for my good and aid my Heavenly Father's glory."

July 29, 1891, Wednesday: "Entered the Deaconess Home. Aunt Emma gave me a lovely pin before I left. She and Uncle have been *so good* to me."

January 22, 1893, Sunday: Her work continued. She began to prepare herself to become a Methodist deaconess. Spent the past two weeks in Oakland distributing invitations to the revival services at the church."

"She spent her whole time, going house to house, finding children for the Sunday school, people for the congregation, and souls for heaven." Emma's life took a new direction. She has been working in the city, in those haunts of misery.

(photo taken 1892)
Emma Hawkins is the second deaconess from the right.

The diary abruptly stops. She died the on the seventh of March, 1893 at twenty-nine years of age of small pox while helping the poor, ill, and those struggling with poverty. Six bishops officiated at her funeral. "Emma who laid down her life in San Francisco for the cause of God, her memory will be an inspiration to us always in our work." She was buried at Cypress Lawn Cemetery, died at 724 Shotwell Street, San Francisco, home of her Aunt Emma Haine Beatty and Uncle B. Frank Beatty, who was also a physician. It is believed that the use of trained, paid deaconesses to do the social services for the Methodist Church was a new development at *that* time and lasted less than half a century.

The invocation mentioned that "her letters to her friends in Ohio were full of California sunshine, flowers, mountains, skies and seas." It was difficult to imagine the loss that was felt by her family and fellow deaconesses. There were six bishops of San Francisco who participated in her memorial service.

A copy of the invocation, her diary, photograph and a gold watch were sent home to her mother, Frances Haine Hawkins, then passed along to Jesse Hawkins upon her death, then Lloyd and, now, to Sue Hawkins Bell.

Her Aunt Emma Haine Beatty died in 1901 at forty-eight years of age and Dr. Frank Beatty died in 1902 at fifty-four years. At some point, they moved to Southern California. Emma Beatty had traveled back to Bloomfield where she died of TB. It was just eight years after her niece Emma Hawkins had died. Emma Beatty is buried in Brownwood Cemetery in Bloomfield. If they had stayed in San Francisco, their home would have been part of the big earthquake and fire of 1908 that killed thousands in San Francisco.

* * * * * * * * * * **

Transcontinental Railroad

Work on the Central Pacific Railway began in 1862 after "The Pacific Railway Act of 1862" was signed by Abraham Lincoln. The bill authorized the construction of the first transcontinental railway. Theodore Judah had the vision to build a railroad across the Sierra Nevada Mountains in California that would link the rails of the West with those from the East. On May 10, 1869, the Central Pacific and the Union Pacific met at Promontory Point, Utah. This railroad helped open up the West.

The railway had been built for twenty-one years when Emma Hawkins went west.

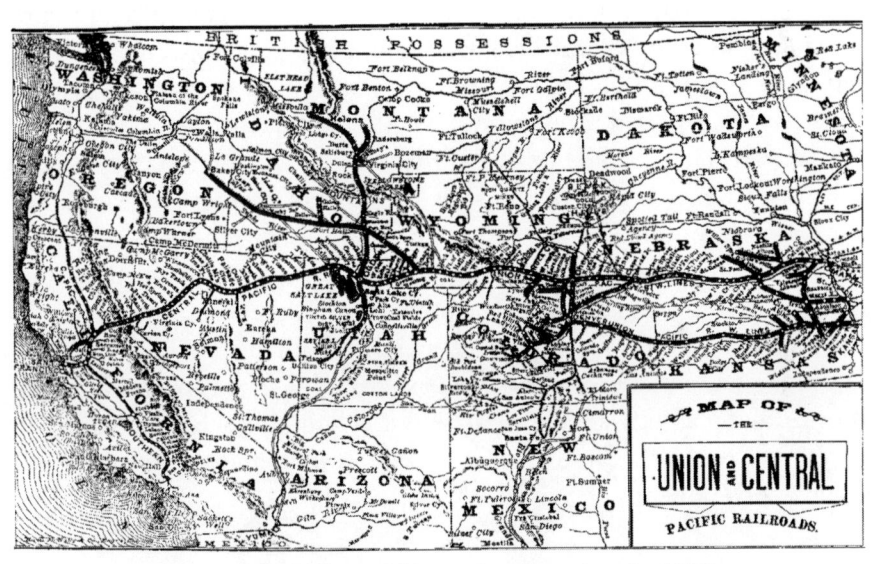

New railroads from Ohio to San Francisco in 1870.

Great-Aunt Bertie

Thomas and Frances's fourth child, Mary Alberta (Bertie, Berta), was born in 1872, followed by her sister Charlotte (Lottie) in 1875. Then Angie was born the following year (1876), but died three months later. In 1880, the twins, Jesse and Jerry, were born.

When I visited Great-Aunt Bertie in 1954, she shared a vivid memory. Bertie remembered when my grandfather Jesse, a twin, was born February 1880. Bertie was only eight years of age and couldn't understand *why* one of the twins was wrapped and taken to the attic. It was freezing cold up there. The reason was that Jesse had lived, but Jerry had not survived. Since it was February, the ground was frozen solid, and it was impossible to dig a grave for the baby. The winter of 1880 broke all records for depth of snow and the near-zero temperatures. Twins were frequently born with a low birth weight and would be more at risk. Jesse's first name was omitted on his birth certificate, and an amended certificate was later produced. The birth certificate also noted that the doctor present was Dr. William Haine, Frances's brother.

* * * * * * * * * * *

In 1909, Bertie and her husband, George Walker, had moved to Forest Depot, Virginia, to be near his family. Frances Haine Hawkins lived with them after the death of Thomas, her husband. Frances had been a widow for three years and had been in poor health for several months. Berta cared daily for her. Frances died on the thirty-first of May in 1911 of what the doctor said was a cancer of the stomach. Berta's brother, Jesse Hawkins, rode down to Virginia to help relieve Berta with her round-the-clock care of Frances, her mother. Upon Frances's death, Jesse accompanied her body back to Bloomfield. They traveled by train, and then he drove her home from the station in a horse-drawn buckboard for her funeral. A cousin, Harold Haine, noted in a letter "how exhausted Jesse was from his journey home." Taking a body across the state-line required much paperwork. Her funeral was held at a family home in Bloomfield, and she was buried in Brownwood Cemetery in North Bloomfield.

Farmington House

Bertie and George Walker are in front of the home where Thomas and Frances had lived for nearly forty years in Farmington Township.

A newspaper clipping from the *Warren Tribune* noted that Bertie and George Walker celebrated their fiftieth wedding anniversary with friends and family. They were married on the twenty-ninth of April in 1896 at the parsonage in North Bloomfield. The article shared that Bertie and George had immediately set up housekeeping at Clover Hill. Her grandfather William Haine had recently died at eighty-nine years of age shortly before their wedding. (Mary Haine had died six years prior on the thirty-first of July, 1890.)

Bertie and her husband, George, moved from Ohio to Montana in 1913 to lease a dairy in Absarokee, Montana. Years later, they moved back East to Meadeville, Pennsylvania. My great-grandaunt Bertie was always very thin and petite, and at times, the family doubted that she was eating properly. She lived to her eighty-sixth birthday and died in 1958. George died two years later in 1960. During those two years, he seemed much relieved of the burden of providing care for Bertie. They were not fortunate in having any children.

Siblings Bertie Hawkins Walker, on the left;
Jesse Hawkins, and Charlotte (Lottie) Hawkins Wolcott,
on the right.
Photo taken in Warren, Ohio, probably in the late 1930s.

Jesse Hawkins
A Good Grandfather

Jesse always remained close to Berta and Lottie. I remember that he visited faithfully. I remember Jesse, my grandfather, as a caring, loving man. He drove us to church each Sunday when Dad was working and took us out for Sunday dinner. Other Sundays, we would visit Great-Uncle John and Great-Aunt Grace Thorp in Parkman, Ohio. Uncle John was the only brother of Mildred, his wife, and my grandmother. The farm in Parkman had over 150 acres and contained many fond memories. This farm is where my grandmother Mildred grew up. Jesse and Mildred lived on the farm with John and Grace Thorp for the first twelve years of their marriage. The farm had cows, workhorses, chickens, pigs, plus several hired hands.

Mildred Phoebe (Thorp) Hawkins and Jesse Thomas Hawkins, married June 22, 1904.

Each February and March at the Thorp farm, they tapped the sugar maple trees and collected sap for making maple syrup. It would take forty gallons of boiled-down sap to make one gallon of syrup. A large amount of chopped wood was required to keep the open fire burning and boil down the sap. Geauga County, Ohio, continues to be famous for maple syrup. (Currently, in 2010, it is selling $80 a gallon.)

During this time, Mildred and Jesse had two sons, Charles and Lloyd (my uncle and dad).

Family photo taken about 1915.
Thorp Farm with barrel for collecting maple sap.

Jesse mentioned in one of his letters to Pliny that he pondered the idea of moving West near his brother Pliny. But instead, he purchased a home in Warren on Parkman Road where he and Mildred reared their sons who attended school in Warren. Jesse made it known that he couldn't make a living farming.

Jesse worked shifts at the blast furnaces at Republic Steel, and then later, he worked night turn as a guard at the steel mill that was located on the south side of Warren. He owned numerous houses and garages that he purchased, rented, and maintained. He was able to repair plumbing, do carpentry and household repairs. "Renting homes was not worth it, if you were not able to keep them in repair yourself." He was active with the Boy Scouts as a leader and enjoyed camping and gardening and was also a trustee at Tod Avenue Methodist Church for numerous years. Jesse and Mildred traveled to California in 1939 to visit Pliny when he was so very ill.

Jesse retired from the steel mill in 1955 at age seventy-five. He lived to seventy-seven years of age and died on the twenty-sixth of October, 1957.

Ernest Hawkins

Yellowstone National Park in the Early Days

Ernest John Hawkins, the youngest child of Thomas and Frances, was born on the twenty-eighth of January 1882. He traveled to Montana to visit his oldest brother, Pliny. He remained single, worked on a ranch, obtained a position as head bellhop at the lodge at Yellowstone National Park, and worked at a hotel during the winters in Billings, Montana.

When visiting with Pliny in California, he became very ill. At the hospital, he was diagnosed with poisoning from an insecticide. It was there that he became critically ill, developed seizures, and became unconscious. The autopsy later noted that he developed an abscess the size of an egg in his brain. His choice was cremation, and his name was added to the backside of the Hawkins's tombstone in the Brownwood Cemetery in Bloomfield. His died on the twenty-fifth of April 1930 at forty-eight. It was not uncommon for him to send newsy messages on picture postcards photos of Yellowstone National Park, tour buses, and black bears to Jessie.

Ernest John Hawkins at the Yellowstone Lodge
1882-1930

CHAPTER 9

Marriage of Sarah Goddard Hawkins

William J. Haine
Soldier and later Doctor

SIX MONTHS PRIOR to Thomas and Frances's wedding in 1863, Thomas's sister Sarah Goddard Hawkins was married to William Joseph Haine on the eleventh of August 1862. She was twenty-eight years of age. The groom was Frances's oldest brother, William Haine. He had just signed on with the 105th OVI (Ohio Volunteer Infantry). William and Sarah traveled to Cleveland before he left for Camp Chase in Columbus, Ohio, for military training. William's younger brother, George Haine, also signed on; and they left for the war together.

A little more than a year later, Sarah and William had a daughter who they named Theodosia, "Dosia," who was born December 15, 1863.

The family Bible sadly noted that Sarah died four years later, on the sixth of August 1867 in Willoughby, Ohio, of TB. She was thirty-three years of age. Dosia came to live at Clover Hill with her Haine grandparents. By the fifth of June 1872, William remarried Cornelia Wolcott. Prior to this, William had been assigned to hospital duty while in Kentucky during the war. Upon returning, he chose to obtain further medical training. (In a *Business Directory of Trumbull County*, found at the Warren Library in Trumbull County, this article was listed.)

Dr. Haine was born in Ohio in 1837. He took a thorough course at the College of Physicians and Surgeons in New York City and graduated from that college in 1869. He started in practice at Mesopotamia, where he remained one and half years. From there he went to the Upper Peninsula of Michigan in the copper and iron regions, where he was in active practice five years, from there he removed to New York where he again engaged in practice. Afterward removing to this place, where he has been practicing for the last six years. During the war he had enlisted in Co. I, 105 O.V.I. in 1862, was commissioned 1st Lieutenant in the 118th U.S. Infantry, and served with honor to the close of the war in 1865.

Cornelia Wolcott Haine, stepmother; Theodosia Haine; and Dr. William J. Haine, her father.

Dosia's New Stepmother

Dosia returned home to West Farmington to live with her father and new stepmother. Her father had been off to war and a year of medical school. From the age of six and onward, Dosia was given many chores to do about the house as seven other children were born in the following fourteen years. From a letter written by Dosia, it appears that there was not much love from her father or stepmother. When she was twenty years of age, she was stricken with a rare ailment called hip-joint disease, which left her unable to walk. She became bedbound for the remainder of her life. It seemed that William's medical practice was questionable. In 1902, her father sold his practice in West Farmington and bought a house in Warren on Adams Street. Dosia's bed was in the front corner of the living room, known as Sunshine Corner due to her sunny disposition.

Much later, in 1914, Dosia wrote a letter to her Uncle George Haine, her father's brother, and told him of the situation and thanked him for the lecture that he had given to her father about not caring properly for his family. William found that he liked to travel south, leaving his family without finances or a father, saying that he had to go because of his "malaria." "After the scolding, he has now been home for the past six weeks and has been well." Upon returning home, William went through their medicine cupboard and took any medicines that he could sell for money.

In the letter that Dosia sent to her Uncle George, she writes,

> Papa told Grace [Dosia's younger stepsister] that he felt awful that you [Uncle George] should talk to him, before me. He forgets that I lost my health caring for his family, while doing too much work. I did not give him much sympathy. After that, he went out to talk to Mama and she sided right in with him. He and mama had a great time talking, how they would take my money away from me. I could hear them talking about it every day or two, but I don't think papa did anything. He was bringing large books home to read after your talk. I thought they might be law books from the library. Then he would go in and talk to Gracie by the hour, on how she ought to have my money and how he would take her for a trip and all sorts of things. He was very loving to her. I can understand all that. He thinks it would be much easier to get the money from Grace. All this talk would get Grace so upset; she was unable to sleep nights. Still, I could not tell for sure, but she seemed less upset when papa was away.
>
> Grace was never a strong girl. You may remember that papa spent the summer traveling, when she was born instead of staying at home as he should have done. Grace was such a tiny child that no one thought that she would live. She was born

before her time and mama had been sick with a fever for many days. I cared for Grace and hardly had her out of my arms as she seemed so cold and lifeless. I have often thought, I kept her alive by holding her in my arms. I remember that nurse saying, "She will not live."

I did not go to school that year, but spent my time caring for Grace and Mary. Grace has always liked to care for me now, since she was sick, Mabel has been real good. She has done more than Grace usually did and papa does not influence Mabel, as he does Grace. I am thankful for this, yet mama tries all the time to turn Mabel against me. I do not think she knows herself why she does so.

It is unknown where Dosia obtained her money, but perhaps it was from her grandparents.

Dosia's stepsisters and brothers are the following:

- Mary Jane Haine born 1874 . . . was divorced.
- Emma Grace born 1876 . . . remained single, stayed at home to care for Dosia.
- George Austin Haine . . . born 1878, had one daughter, Marie Haine.
- William Jay Haine born 1880, no children.
- Clarence Haine born 1882 . . . single.
- Mabel Haine . . . born 1884 . . . no children, died in Ashville N.C.
- Theodore Haine born 1888, died in infancy.

Dr. William Haine died in 1923 in Ashville, North Carolina, at eighty-six years of age. His obituary was very short, and when his wife Cornelia died, her obituary didn't even mention William.

An English proverb: The doctor is more feared than the disease.

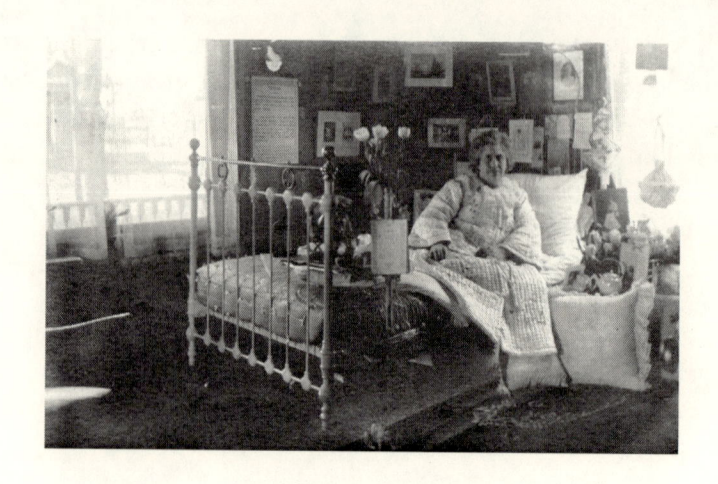

Sunshine Corner

Dosia Haine

Photo taken by Harold Haine in the late 1920s

Dosia seemed to be a very loving person, living on Adams Avenue in Warren with her stepmother and siblings. During her adult life, her bed was on the first floor of the living room and was known as Sunshine Corner. She was an active member of the First Methodist Church in Warren. From her bed, she wrote to shut-ins and prisoners to give encouragement and advice and the message of Christ. She loved to do crafts to earn money for missions. I heard it said that Jesse Hawkins would collect milkweed pods along the roadside that were used in her crafts.

She supported three missionaries in China with her sale of bookmarks containing cheery poems and verses from the scriptures. After their release, many prisoners would come to visit. She had an early communication system from the church to keep in touch and hear the Sunday sermon. Gracie, her one caring stepsister, provided for her needs.

Dosia died on the tenth of August 1930 at sixty-seven years of age. Her death certificate stated that the cause of her death was carcinoma, with no mention about her hip or inability to walk. Some years later, her nephew Harold Haine, son of Charles Haine, the youngest Haine son, purchased a tombstone for her. The stone was placed between her Hawkins and Haine grandparents at Brownwood Cemetery. Harold stated in a letter to me that

"Dosia was an important person in the Haine-Hawkins family. She was a good listener and we would go to her for comfort and sound advice." "Sunshine Corner" was engraved on her tombstone.

* * * * * * * * * * *

The Haine Family Reunion

The reunion was held on Adams Street at the home of Dosia in 1907. Those seated in the photo, from left to right, are children of William and Mary Haine, starting with Dr. William Haine; and the remainder are labeled on the outlined diagram. (Placement and naming completed by Carrie Jean Cox.)

HAINE REUNION -- WARREN, OHIO -- JULY 4, 1907

PHOTO TAKEN JULY 4th 1907

WARREN, OH   ADAMS STREET

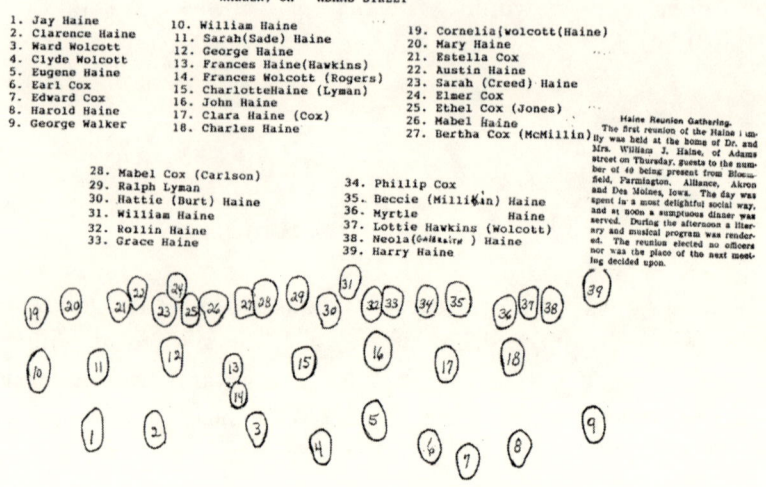

1. Jay Haine
2. Clarence Haine
3. Ward Wolcott
4. Clyde Wolcott
5. Eugene Haine
6. Earl Cox
7. Edward Cox
8. Harold Haine
9. George Walker
10. William Haine
11. Sarah(Sade) Haine
12. George Haine
13. Frances Haine(Hawkins)
14. Frances Wolcott (Rogers)
15. CharlotteHaine (Lyman)
16. John Haine
17. Clara Haine (Cox)
18. Charles Haine
19. Cornelia(Wolcott(Haine)
20. Mary Haine
21. Estella Cox
22. Austin Haine
23. Sarah (Creed) Haine
24. Elmer Cox
25. Ethel Cox (Jones)
26. Mabel Haine
27. Bertha Cox (McMillin)
28. Mabel Cox (Carlson)
29. Ralph Lyman
30. Hattie (Burt) Haine
31. William Haine
32. Rollin Haine
33. Grace Haine
34. Phillip Cox
35. Beccie (Millikin) Haine
36. Myrtle   Haine
37. Lottie Hawkins (Wolcott)
38. Neola (Galloway) Haine
39. Harry Haine

Haine Reunion Gathering. The first reunion of the Haine family was held at the home of Dr. and Mrs. William J. Haine, of Adams street on Thursday. guests to the number of 40 being present from Bloomfield, Farmington, Alliance, Akron and Des Moines, Iowa. The day was spent in a most delightful social way, and at noon a sumptuous dinner was served. During the afternoon a literary and musical program was rendered. The reunion elected no officers nor was the place of the next meeting decided upon.

Haine Reunion Gathering

July 4, 1907

"The first reunion of the Haine Family was held at the home of Dr. and Mrs. William J. Haine of Adams St. on Thursday. Guests numbered 40, being present from Bloomfield, Farmington, Alliance, Akron and Des Moines, Iowa. The day was spent in a most delightful social way and at noon a sumptuous dinner was served. During the afternoon a literary and musical program was rendered. The reunion elected no officers nor was the place of the next meeting decided upon", from the Warren Chronicle Newspaper.

SECTION FOUR

CHAPTER 10

The Younger Generation:

Riding the Rails West

DURING THE SUMMER of 1933, with the depressed economy still very real, Lloyd Hawkins, my father, planned to head west to visit and work for his uncle Pliny in Absarokee, Montana. Hitchhiking was a common way to travel, but Lloyd started out by train. I was in disbelief when my father told how he rode the freight train.

He would climb the ladder at the end of the boxcar and then lie on top. He would secure himself by fastening his belt through the ladder on the top of the boxcar. I asked, "Why didn't you ride inside the boxcar?" He answered, "The men inside would rob you blind, take your money, shoes, or coat." I asked, "What about going through the tunnels when you are laying on top of the train?" He said, "They had low clearance so I would just lie flat. It would be cold and dirty, plus there would be the choking black smoke from the engine."

In the book *Riding the Rails—Teenagers on the Move—During the Great Depression*, the author writes "that riding the rails was always the alternative to hitchhiking. Many train hoppers resorted to thumbing for a lift for short distances, particularly when they had to make their way to a main line. It was impossible to hitchhike at night, which meant that you had to sleep in the open. You could ride all night on a train and be a lot farther down the road.

"Most traveled alone and more common was the danger of being locked in a boxcar as you slept, or by misfortunate." The book tells of "a fifteen year old, Chester Siems and a friend, riding from New York to Pittsburgh in a steel boxcar when they were lulled asleep and didn't hear the door slide shut. They awoke in total darkness and panicked, fearing that they would be shunted into a holding yard and left to die of thirst and starvation. My buddy was crying hysterically and beating his fists on the doors of the railroad car, yet we didn't know how long we rode or whether it was dark outside. Now and then the train stopped and we would pound frantically to no avail. Finally the train made a halt and we heard voices. We banged on the doors and screamed and pleaded to be let out. When the door slid open, I remember seeing frost on the ground. To this day, I give thanks but I also suffer from claustrophobia," the author told.

"It was dangerous riding the freights. You had to be careful not to stumble and fall under the wheels when you climbed on the cars. You had to jump off at the right time too, because once the train picked up speed you had a hard time getting off.

"Sometimes you slept in a boxcar in a rail yard, the next morning when you woke up, the train would be taking off with you. It was scary and dangerous, but you had to do it to survive."

By 1933, 25 percent of the work force was unemployed. There was no "golden parachute," no welfare, nor unemployment in those days. Riding the rails was the only way to go.

My dad, Lloyd Hawkins, rode the rails from Ohio to Montana and hitchhiked on to Pliny's ranch. Pliny owned a five-thousand-acre ranch at the junction of the road to Big Timber and the road into the mountains. Lloyd and two other hands lived in a cabin there. Pliny often stayed there too and did the same work as the others. The land had no cattle during the summer, but was used for grazing during the winter. There was no electricity in "Leafy Lodge," Pliny's place. Lloyd offered to wire it for him, but Pliny turned him down. Lloyd sometimes joined Pliny, Grace, and Milner in Absarokee; but then Lloyd told how his stay was unexpectedly cut short.

"Pliny and I heard shots while out mending the fences. Upon investigation, we and another hired-hand, discovered the sheriff and his deputy had been shot nearby. The deputy was dead and the sheriff had a bullet lodged below his heart. A criminal they were pursuing had apparently ambushed them," Lloyd remarked.

"Through a phone call to a doctor in Big Timer, we arranged that we would bring the wounded sheriff to the doctor in Pliny's Oldsmobile. The doctor would meet us on the highway to take the sheriff the rest of the way to the hospital. Pliny drove, holding his arm out the window, waving a white handkerchief as a prearranged signal to the doctor to know that it was our car. Meanwhile, I tried to aid the wounded sheriff by holding my finger in the bullet hole to stop the bleeding . . . He was taken to the Big Timber Hospital, but he died the following day.

"Upon the sheriff's death, a notice was issued offering a reward for the killer, *Dead or Alive!* At that time, it was still possible for someone to kill a stranger who was in the vicinity and bring him in for the reward with no questions asked. Because of this possibility, and that I was a newcomer and not knowing anyone, Pliny urged me to leave town immediately. He drove me as far as Livingston, Montana, where Pliny wrote occasionally for the local newspaper. He wanted to report the ambushing story accurately. Pliny said goodbye and I set out hitchhiking south, and from there, I went onto California."

Dr. Robert Hawkins, Pliny's grandson, initiated the interview of Lloyd's trip to Montana. This interview was while he was visiting my father on September 29, 1979, two years before he died.

Several years later, Pliny and Grace retired to a home that they had built in Southern California, in Palos Verdes, which overlooked the Pacific Ocean, with views from each window. They named their home Broadview.

Pliny's health over the next several years was failing. The X-ray showed a large malignant tumor in the marrow of the femur, close to the ball and socket. It was probably a progression of the melanoma, a skin cancer that had appeared on his back. In May 1939, his brother Jesse and Mildred Hawkins drove from Warren, Ohio, as they hadn't seen Pliny for thirty-three years.

In the fall of 1939, his sister Bertie and her husband, George Walker, came from Meadeville, Pennsylvania, to visit him and his wife. About this time, he had his leg amputated, but he had his car especially adapted, so he was still able to drive. He remained fairly cheerful despite his suffering. When the pain became unbearable, he needed morphine.

A letter that Aunt Clara Cox received from Pliny on the eighteenth of December 1939 shared that "Jesse's and Berta's visits gave us great pleasure . . . At Christmas time one always remembers the old house at Grandpa Haine's—the long table loaded with the many good things that Aunt Sarah certainly knew how to cook—and family sitting around enjoying everything. Grandfather and Grandmother were as near to me as my own family."

Pliny died on the fifteenth of September of 1940, leaving his wife, Grace, and daughter, Frances, joint executors of his estate. In his last will and testament, he had one wish that Milner would finally forgive him (Pliny) for committing him to the mental hospital as he had no choice. Pliny made this one plea on 27 July 1940.

Pickets, Airplanes, and Machine Guns

The Big Steel Strike of 1937

Letters Written by Lloyd Hawkins

Lloyd had known Martha Schout for some time as they both were members of their parents' church Tod Avenue Methodist Church. Lloyd and Martha had mutual friends and enjoyed activities together.

After returning to Ohio from Montana and California, Lloyd started working at Republic Steel in Warren where his father Jesse worked. In June 1936, the Amalgamated Association of Iron, Steel, and Tin Workers and the Committee for Industrial Organization agreed to a joint effort to organize the steel industry for better hours and pay. In March of 1937, the organizing committee started efforts to form a union in the Mahoning Valley. This resulted in the talks breaking down and twenty-five thousand steelworkers nationwide walking off their jobs from Republic Steel and Youngstown Sheet and Tube on May 26, 1937. The 2,300 workers in Warren and Niles were locked inside.

Most of the mills were shut down at the start of the strike. However, Republic Steel kept their Warren and Niles plants open using nonstriking steelworkers. This led to a number of violent confrontations outside the mills. No end to the strike was in sight.

The *Warren Tribune* newspaper's headline noted on June 1, 1937, "Planes land frequently in the mill yard of the Republic Steel since the mail trucks are being stopped. Food was hauled into the plant by ships [single-engine airplanes], which were greeted by bullets as they entered and left." The Union was trying to enforce their "quit work or starve" policy against the men remaining in the steel mills. Pickets are demanding inspection of each load.

On June 15, the Tribune reported, "Pennsylvania Railroad track in Niles was dynamited after 35 car loads of steel left from the Warren Plant."

By June 21, 1937, it was announced that the mills at Youngstown Sheet and Tube and Republic Steel would be reopened for those workers who wanted to return to work. Fearing the violence that would follow, attempts were made to reopen the plants and the governor of Ohio, ordered in two thousand National Guardsmen to maintain safety.

By June 25, the striking steelworkers began returning to work under the protection of the National Guard that was brought in to keep the peace. Not until 1941 did Republic Steel and Youngstown Sheet and Tube sign agreements recognizing the union.

Letters Written to My Mother, Martha Schout, During This Time

In June 1937, Lloyd was pulled into the union fighting that was taking place in Warren.

Carnegie Steel Co., Niles Blast Furnace, Niles, Ohio

(Photo postcard of Steel Mill dated 1937.)

A JOURNEY FROM SOMERSET, ENGLAND TO OHIO

Dear Martha,

I am in good health and working 8 hours per day. The Co. gives us meal tickets so we can eat free. We are getting paid time and a half. There is between 2800 and 3400 men in the plant. Our mill still has more than two crews and it starts at 7 and stops at 11. I usually get up at 5:30, go over and stand in line for about 20 minutes before eating, we get enough to eat and I have learned to like cabbage, sauerkraut and milk. As long as the mail is shipped Parcel Post, we have pop and ice cream and I prefer to read but that was stopped. We now get our food by plane. The first day the P.R.R. [Pennsylvania Rail Road], would spot cars on the siding and we would go out with clubs and chase the pickets and they would bring food in. The planes have landed about 13 times today. The A.P. Photographers were in here today, taking pictures and when they left they shot 2 times at the plane. One plane that comes in here now has 13 bullet holes in it, they tell me. I have read 3 Plain Dealers and I believe they try to tell the truth. The Tribune is a . . . liar. 1200 men in the plant signed a petition today to have it stopped. They have cots for us to sleep on and blankets. I am at 158 pounds at present. The majority of the men like gambling and they have a great time every evening. They have a number of radios in the plant and a large number of autos which we ride around in. The men were discouraged the first 3 days and a number went home but since then the men have begun to like it and men are beginning to sneak in nights. They are fixing the landing field now so that the Tri-motored planes can land. If this gang ever gets forced out of this plant, there will be a lot of things that will be personally attended to. There is only about 7 guys hanging around this space and this pencil is only about 1 inch long and I doubt if you can read it. We are having a good time. Your letter reached here at 9 p.m.

With love, Lloyd

June 3, 1937

Dear Martha,

We had a swell supper, baked ham, string beans and baked potatoes with peaches. I was down to the landing field to watch the planes come and go. Some of the planes were hit by bullets. They are all new planes and they carry between 600 and 1000 lbs. each. The person that is backing this strike sure has a lot of money. I am making more money now than I ever made before. There are a lot of fellows outside that are wanting in. Lots of times I think they put stuff in our food to keep us quieted down. They sure were afraid that we were all going uptown. The way things look now I don't believe I will be going anywhere for a week, unless I walk over to the blast furnaces to see dad. I like to listen to the radio and they have a lot of new men. The spirit of the men is running high and they seem to be having a wonderful time gambling and playing cards. You should see the washing machines the men made. I think the mail is all well aged in the post before it is sent out.... I don't believe the men outside will be hired back after the strike is settled without a physical examination and that will be where they get rid of all they don't want. They have a glass that they can check the pickets over and I'll bet that no one in the picket line gets a job. Tuesday is our payday but it won't do us any good. I don't know when the pickets will be paid off.

With love, Lloyd

June 23, 1937

Dear Martha,

It seems like time has just stopped since we came in here, yet the days go fast. There is not a picket to be seen and I have been setting here an hour. If they don't do better, we may get a cut in pay. I walked over to Trumbull Cliffs Sunday, to see my dad [Jesse Hawkins] and we came to the conclusion that all those that want to come to work could come, if they had a little nerve and was willing to run in. I watched the Open Hearth pour two heats. They handle that steel like you would soup, except it is done with a 250 ton crane holding this soup.

The pickets must be disgusted. The bosses do a lot of looking through the telescopes, like the type that the surveyors use. I don't believe that anybody that is seen in the picket line will even get a job back. If they can get the R.R. open, we will be all set, if not, things are going to be bad. I don't see where I am going to loose anything. I think that I will be careful where I park my car for awhile after this is over. The first few days it was nice to watch the planes come and go, but no more. I am working 3-11 and I can't go to the show in the evening. I got the biggest pay Tuesday that I ever got for 2 weeks. We have wash boards and machine, also free barbershops. I am holding a piece of tin to write on. This makes two weeks for me at 5 o'clock tonight.

I think the C.I.O. is pretty small when they picked on women and children at home. Personally I think they are afraid to do any damage to any property because it would be bad publicity. We get to read the [Cleveland] Plain Dealer and the Pittsburgh Sun Telegraph and to listen to the radio. I don't think we are missing much. I think that a little raid, would clean out those pickets at night but the Company doesn't want that and if we did we would get a little more medicine the next meal. Our meals are good. How are the merchants up town getting along?

Lloyd

This is the sixth and last letter postmarked June 26, 1937.

Dear Martha,
Things look a little more optimistic for the fellows in the mill this morning. We are in hopes of getting a pass so we can get back and forth to work. I was up to the front gate looking to see what I could see about one hour ago. When you look out the front gate you are looking right into the barrel of a machine gun. I'll bet the rifles the men are carrying are heavy at night. The R.R. police are all lined up along the tracks expecting the freight to come in. I just doubt if it will be safe for the fellows that are in the mill to hang around uptown for some time. I just heard that the men in the restaurants are going home tonight. Boy that is good news. Today is payday. This is the day we all look forward, even though the money is no good in here. We went without our lunch hour last night, so we could have the freight. I'll bet this is the first time this mill ever shut down for a freight [train]. I was hoping that I would get a couple of days off after this thing was settled but I just doubt it now. I must close if this is to get in the morning mail.

Lloyd

On June 18, 1937, the *Warren Tribune* noted that Judge Griffith "took the case under advisement." Both sides awaited the ruling of whether or not to restrain striking pickets from interfering with its plant operation in Warren and Niles. The question was a serious one. The issues were national in scope and involved the general public as well. The judge restricted all roads into Warren. Roads were blocked and searched by deputies for arms and liquor, items prohibited in Warren. The Ohio National Guard was also called in to enforce the injunction.

I am not sure of the date when the strike was finally settled, but I remember that Dad earned sufficient money to purchase a duplex home and become engaged to Martha shortly afterward. Lloyd and Martha were married on January 8, 1938. They lived on the lower level of the duplex and rented the upper floor. Within two years, Dad purchased the empty lot next door and built a two-bedroom home. Eight years later, Dad built a three-bedroom home on Laird Avenue where we lived until I left home in 1959.

In 1941, shift work at the mill became difficult as he and Martha were expecting a second child. Lloyd joined the Warren Fire Department and retired from there thirty-five years later. He made it known that he was never interested in holding a position such as lieutenant or chief at the fire department because he felt that it was all politics.

Dad's real love was building homes. He would start a home each spring, have it enclosed by fall, and spend the winter finishing the interior. He did the plumbing and wiring but always had the plastering done by a professional. He built approximately twelve homes for others besides three of his own. Frequently, other fireman would assist on their days off.

In 1960, Dad developed leukemia. After requiring nineteen units of blood that year, plus the new miracle medication from the Cleveland Clinic, he went into remission and did very well. After twenty years, one doctor said that he was his oldest living patient (with his diagnosis of leukemia). My father changed doctors as he wanted one with a better record. He was very fortunate to live and enjoy life for twenty-two additional years to the age of seventy-one. He died on August 1, 1982.

His love of camping and traveling continued for forty-five years with Dad and Mom making it to all forty-eight states, Hawaii, South America, England, Spain, and much of Europe.

Brother Charles Marries

Charles Hawkins and Nancy Buckingham
on their wedding day.
(June 18, 1938)

Charles was born on the twentieth of March 1910. He and Lloyd both attended Warren G. Harding High School in Warren. Charles graduated from Ohio University in 1929, majoring in accounting. After graduation in 1933, he traveled to California to visit his uncle Pliny. He found a job working in a bank in California.

He decided to return to Warren where he married Nancy Buckingham in June of 1938, six months after Lloyd and Martha married. Charles started work in the accounting department at Packard Electric in Warren, Ohio, and worked there for thirty-three years, retiring at age sixty. Uncle Charles always loved boating. He and Nancy had a summer home at Lakeside, Ohio. Nancy and their sons, Thomas and Robert, spent every summer there. Charles would drive to Lakeside each weekend after work.

Charles and Nancy moved to Penny Farms, a retirement community near Jacksonville, Florida. Nancy died on 24 April 1987. Charles remarried another resident, who was a widow named Grace. They continued to enjoyed life at the Florida retirement community. Charles died on the eighteenth of December 1999 at eighty-nine years of age.

Thomas Hawkins and Robert Hawkins, sons of Charles T. Hawkins

Thomas F. Hawkins married Janet Sue Breystpraak on June 1967.

Robert C. Hawkins married Mary Kay Branfield on June 1966.

1. Katherine Hawkins married Kevin Boardman
   a. Meredith Boardman, born 1997
   b. Chase Ivan Boardman, born 1999

2. Robert Hawkins married Teresa Coppola in 1997

On left: Martha Hawkins talking with family at Clover Hill.
On right: Hazel and Charles Cox with daughter Carrie Jean Cox in 1979.

Martha and Lloyd Hawkins (1978)
in the parlor at Clover Hill.

SUE HAWKINS BELL

Dr. Charles Haine Hawkins (Pliny's grandson), Sue Hawkins Bell,
Millie Hawkins; Sue and Millie are sisters,
Lloyd B. Hawkins and Jennifer Bell, Lloyd's granddaughter in 1981.

CHAPTER 11

Hawkins—Haine International Reunion 2005

HAINE FAMILY REUNION
AUGUST 2005 - PUNDERSON MANOR, OHIO

Standing: 1. Roger Bell 2. Deirdre Dawson 3. Laura Keller 4. Leah McMillan 5. Nona Bonheimer 6. Susan Jean Haine 7. Pat Hawkins 8. Haidi Haiss 9. Tom King 10. Roberta King 11. Jonathan King 12. Adrienne King 13. Douglas Bell 14. Tisha Goss 15. Charles Hawkins 16. Clara Talbert 17. Marilyn Miller 18. Ron Miller 19. Carrie Jean Cox 20. Ruth Jones 21. Evelyn Manning 22. Willard Jones 23. Connie Alexander 24. Carol Ann Cox Sasey 25. Carol Hawkins 26. Dean Haine 27. Susan Haine 28. Lynne Detweiler 29. Paul Melnick 30. Dave Detweiler 31. Larry Hawkins
Seated (Chairs): 32. Matt Haine 33. Debbie Talbert 34. Vera Willson 35. Delbert McMillin 36. Millie Hawkins 37. Martha Hawkins 38. Sue Bell 39. David Walsh 40. Hazel Cox 41. Marian Cox 42. John Cox 43. Tom Hawkins
Seated (Floor): 44. Jim Haine 45. Frances Haine Dawson 46. Nola M. Haiss 47. Hanna Nicholas 48. Ginger Jensen 49. Jan Hawkins 50. Meredith Melnick 51. Jennifer Bell Shipman 52. James Cox 53. Lillyan Detweiler 54. Samantha Sasey 55. Theodore Melnick 56. Kelly Melnick 57. Elizabeth Shipman

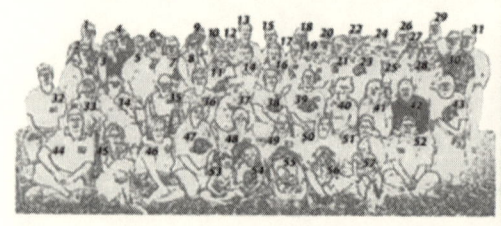

Photo and labeling by James Haine
(seated front row, first on the left).

*All the flowers . . . of all the tomorrows
Are in the seeds of today.*
—*Indian proverb*

Jonathan King, Adrienne King, Roberta (Hawkins) King (above).
David Walsh, Ron Miller, and Marilyn Miller at Clover Hill.
(Photos taken by James Haine)

Roger Bell, Jennifer Bell Shipman, Douglas and Tisha Bell
Group gathering for the reunion.

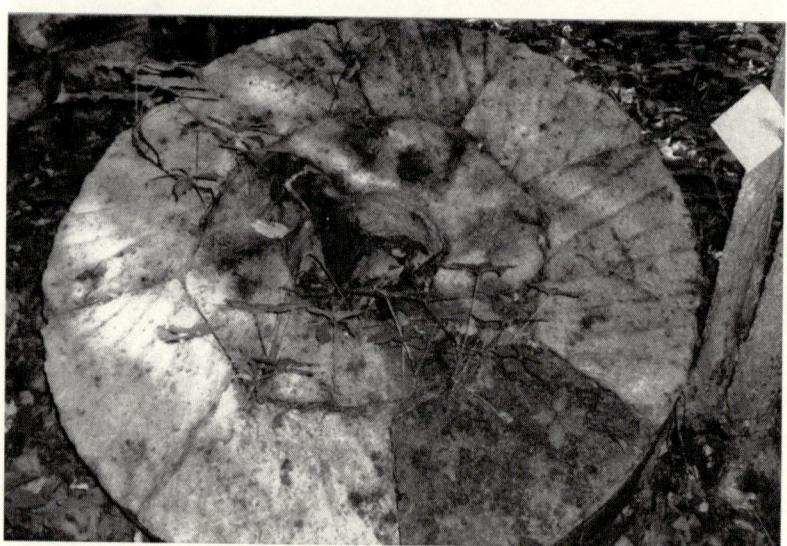

Pat (Heiple) Hawkins, Hanna Nicholas, (from London), Jan Hawkins, Millie Hawkins, Meredith (Hawkins) Melnick, and Paul Melnick. Lt. to Rt. Millstone from gristmill at Clover Hill.

SECTION FIVE

The Somerset Generations

CHAPTER 12

Traveling Back in Time

OUR IMMEDIATE ANCESTORS may have kept a diary or journal to keep track of events or stories, but before the 1800s, ways of documenting important events and family stories were limited. The written word of family history was scarce due to the lack of skills in reading and writing. In England, much of the information was documented in the church parish records. This began in the late 1580s with recording of baptismal records, marriages, and burial dates that were mandated by law. These became the major sources for historical family information.

Tombstone inscriptions, another source of records, would become weathered and difficult to read over time. Monument inscriptions in the church were costly and space available in the church was limited. Consequently, local histories and diaries before 1800 seemed rare. Many families were just coping with the large numbers of children in the family, contagious diseases, and the loss of women during childbirth.

Transportation

It is difficult to imagine how transportation changed during the 1800s. For centuries, people would use horses for riding, pulling carts, and pulling coaches. For generations, most people lived close to the area where their family had lived or move to nearby villages.

If a person lived in Somerset or Cornwall in the early 1800s, London was almost as foreign as it had been in the 1600s. A log kept for the toll roads gave an idea of the use of the roads. Passing by were coaches, chariots, barouches, chaises, chairs, hearses, wagons, wains, and droves of oxen, cows, hogs, sheep, and lambs. All were subject to charges. Those who were able to pass without a toll were the royal family, road menders, the mail, prisoners, and the local clergy. The improved road surfaces led to more travel. By 1816, J.L. McAdam, a Scotsman, was employed to resurface what became known as Macadam Roads that were constructed from Bath to Bristol.

Regular mail coaches would carry both passengers and mail between all the towns and cities of Britain. From around 1840, the use of stagecoaches started to decline due to the competition with the newer railways.

The expansion of the British Steam Railway in 1841 made travel possible to many areas of Great Britain. The Great Western Railway opened a Somerset route from London to Bristol and families could travel south to the seaside for the first time. Travel by train was still problematic, however, because of the lack of standardized time. Each town or place had a different system for telling time. This made train schedules difficult to maintain. By 1847, in Greenwich, England, time was standardized to keep clocks over the world consistent with "Greenwich Standardized Time."

At the same time, as railroad travel expanded, new rules and regulations improved the safety on ships. Schedules for departure became more reliable for ocean voyages. Safety improved along with the surge of emigrants. During this time, sailing ships remained popular into the 1880s.

In his letter written to a friend in 1842, Charles Dickens describes his travels across the Atlantic. He—along with his wife, her maid, ten children, and his two associates—left Liverpool on the steam ship SS *Britannia*. On their return trip home, he chose *sail* rather than *steam*. He described the steamship as having "a tall funnel extending 40 feet above the ship, with a fire blazing 2-3 feet above the top of the funnel." Dickens felt that if the funnel blew overboard, the vessel would be instantly on fire. The steamship required coal. The trip from London to Halifax, Canada, required seven hundred tons of coal. When it left port, it would be too heavy, and it would be too light when it returned. His other concern was that "they carried no (life) boats." Because of these limitations steam-powered ships of the 1840s were being used mostly on lakes, rivers, and in harbors.

Travel by rail became popular in the United States. Because of large populations in the bigger cities, people used streetcars or trolley cars for travel. Additionally, Abraham Lincoln signed the Pacific Railway Act in 1862, which made coast-to-coast travel possible. The Sierra Nevada Mountains, which had been nearly impossible to cross, was able to be traversed when the Great Pacific Railroad was completed.

Foods and Preserving

Planting, growing, and preparing food was not easy in either England or Ohio. Preserving foods was very time-consuming. People would dry, smoke, or salt meats and preserve root vegetables such as carrots, potatoes, and parsnips in a root cellar. Fruits could last the winter when they were canned in glass containers that were sealed airtight. People would slice dry apples and pickle some vegetables such as turning cabbage into sauerkraut. Making cheese allowed for milk products to be preserved. Farming and food preservation were major occupations for the majority of the population in the 1800s and well into the 1900s. Having a variety of foods available played an important role in Charles Dickens's *A Christmas Carol*. In 1843, his description of a wonderful "Christmas dinner" describes Scrooge's when he feasts his eyes "on roast goose and red hot chestnuts to plum puddings and juicy oranges, also mince pies, oysters, apples, raisins and figs are laid out." Dickens's description of these foods set a standard menu for Christmas dinners on years to come. Variety is the spice of life.

Tithe Barns

After being restored, several tithe barns from the fourteenth century remain in Somerset, England. During medieval times, the farmers would tithe 10 percent of their grain to the church. This grain was to be stored for the abbey. The tithe barns of Pilton, Glastonbury, and Doulting parishes remain to the present.

Pilton Tithe Barn

Arrow Slits decorate the exterior
allowing for light
Recently restored and reopened in 2005

(Carole Welch and Roger Bell)

Interior of Pilton tithe barn.

Education

Charles Dickens firmly believed that *education* was a remedy for the poverty in England. Poverty in the countryside was reason given for absence of children from school. The children often had to earn money and work to supplement the family's food supply. The crimes associated with poverty that Dickens and his father witnessed during his childhood living in the workhouse was always a part of his life and writings.

Gloving (a home industry), potato planting, gleaning, and fruit picking were standard excuses for missing school. For the girls, they had chores of carrying meals to the men in harvest fields or staying home to sew buttonholes on shirts. Girls as young as nine were employed as silk winders and weavers. Unfortunately, by 1830, the silk industry was on a steep decline. The family income relied upon any money that the children could add.

The importance of a good village school in the nineteenth century in Somerset can hardly be overestimated. They had an endowed school for ten boys, along with a national school, but there was a real need for more and better schools. The privilege of an education was not always available in England, but Ohio provided schools for girls *and* boys and was funded by property taxes starting in 1853.

Childbirth

A woman's life was not easy. Women had the fear of dying in childbirth, and after the birth of the baby, they were anxious over the health of the baby. Mothers might have to tolerate "morning sickness," followed by a growing pregnancy, followed by nursing the baby for months. Life was nonstop. The woman would do the laundry, cook, bake, sew, and then probably have another child the following year. Some mothers felt that as long as she were nursing the infant, she would not become pregnant, but this was not an effective method of birth control.

The birth of an infant would be followed by another baby every two years, sometimes continuing in this pattern for the next twenty years. Of course, in time, the older children would be taught to help with chores and the caring for the younger siblings. Sleeping quarters grew tight as more children joined the family. Sleeping space went from cradle, to cot, and then a shared bed with two or three brothers or sisters. Sometimes the space up in the loft was used for the older children.

SECTION SIX

CHAPTER 13

The Village of Pilton and Evercreech

William Dredge Hawkins

One of the
Twelve Children of Peter and Nancy Dredge Hawkins
(Great-Great-Great-Grandparents)

Peter Hawkins, who was born on 28 April 1772 (father).
Nancy (Ann) Dredge, born on 5 October 1777 (mother).

1. *Thomas Hawkins* was born in Pilton on 21 Dec 1798. He died the twentieth of November in 1880. He married Sarah Haine who was born on 1799 and died on the eighth of May 1867. They resided at Westbrook Farm, Evercreech, Somerset, and had no descendants.
2. *George Hawkins* was baptized Evercreech on 15 September 1799. He died on the thirtieth of July 1863 and married Ann Creighton and had one daughter, Sarah, who married Richard Ashman.
3. *John Hawkins* was born in Pilton and baptized in Evercreech on 12 April 1801. He was a carpenter by trade in Doulting Parish and married Ann Parfitt in 1830 and had a daughter, Matilda. He died in 1851.
4. *Jane Carey Hawkins* was born in Evercreech born on 16 September 1803 and was buried at Evercreech, Somerset, on 16 September 1803. Carey was her maternal grandmother's last name.
5. *William Dredge Hawkins* was born in Evercreech at Chesterblade Hill on the seventh of August 1804. He married Mary Ann Goddard, a dairymaid, on the tenth of November 1831 in Batcombe. Various occupations have been noted for William, that of carpenter,

wheelwright, butcher, and that he worked in the lumberyard in Bristol. They had four children when they immigrated in 1844 to Ohio.

6. *Mary Hawkins* was baptized in Shepton Mallet on 17 August 1806. She married William Dredge on 5 April 1826.
7. *James Hawkins* was baptized on 22 Aug 1808. He married Dorothy Goddard, sister of Mary Ann Goddard. James died on the eleventh of December 1840. She, a widow, and her children immigrated to Minnesota and then to Wisconsin. Their son James married Mary Ann Hawkins, his first cousin in Bloomfield, Ohio.
8. *Benjamin Hawkins* was born in Evercreech on 16 May 1810. He resided in Glastonbury, Somerset. He married twice—first, Louisa Jane Millard and the second marriage was to Ann Cottle. He died in 1883 at seventy-three years. He was a builder and stationer in Glastonbury. His son Henry was mayor, alderman, councilman, and builder. Both, father and son, were very active in the Glastonbury Methodist Church, with their names clearly marked on the stained glass windows.
9. *Elizabeth Hawkins* was baptized in East Lydford on 12 Aug. 1813. She married Thomas Biggin on the twenty-third October 1832 in Evercreech and resided at Westbrook Farm for a period of time with her widowed mother. They immigrated to Bloomfield, Ohio in 1856. They had 11 children and later purchased property in Vernon Township, Trumbull County that was later known as Biggin Corners. Elizabeth died on 28 December 1891. They socialized less in that they were now twenty miles apart.
10. *Daniel Hawkins*, at the public records office, it is noted that he attended school for three years in Evercreech. He was born about 1815, no documentation in the parish records, but in Ann Dredge's *will* (his grandmother), Daniel, Job, and Andrew were mentioned as being one of "Nancy's boys."
11. *Job Hawkins* was born in E. Pennard/Ditcheat about 1818 and married Eliza Pike on 25 February 1862. He resided at Moore's Farm in Holcombe, Somerset. They had four daughters. Job died on December 1910 in West Pennard.
12. *Andrew Hawkins* was born in Somerset, England, about 1819/1820; it appears that he emigrated and settled in Ste-Armand, Quebec, Canada, where he married Hannah Elizabeth Merick on 26 June 1844. They had three daughters and a son, Hobart B. Hawkins.

This area of Canada is approximately seven miles from the state of Vermont.

Genealogy isn't just about looking for ancestors who were historically noteworthy, but the fact that they are family and have survived migration, ocean voyages, economic depressions, flu epidemics, wars, and so on. Many have lived well into their seventies, eighties, and nineties and most without surgery or medical care.

* * * * * * * * * * **

Somerset: Home of the Hawkins, Haine, and Goddard Families

Somerset is a county located in the southwest of England, known as the West Country in the Mendip Hills, just south of Wales. The landscape is hilly, green, and irregular, with hedgerows running across the fields and along the road. A farmhouse here and there can be seen dotting the countryside with an occasional pheasant scampering across the road. My husband and I first visited Somerset in 1980.

My second cousin, Charles Haine Hawkins from Ellensburg, Washington, had visited several cousins in the Somerset area the year before. I wrote a letter to Frances and introduced myself and shared our plans of visiting the area. *Frances Goddard Dowding*, a retired schoolteacher who was eighty-four years of age at the time, kindly invited us to stay at her home. We were first cousins three times removed. She was a first cousin to Thomas Goddard Hawkins, and I am three generations removed.

Her farm was called Lower Eastcombe in Batcombe. The word *combe* means narrow valley. Their home was built on 1619, documented in writing on the top gable. Her farmhouse was partially ivy covered, two storied, and made of gray-brown stone with a rust-colored roof. There were two fireplaces on each floor with a steep curving staircase to the second floor. To the rear there were several buildings and a paddock Pugh's Bottom; the farm next door was the birthplace of Mary Ann Goddard Hawkins. She lived there with her parents, Thomas Goddard (1762-1834) and her mother Dorothy "Dolly" Ryall Goddard (1771-1847). In the 1841 Census of Batcombe, Somerset, listed Thomas (Goddard) Hawkins, age eight, living there with his grandmother Dorothy Goddard, age seventy years, and his uncle William Goddard, age thirty-five years, and Sarah Goddard, age sixty years, and Betty Ryall, age twenty.

Frances introduced us to the sights of Somerset, Glastonbury Abbey, the Glastonbury Tor, the alleged burial site of King Arthur and Guinevere; and then we visited the spectacular and unique cathedral in the town of Wells. The cathedral has an early English gothic exterior, with medieval sculptures of saints and kings on the west side. The interior nave features a magnificent "scissor arch" architecture that was completed in 1348.

Frances was such a delight as she was very knowledgeable about the area and the Goddard Family. Frances had graduated from a teachers' college in 1916. A teaching certificate was a new educational requirement that had not been required prior to this time.

She is the one who discovered the diary written by Thomas Goddard detailing their trip to America in 1831 in the attic of her home in 1976. Frances gave me a copy of the news article from the *Somerset Gazette* written in 1978 about finding the diaries.

We drove around Somerset, enjoying the lush green countryside bordered by hedgerows that was dotted with trees, stone fences, and iron gates in the prettiest countryside of England. She offered to treat us to "tea," but after stopping at a pub and looking at the menu, she felt that the tea (England's evening meal) was too costly. We returned to her home where she served cheddar cheese on bread, tea with milk and sugar, and moist plum cake, safely kept in a tin. This was probably her usual meal.

Frances told of her memories of Queen Victoria's death in 1900. She was four years old at the time and remembered the church bells ringing and the feeling of sadness when her family heard the news.

Her father, John Gibbons Goddard, was born on the fifth of September in 1830. He lived to the age of eighty-six and was sixty-six years of age when Frances was born. Frances's mother, Edith, was born in 1853. She was forty-one years of age when Frances, their only child, was born. This meant that her parents were much older than the parents of any of her schoolmates.

Young Frances Goddard

A story was written about Batcombe and life at the time. Frances Goddard was a neighbor and girlhood friend of the author's family. The book was called *Beyond the Beeches, a Somerset Girlhood 1900-1922* by Diana Hargreaves. The book was written in 2001. Frances Goddard was a ten-year-old girl in 1907.

Afternoon Tea

"Good afternoon, what a beautiful tea," cried a voice. It was Mrs. Goddard and her daughter Frances. Mrs. Goddard was a lot older, but Frances was the same age and had recently come into my class at school. I did not usually speak to her because Frances wore old-fashioned clothes and spoke in a quaint precocious way. Mrs. Goddard, her mother, was almost old enough to be her grandmother, as she dressed like a former generation. She was dressed in black satin, and unlike the other mothers, she wore a bonnet. The bonnet was also black satin with a frilly edge, interwoven with purple flowers. Frances wore long red flannelette drawers, edged with lace that came down to her calves with embroidered flowers beneath her long skirt. Consequently nobody talked to Frances at playtime unless it was to torment her.

At school, Frances was very clever and had an uncanny way of knowing all the answers without even learning them. Nobody talked to Frances at playtime, but now I found myself confronted by the girl and her mother with no escape route and under my mother's sharp eye.

Frances now became bolder at school. One day at playtime, two older girls were drawing pictures of nude females with protruding stomachs and whispering to us inquisitive juniors, "That's where babies come from," pointing to the navel. This seemed absolutely correct until Frances suddenly spoiled it all by saying it was nonsense, and she knew about babies because her mother had told her. She then gave us an exact description of a baby's conception and birth, as correctly passed on by her elderly mother and to our open-mouthed amazement; I had become her new friend.

Frances became a schoolteacher after completing teachers' college. She married later in life and had no children. Her husband, Henry Dowding, died in 1944, and she had been a widow for over thirty-five years when we visited her.

When talking with Frances, I found her memory to be very sharp. She was pleased to be able to share information about her family history, plus she was also an avid Scrabble player.

It was time for us to go, and we needed to catch up with our tour in Chester in the north of England. On our next trip to Somerset, ten years later, I was sorry to see her tombstone in the small graveyard at St. Mary's Church in Batcombe.

"Frances Goddard Dowding 1896-1985"
(She died at eighty-nine years of age.)

CHAPTER 14

Time Marches On in Evercreech

IT WAS 1990 before we had the opportunity to return to England. On the next trip, we meet with Beryl Hawkins, our third cousin. She was related through William Dredge Hawkins's brother Benjamin. We visited the villages of Evercreech, Pilton, and Batcombe. In Evercreech, the St. Peter's Anglican Church, with gargoyles on the roof edges, has a history dating back into the 1400's. The interior of the church had been restored to the original brightly painted beams, with wooden angels in the center of the beams. While walking around the perimeter of the church, we found a tombstone that was about thirty inches tall and made of a gray-black stone. The stone was leaning against the outside edge of the church on the left side of the front door and contained the names Thomas Hawkins, Westbrook House, Evercreech, who died on November 20, 1880, age eigty-two; also his wife, Sarah, who died on May 8, 1887, age sixty-eight. It was later found that Sarah's maiden name was *Haine*, a name that would be part of the family.

Evercreech, Somerset, St. Peter's Church
with unusual clock and village cross.
(Sketch on a postcard received in 1978.)

St Peter's Church has a clockface with a mistake on the front of the tower, as it is missing the number 10. The roman numerals are IX, XI, XII, and XII (9, 11, 12, and 12). This has given rise to many village stories, including "the clock painter who had too many visits to the pub," as nearby is the Bell Inn, or "the husband that told his wife that he would be home from the pub by ten . . . as there was no "10 o'clock."

Thomas, the name on the stone, was the oldest brother of William Dredge Hawkins and resided at "Westbrook Cottage" or Farm. William's father and mother, Peter and Nancy, also lived at Westbrook Farm. Thomas's tombstone was the only family tombstone that we found in Evercreech.

The village cross in front of St. Peter's Church in Evercreech is believed to date from the fifteenth century. The cross was moved in 1781 from the right side of the churchyard to its present site in front. Churchwarden's accounts also show that they fenced the area with iron posts and chains. This encircles the village cross.

The Westbrook Farm is an area dotted with trees on the lower
left-hand corner.

CHAPTER 15

Pilton's: St. John the Baptist Church

ON SUNDAY, BERYL Hawkins; my husband, Roger; and I attended the Sunday morning service at John the Baptist Anglican Church in Pilton. Following the morning service, we walked up the aisle to look at the windows and monuments. We happened to see a four-foot-tall monument inscription high up on the wall to the right of the pulpit. The inscription was all in Latin, but one name stood out in English, Peter Hawkins. We could see dates and several other names and a place called Boxwell, Gloucester.

Other than the name *Hawkins*, the other names didn't ring a bell. Little did I realize that this would be the clue to the next two generations.

At a later time, Beryl found the translation in the Somerset Record Office in Taunton where she lived. This information grew in importance, and after further research, the names and dates were the missing pieces to the puzzle. The monument inscription read, "In memory of *Mary Huntley*, her husband, *Rector Wykes Huntley* of Boxwell, Gloucester, and their daughter *Frances* who married *Peter Hawkins*." It also mentioned their death dates and ages. Later, this would prove to be a very important piece of information as they were the great-grandparents of William Dredge Hawkins, who immigrated to Ohio.

(Translation of Latin by Richard Welch, descendant of Job Hawkins.)

Joining of the Huntley and Hawkins Families

Memorial in Pilton Church (Somerset) - *with rough translation*

Subter recondunter Gêneres	The [relations?] have been set down below
Dn~æ Mariæ Huntley	of the [??] Mary Huntley
Viduæ quæ duro occubit Fato	widow, who rests by a harsh destiny
decimo nono die Augusti Anno	on the nineteenth day of August in the year
Dom~i 1728 Aetatis Suæ 79	of the Lord 1728 of her age 79.
Atiam Mariæ filiæ Reverendi Wykes	[Also?] of Mary the daughter of the Reverend
Huntley et supra dictæ Mariæ Uxoris	Wykes Huntley and the above Mary his wife
Ejus Quæ obiit 23rd Julii Anno Domini 1779	who died 23rd July in the year of the Lord 1779
Aetatis Suae 86	of her age 86
Item Francescæ Hawkins filiæ	Also of Frances Hawkins the daughter
Supra dicti Reverendi Wykes Huntley	of the above Reverend Wykes Huntley
Uxorisque Ejus Quæ obiit 8th Maii Anno Domini	and his wife who died 8th May in the year of the
1781 Aetatis Suae 81	Lord 1781 of her age 81.
Etiam Peter Hawkins mariti	Also of Peter Hawkins the husband
Francescæ Hawkins qui obiit 5th Aprilis	of Frances Hawkins who died 5th April
Anno Domini 1758 Aetatis Sui 71	in the year of the Lord 1758 of his age 71

Summary:

Rev Wykes Huntley married Mary	she died 19 August 1728 aged 79
their daughter Mary	died 23 July 1779 aged 86
and their daughter Frances Hawkins	died 8th May 1781 aged 81
whose husband was Peter Hawkins	who died 5 April 1758 aged 71

To clarify the generations:

1. John Hawkins married Hana Brooks (1674), d. 1684, married again before 1687 to Gertrude (-).
2. Peter Hawkins married Frances Huntley (ca. 1721).
3. George Hawkins married Mary Stokes (1759).
4. Peter Hawkins married Nancy (Ann) Dredge (1787).
5. William Dredge Hawkins married Mary Ann Goddard (1831).
6. Thomas Goddard Hawkins married Frances Haine (1863).
7. Jesse T. Hawkins married Mildred Thorp (1904).
8. Lloyd B. Hawkins married Martha Schout (1938).
9. Sue Hawkins married Roger Bell (1962)

CHAPTER 16

Grandfather Peter Hawkins
1687-1758

Young Peter Hawkins,
His Grandson, 1772-1846

PETER HAWKINS (GRANDSON) was born on 28 April 1772 and married Nancy (Ann) Dredge on March 1, 1797, in Pylle, home of Nancy's family. Pylle (pronounced Pill) is less than three miles west of Evercreech. Peter died young on the twenty-sixth of April 1822 at the age of fifty.

Nancy Dredge was born on the fifth of October 1777 and died on the sixth of September 1846 at the age of seventy-one. She was still living at Westbrook Farm. In the 1841 Census of Evercreech, "Ann Hawkins" was living with the Thomas and Elizabeth Biggin family at Westbrook Farm. Elizabeth was a Hawkins and also a daughter of Peter and Nancy Hawkins. She used "Nancy" as her name, while her mother Ann Dredge was still living.

There was confusion between the names Nancy and Ann as both names were listed in the IGI (International Genealogical Index) in the St. Lake City records with the same birth dates, plus the name Nancy is a derivative of the name Ann. So the conclusion is that Nancy Dredge and Ann Dredge is the same person.

Children of Peter and Nancy Dredge Hawkins

Third Great-Grandparents
and Siblings of William Dredge Hawkins

1. Thomas Hawkins was born on 21 December 1798 in Pilton and died on the twentieth of November in 1880. He married Sarah Haine, who was born on 1799 and died on the eighth of May 1867. They resided at Westbrook, Evercreech, Somerset, and had no descendants.
2. George Hawkins was born on 15 September 1799 in Pilton and baptized in Evercreech. He died on 30 July 1863, married Ann Creighton, and had one daughter, Sarah, who married Richard Ashman.
3. John Hawkins, born 12 April 1801, was baptized at Evercreech. He was a carpenter by trade in Doulting Parish; he married Ann Parfitt in 1830.
4. Jane Carey Hawkins was born on 16 September 1803 and died young and was buried at Evercreech, Somerset.
5. William Dredge Hawkins was born on 7 August 1804 in Chesterblade Hill Evercreech. He married Mary Ann Goddard on 10 November 1831 in Batcombe; they had four children, and they emigrated in 1844.
6. Mary Hawkins was baptized on 17 August 1806 at Shepton Mallet, Somerset, and married William Dredge on 5 April 1826.
7. James Hawkins was baptized on 22 August 1808. He married Dorothy Goddard, sister of Mary Ann Goddard. James died on the eleventh of December 1840. She, a widow with children, immigrated to Bloomfield in 1850, then onto Minnesota and later Wisconsin.
8. Benjamin Hawkins was born on 16 May 1810 in Evercreech and resided in Glastonbury, Somerset. He married twice—first, Louisa Jane Millard and had five children and his second wife, Ann Cottle, had two children. He died in 1883 at seventy-three years.
9. Elizabeth Hawkins was baptized on 12 August 1813 in East Lydford, Somerset. She married Thomas Biggin and they immigrated to Bloomfield, Ohio, in 1856. They had eleven children.
10. Daniel Hawkins is undocumented—born about 1815 in Somerset. Has a record of going to school in Evercreech for three years.
11. Job Hawkins was born about 1818 in E. Pennard/Ditcheat and resided at Moore's Farm, Holcombe; a farmer of 156 acres, he married Mary Pike and had four daughters; he died in 1894 at seventy-six, and she lived up to ninety-one years of age.

12. Andrew Hawkins was born about 1819 in Somerset, and emigrated in 1843 while single, to Quebec, Canada. He married Hannah E. Merrick, and they had three daughters and a son, Hobert, in Mississquoi, Quebec. This area is about four miles from the state of Vermont.

History of Parish Records

Parish registers can be found in each county record office. The Mormons copied the records and kept them on file at the Family History Library in Salt Lake City, Utah. In general, births were not recorded, but children were generally baptized within two to three months from birth and the baptism records usually gave the name of the parents.

Thomas Cromwell, vicar general of King Henry VIII, first ordered the parish registers in England in 1538. Cromwell ordered that every parish must keep a register, noting the baptisms, marriages, and date of burials of all in the parish. The register was to be kept in a coffer or chest with two locks. Failure to comply would impose a fine. People received the order with much suspicion. Most people believed it would lead to a new tax. Consequently, many parishes ignored it.

The order was repeated in 1547, but this time, the fine was to go toward assisting the poor. It was not until 1597 and 1603 that the act was enforced throughout the county. The entries were to be read each Sunday after Evensong and kept secured in a chest with three locks.

Registers were poorly kept during the English Civil War (1643-1647) and the commonwealth period that followed it. Many were abandoned or hidden by the clergy and some were completely lost. Registers were returned to churches after the restoration of the monarchy in 1660. The register book for each parish was kept and secured in a locked chest at each church.

In 1711, an order was decreed that parish registers should be of parchment, ruled, and on numbered pages. This too was generally ignored. The records were difficult to read, the ink was poor, and the paper became stained from mold. The year 1738 marked the beginning of Methodist registers as they had to be hidden since they were not recognized by the established Church of England.

The calendar was adopted in 1751. Prior to this, the year commenced on the twenty-fifth of March. In previous registers, December 31 of 1750 would have been followed by January 1, 1750 and not 1751.

The change to the Gregorian calendar made it difficult in keeping records of baptisms, marriages, and burials. In 1763, a person below the age of twenty-one was required to have consent of parents to be married in England. Burial dates rather than death dates were noted.

The spelling of names varied tremendously, such as Hawkins, Hawkings, Hakens, and Hawkens, and the same with Haine, Hain, Hayne, and Hains. Usually, the name was spelled the way it sounded to the writer.

* * * * * * * * * * **

Somerset

In this Mendip area of Somerset, the soil was difficult to plow, but the land was excellent for grazing sheep and cattle. The wool trade, along with the sale of dairy products—such as cheese and butter—became lucrative during the late eighteenth and early nineteenth century.

Stone was quarried from the Mendip Hills in the Evercreech area. This stone, used for building churches, villages, and manor houses, had been used since Roman times as this stone could be easily carved for building, bridges, headstones, and gargoyles. The Doulting stone was quarried and used in the building of Glastonbury Abbey and the west facades of Wells Cathedral.

George Hawkins
Fourth Great-Grandfather

(George is the son of Peter Hawkins (b.1687) and father of Peter (b.1772)

George Hawkins was baptized on 14 April 1737 in Pilton and married *Mary Stokes* on the twenty-sixth of February 1759 in Pylle at eighteen years of age. She is the daughter of John Stokes. She was baptized on 28 February 1741. They had a family of seven children:

1. Robert Hawkins was born in 1765 in Pilton, Somerset.
2. Sarah Hawkins was born in 1767 in Pilton, Somerset.
3. George Hawkins was born in 1769 in Pilton; occupation of glazier.

4. Peter Hawkins was born in 1772 in Pilton; he married Nancy Ann Dredge.
5. John Hawkins was born in 1774 in Pilton.
6. Thomas Hawkins was born in 1779 in Pilton.
7. Elizabeth Hawkins was born in 1781 Pilton.

John Stokes, her father, died on 19 December 1801.

CHAPTER 17

Somerset-Gloucester Generations

Peter Hawkins (1687-1758)
Frances Huntley (1699-1781)

Children of Peter Hawkins and Frances Huntley

1. John Hawkins was baptized in 1722 in Boxwell, Gloucester, England. He married Martha; they had eight children: Jane Huntley in 1754; Samuel, born on 1756; Eleanor, born on 1758; Sarah, born on 1760; John, born on 1762; Joseph, born on 1764, married twice; George, born on 1765; Sarah, born on 1767; and Mary, born on 1769.
2. Richard Hawkins was baptized on 7 February 1725 in Pilton, Somerset.
3. Robert Hawkins was baptized on 11 October 1727 in Pilton, Somerset.
4. William Hawkins was baptized on 8 December 1731 in Pilton, Somerset. He married Mary (Reeves), and their children are Fanny, baptized on September 1761 and James baptized 1765.
5. Mary Hawkins was baptized on 25 June 1734 in Pilton, Somerset.
6. George Hawkins was baptized on 14 April 1737 in Pilton, Somerset. He married Mary Stokes on 26 February 1759 by license. She was baptized on 28 February 1741 of Pylle, and her death date is unknown. George was buried on 19 December 1801.

* * * * * * * * * * *

Photo on postcard, postmark date 1906.
Postcards first available in 1906.
John the Baptist Anglican Church in Pilton.

Children of John Hawkins
(Sixth great-grandparent)

John Hawkins first married Hana (Hanna) Brook who died in childbirth in 1684. Second marriage was to (Garjhad) or Gertrude (?) in Pilton, Somerset. John was a sexton and caretaker of the church.

1. Peter Hawkins was baptized on 4 November 1687 and was buried on 26 April 1758. He married Frances Huntley before 1721.
2. Flana Hawkins was baptized on 25 November 1691 (or Hana).
3. Gertrude Hawkins was baptized on 24 October 1693 and was buried on 30 Sept 1728.
4. John Hawkins was baptized on 3 ? 1697. He was buried on 12 Aug 1778.
5. Elizabeth Hawkins was baptized on 25 January 1699; she was buried on 15 May 1702.
6. Samuel Hawkins (1699).
7. George Hawkins was baptized on 1 October 1704.

Order of children is unclear, but it is clearly marked in stone that Peter Hawkins died in 1758 at seventy-one years of age, making his birth year 1687. Register records reflect baptismal date is the fourth of November 1687. I strongly suspect that John Hawkings's first wife died in childbirth as death date for Hana is July 11, 1684. Second marriage to Gertrude (?) in Pilton, Somerset. John was sexton and caretaker of the church.

The Siblings of Peter Hawkins

Peter Hawkins was baptized on 4 November 1687 in Pilton, the son of John and (probably Garjhed, which was very difficult to read) Gertrude Hawkins. Peter was buried on the twenty-sixth of April 1758 at seventy-one years of age. He married Frances Huntley before 1721 in Gloucestershire or Pilton, Somerset. No marriage record could be found.

The early Pilton parish records are a challenge to decipher due to the variety of penmanship and heavy ink used. When listing the baptismal records during the early 1700s, only the child's name and that they are a son or daughter, and the name of the father is included, not the child's mother.

The church warden records of Pilton, which is different from parish records, report that Peter Hawkins was paid for rethatching the vicar's roof, and on another date, he was paid for work "removing snow from the leads." Supposedly, this was the roof gutters or down spouts.

Notes in the parish records record that Peter Hawkins, who married Frances Huntley, was the son of John Hawkings and was baptized on the fourth of November 1687. The parish record also suggests that John Hawkings is the son of Pettor Hawkings, baptized on 1650.

The monument inscription on the wall at Pilton clearly states that Frances Huntley and Peter Hawkins are man and wife. One question that remains is, "How did they meet if her family was in Boxwell and Peter is in Pilton? The two villages are nearly 75 miles apart." There must have been a reason that the monument was placed in the church at Pilton. The bishop's records noted that "upon his death, Rector Wykes Huntley served faithfully for 37 years at Boxwell Parish in Gloucester." At the Pilton church, the amount listed on the accounts for the church recorded that Mrs. Mary Huntley (wife of Wykes Huntley) was one of the larger contributors that tithed to the church.

"John the Baptist" Anglican Church in Pilton

The church has been at this location for over one thousand years.
The Hawkins family attended from before 1650s to 1801
(photo taken in 2008).

CHAPTER 18

Joining of the Hawkins and Huntley Families in 1722

BOXWELL IS A parish and a village. The parish register dates from the year 1548. The old manor house was the court or house of the abbot of Gloucester. The Huntleys leased and then purchased the freehold of Sir Walter Raleigh, to whom it was granted by Queen Elizabeth I. Henry Huntley, Esquire, was the lord of the manor in 1615 and principal landowner. The land area is 2,266 acres.

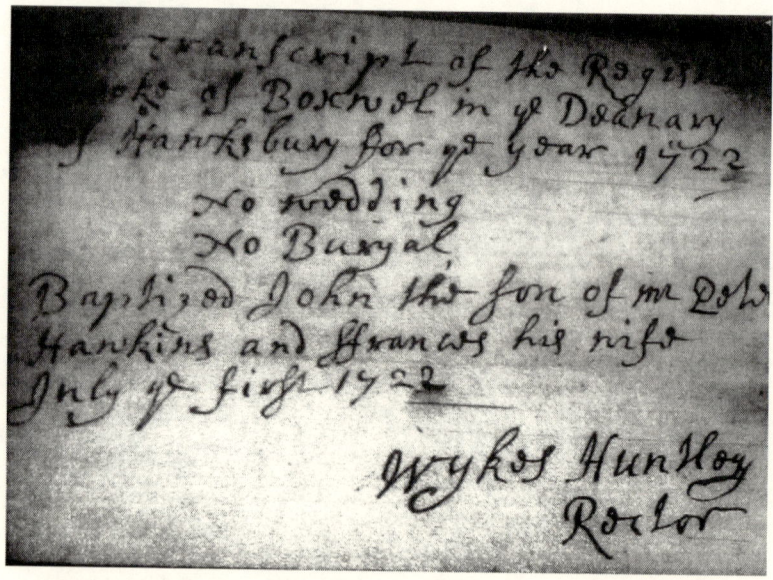

Bishop's record: "Script of the Register of Boxwell."
No Weddings, No Buryal and Baptized John the son of Mr. Pettor Hawkins and Frances his wife, July ye first 1722 . . .
—signed Wykes Huntley, Rector."

Peter Hawkins and his wife, *Frances*, baptized their first child, John Hawkins, July ye first,(Old English lettering S's appear as f) 1722. Records noted that the rector officiating at the baptism was Frances's father and John's grandfather, *Rector Wykes Huntley* from Boxwell, Gloucestershire. The baptism was noted in the parish records that was found at the Family History Library in Salt Lake City. The parish records also included the following four children of Peter and Frances were Richard (1725/26), Robert (1727), William (1731), and Mary (1734); they were all baptized at the church in Pilton, Somerset, as opposed to Boxwell, Gloucester. It was not uncommon for parents to return to the mother's home church to baptize their first child. It is assumed that they married about 1721.

The "Baptismal Record of John Hawkins," their first born,

Rev. Wykes Huntley, father of Frances (Huntley) Hawkins, graduated from Oxford University in 1688 and was rector at Boxwell and Leighton parishes in Gloucester, for nearly thirty-nine years until the year 1727. He married *Mary Codrington*, who had been the widow of William Morgan. She and Wykes were the parents of all eight of their children. Records for the children found are as follows:

1. Job Huntley, christened on 1681.
2. William Huntley, christened on 1684 at Boxwell/Leighterton.
3. Robert Huntley, christened on 1687 and buried on 1737.
4. Mary Huntley, christened on 1693.
5. John Huntley, christened on December 1694.
6. Samuel Huntley, christened about 1694.
7. Elizabeth Huntley was born on the eighth of May 1698. She died in 1720 in Pilton. A monumental stone for Elizabeth is in the floor, in an aisle, of St. John the Baptist Church in Pilton, Somerset.
8. Frances Huntley was born. The Boxwell parish record states, "Frances daughter of Wykes Huntley, Clerk, and Mary, his wife, was baptized February 29, 1699." (Despite the fact that there is no twenty-ninth in February.)

Frances died on the eighth of May 1781 at eighty-one years of age in Pilton, Somerset. Frances, Elizabeth, and Mary—along with their mother, Mary—all lived in Somerset and attended the church in Pilton.

The *bishop's records* are on file at the LDS Library in Salt Lake City, for some of the parishes, recording the baptisms, marriages, and burials for each parish. Each rector would send a monthly report to the bishop.

In 1722, Rector Wykes Huntley noted in his own handwriting that he baptized his grandson John Hawkins.

After reviewing a copy of the original records each month, I noticed that *Rector Wykes Huntley's* handwriting by 1727 appeared very unsteady, before that, his handwriting had been very legible. The following month, it was noted that he died on the twenty-ninth of January 1725 at Wells, Somerset, after being rector for thirty-nine years. Frances was the youngest of his eight children. Her mother was *Mary Codrington*, widow of William Morgan, according to the Gloucester Archives (Huntley File).

It is difficult to believe that there is not a marriage record to be found for Frances and Peter Hawkins despite her father being a rector. The records were thoroughly reviewed for Boxwell, Gloucester, and Pilton, Somerset. Another question was, how did Peter and Frances meet? In searching the list of rectors at the Pilton church, I did not find a listing of any *Huntley* as rector. The monument on the wall at John the Baptist Anglican Church in Pilton notes the names and dates for Wykes and Mary and their daughters Mary, Elizabeth, and Frances and her husband, Peter Hawkins; that they were all there in Pilton.

> A Register Book for the parish of Pilton in Somerset begining the 26:th day of March Anno Dm 1692

Records for Pilton are from 1692 to 1743.

Burial Transcript
for Rector Wykes Huntley
(a sixth great-grandfather).

"Burials of Boxwell for the year One Thousand Seven hundred Twenty Five . . . Wykes Huntley Rector of Boxwell was Buried January the Twenty Ninth."

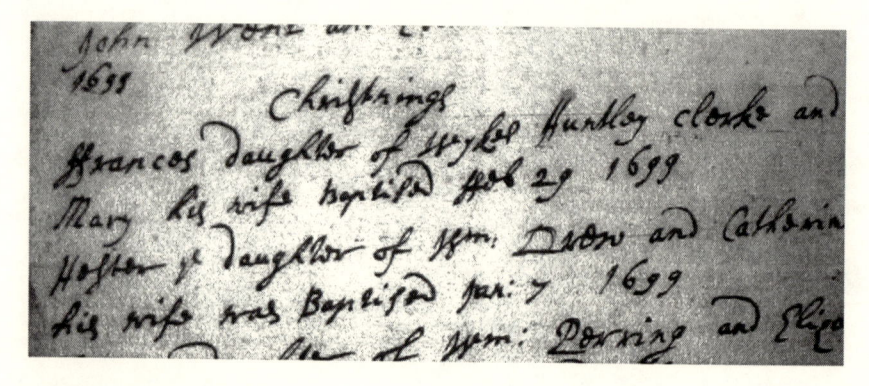

"Christenings:

Frances daughter of Wykes Huntley, clerk and Mary his wife baptised Feb 29 1699" (next entry).

These Bishop's Records are on file at the LDS Library in Salt Lake City; for only some of the parishes, recording the baptisms, marriages, and burials, the rector would send a monthly report to the bishop.

SECTION SEVEN

CHAPTER 19

A Visit to Boxwell Court

IN MAY OF 2006, while planning a trip to England, I was hoping to drive up to Gloucester to see if we could find Boxwell, the place noted on the memorial plaque in the Anglican Church at Pilton. My third cousin, Richard Welsh, a descendant of Job Hawkins, who lives in Gloucestershire, invited us to visit. I explained that our time was limited, and I hoped to find the area called Boxwell in Gloucester. He did some detective work a couple of weeks before our arrival, and he found that Boxwell was less than thirty minutes from his home in Gloucester. He gave us specific directions, and we planned to meet him at two o'clock at the church. Surprisingly, we arrived within minutes of each other, then walked through the gate and into the small St. Mary's churchyard.

Just outside the church door on the left, we noticed six or seven beautiful tabletop tombs from the sixteenth century. Unfortunately, the inscriptions were no longer readable. We entered the church through the portico into the chapel that had many monuments on the walls. I also saw and marveled at all the tombstones with the last name of Huntley that were lying flat throughout the floor.

Huntley Family Crest

St. Mary's Chapel at Boxwell Court.

Boxwell Court in Gloucester, England; chapel is on the left.

It wasn't long before a man entered the chapel and began asking us who we were. I stated that my maiden name was Hawkins and a Hawkins had married a Huntley centuries before. This handsome tall gentleman in his sixties, with his perfect Oxford accent said, "Well, my name is John Huntley." This very informative relative described the massive stone baptismal font in the chapel as one constructed in the twelfth century. He also shared that the Bellcote on the roof of the church dated from the early Saxon times. He described the three church pews along the back wall as being made from thirteenth century elm. After talking for some time, John gave me a pamphlet with the history of the church written by his father.

John went inside his home and soon returned to ask if we would like to come in for a cup of tea. His wife, Bridget, was very cordial; and we were encouraged to have a seat around their large kitchen table. John shared that their kitchen had been added onto the home when the house was updated about 1900. The kitchen was a perfect country kitchen. Bridget brought out a book on the "Huntley Family" perhaps assembled by another family member via the computer. Bridget complained that the book was difficult to use as "one gets lost in the different generations." I copied several very early names from the beginning of their family book:

Baderon came along with his brother *Wythenic* and his five sons".

John stated that it is felt that the Huntley family originated in Wales, near Monmouthshire, close to the English border, north of Cardiff, Wales.

Walter de Huntley [Sir], spouse de Hastings, living *1299*.
Thomas de Huntley, married Grudour, land of St. Britts, Netherwent, South Wales.
Thomas' son Thomas, called "Tomlyn" of the Welsh, his spouse Alice Wallis

The earliest John Huntley married Elizabeth Adam, but few dates were noted.
Boxwell Court (their family home) is attached to St. Mary's Chapel. The court was large from the outside and appeared to have seventeen stone chimneys.

Family crest above back door at Boxwell Court.

George Huntley (1563)
High Sheriff of Gloucester

Constance Ferrers, George's wife on her fortieth birthday.

Matthew Huntley, born 1580
Son of George and father of
Wykes Huntley

Carol and Richard Welsh
Bridget and John Huntley
Sue Hawkins Bell

The Early Huntleys

After tea, John asked if we would like to see some family paintings. I was delighted. The large framed oil paintings were on the wall at the top of an amazing staircase that led from the center hall. Immediately, I recognized the names on the picture frames from my research of the Huntley name. Each name was attached on the bottom edge of the picture. George Huntley (1563), high sheriff of Gloucester, pictured in black. The painting to the right was his wife, Constance Ferrers, in her fortieth year; and the lower painting was Matthew Huntley, their son, who was born about 1580, and Sylvester Wykes. She was born in 1622. Their son, Wykes Huntley, was the father of Frances Huntley, who married Peter Hawkins.

I asked if I could take a photo of the paintings, and John nodded yes. Constance was wearing a starched ruff collar of lace gathered into full folds. Men and women would both wear a ruff collar, which were all the fashion during the sixteenth and seventeenth centuries. George Huntley, the man in the painting, was wearing a goatee and mustache, a ruff, and an embroidered sash over a black jacket. George is the one who purchased the court and land from Sir Walter Raleigh in the early 1600s. George's father was Henry Huntley, a gentleman who also lived here. Henry's will was dated 1554 with no other dates known.

Above the hallway door were parts of a suit of armor. These included the gauntlets that would cover the hands and a metal helmet. John also pointed out the arched doorway in the hall dating from the Norman period. The door had once been an exterior doorway before the kitchen was added.

John Huntley explained that in the past, there was a need for a chain and lock on the baptismal font in the church because stealing the holy water had become a problem. Some felt that the water had healing powers. John also told us that the church and court were in disrepair in the early 1900s. Shortly after some renovations, his grandfather Huntley moved back into the house. John stated that his father was born in 1907 and that he is one of five children that included two brothers and two sisters. John has lived house since 1962 when his grandfather died.

I found Wykes Huntley's name in their family book. The records stated that he was born on the fifteenth of April in 1656 and that he died on the twenty-seventh of January in 1726. He matriculated (started) at Oxford University in 1672 at seventeen years of age. Their records note that his wife was Mary and that they did not know her last name. (Since that time, the Gloucester Archives revealed that it was Mary Codrington, the widow of William Morgan.) The only children noted of Wykes Huntley in their book were William, Samuel, and John, but no Frances. (Parish registers contained Job, Robert, Mary, John, Elizabeth, and Frances—a total of nine. I found it interesting that the girls, Mary, Elizabeth, and Frances, all lived later in Pilton, Somerset.)

John also told about his grandfather who, at the age of thirty-four, had a strong dislike of the Germans, so he volunteered and served in WWI. After the war, he returned to Boxwell to raise his family.

We entered the dining room, showcasing a magnificent Huntley coat of arms above the fireplace. There were more portraits along the wall in the dining room of more recent family members dating from 1840. The center of the room had a long table with eight Windsor-type chairs. John also pointed out that the door casement in the foyer was originally Norman in architecture.

John shared the reason why the neighbor called him upon our arrival. One night, an intruder in a pick-up truck attempted to steal some of the Cotswold stone from the roof of a side building. A couple of other attempts of stealing the roofing material from their property recently occurred as well. They were being very cautious of strangers since the Cotswold stone can bring in a hefty sum.

When it was time to leave, we took a minute to take several photos outside the front door. Immediately across from the front door was a lush green vale full of sheep and lambs. All that we could hear was the quiet *baaa*-ing of the sheep and chirping of birds. What a serene and peaceful landscape.

We all got back in the car and were on our way. What a wonderful memory!

Boxwell Court occupies 2,266 acres of lush green rolling hills that are dotted with over two hundred sheep. Ancient straddle stones lined the driveway. Originally, these mushroom shaped stones, about twelve to fourteen inches in height, were used to elevate small buildings. They were placed at each corner of the building for support to store grain and keep it dry and free of rodents.

The Ancient History of the Huntley Name

The Huntley family is of Anglo-Saxon origin. The Manor of Boxwell is mentioned in the *Domesday Book* in 1086. Later, it was monastic land for the Abbey of St. Peter, Gloucester, and it has been farmed since that time. For over six hundred years, since the dissolution of the monasteries and at the time of King Henry VIII, the Huntleys have been at Boxwell. In 1555, George Huntley, a family ancestor, acquired the manor and freewarren of Boxwell from James I. He purchased it from Sir Walter Raleigh, and it was granted by Queen Elizabeth I. During the Civil War, Boxwell was frequently the resting place of Prince Rupert, a nephew of King Charles I. The family members were strong royalists during the English Civil War. Walter Raleigh had possession of part of the estate of Boxwell at the beginning of the 1600s. It reverted to the crown and, later, sold to George Huntley in 1612, granted by Queen Elizabeth I, during the English Civil War. Henry Huntley, George's father, became the lord of the manor.

In the earlier centuries, the historic boxwood was a serious crop, making a useful contribution to the farm accounts. In 1793, with fifty-nine tons of large boxwood, an English shrub, was sold for over three hundred pounds. More recently, metal has replaced the role of the boxwood.

"Box is very slow growing and very fine-grained wood. Its use historically was for making rolling pins, nutcrackers, pestles and weaver's shuttles. The last serious cut of the boxwood was prior to WWI. Beyond the boxwood, a rare breed of sheep were raised and pheasants were in plentiful supply." John Huntley said that sparrow hawks and barn owls are still prevalent.

Legend states that there was once a nunnery at Boxwell and that it was sacked by the Danes during the 600-800 AD period. Old maps indicate that there was a holy well and a fish pond. The nuns would have been the doctors and nurses of their day.

More recently, people would come to collect water, which was thought to cure diseases of the eyes, from the holy well. This practice ceased about 1920.

Architectural and Historical Tidbits

Many of the surrounding towns and villages, as well as Boxwell, Evercreech, Pilton, and Batcombe, date back into the 1400s and had been previously recorded in the *Domesday Book* in 1086. William the Conqueror ordered this first census of England. In 1586, King Henry VIII ordered that every parish will document each baptism, marriage, and burial of the parish. This decree has made the parish record books available to the present time.

The bell turret on St. Mary's Church at Boxwell is unusual. Originally, the turret was thought to be a chimney from a Saxon farmhouse. Later, it was moved to the church when that house was rebuilt. A bell was added when the turret was placed on the church. This is speculation as there is a similar turret at Great Chalfield in Wiltshire.

Tabletop Tombs at Boxwell

Early Huntley's

Henry Huntley, Esquire, was the lord of the manor and principal landowner and was born in 1516, married in 1541, followed by the birth of their son *George Huntley*. In 1553, he became the high sheriff of Gloucester. He married *Constance Ferrers* in 1599, the daughter of Edward Ferrers, a coheir.

Their son *Matthew Huntley* was born on the thirteenth of January 1583. He first married Ms. *Algini*; she had a son by his half brother, and then he married *Frances Snigge*, daughter of Sir George Snigge, baron. They had eleven children, and George was their eldest son.

Their son *George Huntley*, who married *Sylvester Wykes*, daughter of Edward Wykes, was an attorney in Wells, Somerset. Their fifth son of thirteen children, *Wykes Huntley*, attended Oxford University at age seventeen, who became a rector. He married *Mary Codrington*, a widow of William Morgan. They had a large family with their youngest daughter, *Frances*, being born on the twenty-ninth of February 1699 and was married before 1722 to *Peter Hawkins* of Pilton, Somerset. (Our calendar does not have a twenty-ninth of February 1699, but that is what is recorded in the bishop's record.)

Boxwell Court (their family home) was attached to the church. The beautifully maintained court was large, with crenellations along the top edge and arrow slits on the side of the tower for decoration.

SECTION EIGHT

CHAPTER 20

Hawkins Cousins

First row, left to right: Roger Bell, Graci and Rodney Cottrell, Sylvia Cottrell, Tina Hawkins, Judy England (daughter of Lena Hawkins), John Cottrell, Graham Salvage.
Second row: Terry and Diane Miller, Ken Aylett, Sheila Savage, Beryl Hawkins, Sue Hawkins Bell, Lorna Aylett, Carole Welsh, Richard Welsh, and Trevor England, husband of Judy.

Somerset Hawkins Reunion

IN MAY OF 2008, a Hawkins reunion was planned in Somerset, England, by *Rodney Cottrell*, who now resides in South Africa and is a descendant of *Benjamin Hawkins*. Rodney arranged for the gathering of cousins in England. We met at the Clavelshay Barn Restaurant, near Broomfield, outside of North Petherton. The restaurant was tucked in among the hedgerows next to a dairy farm. Eight Hawkins cousins, plus spouses, joined in the fun. It was a day of sharing information. The following day, several of us drove to Evercreech and had an opportunity to tour the Westbrook Cottage, the ancestral home of the Hawkins family from before 1798 to 1857.

Rodney descends from *Benjamin Hawkins*, a brother of *William Dredge Hawkins*, my great-great-grandfather. In addition to Rodney, his brother John was present. *Richard Welsh*, a descendant of *Job Hawkins*, another brother, was also present. Judy, Shelia Savage, and Beryl Hawkins were all first cousins, also descending from Benjamin.

On Sunday afternoon, a "tea party" was held at the newly renovated Pilton Tithe Barn. This fourteen-century building had deteriorated and, after being renovated, is open again for community events. Originally, it had been used as a tithe barn to hold produce from farms in the area, for the Glastonbury Abbey, one of the largest abbeys in England

Sunday evening, we joined Rodney and Graci, his wife, for dinner with friends in their home in Bridgewater. We had a lovely time and a beautiful elegant meal with many good laughs.

Traveling with Our Australian Haine Cousins

In 2006, we traveled to Sydney, Australia, and met my third cousin, Michael Haine, and his wife, Cleo. While we were in Australia, they gave us the grand tour of Sydney. In 2008, we once again joined up with them, but this time, we met in Prague. We were booked passage on a twelve-day cruise on the Danube River.

Michael's branch of the Haine family had emigrated from Over, Gloucester, to New South Wales, Australia. Michael's great-grandfather, George Haine, was brother of Mary Haine, my great-grandmother. They were brother and sister four generations ago. George's son, Ernest, immigrated to New South Wales, Australia, in about the 1880s.

After our Danube River cruise, Michael and Cleo continued their trip and traveled to Greece and Turkey before flying to New York City. They had an around-the-world ticket. From New York, they traveled across Pennsylvania by train to Pittsburgh, where we met up again for a week in Canfield, Ohio. What fun, meeting up with family from halfway around the world!

Cleo and Michael Haine, family from Sydney, Australia, at Clover Hill in Ohio, 2008.

Fellow Researchers

David Walsh and Hanna Nicholas, Londoners, are two cousins who have been key in the Haine family research. Their enthusiasm and knowledge have been an inspiration. In 1999, David was a college student conducting a family research project. In hopes of finding an Ohio branch of the Hawkins-Haine family, he sent a letter to my mother and father's home in Warren, Ohio. David questioned what might have happened to this branch of the family. Through his cunning research and the 1920 census records, he found a Lloyd Hawkins on the computer. My father had died seventeen years prior to this, but the address and phone number had remained the same in the whitepages.com section on the computer. My mother passed along his letter, and I immediately e-mailed and shared the information that I knew. David has since visited us twice in Ohio, first in the year 2000 and then again in 2005 for our Haine and Hawkins reunions.

Together, we joined in researching death records, wills, and estates at the archives and census records at the Warren-Trumbull County Library. David is the author of a hundred-page book titled *The Haine Family—2000*. It is a remarkable piece of work that traces Haine lines of the family to Canada, United States, Australia, New Zealand, India, Africa, England, and the West Indies. He also contacted numerous Haine relatives who were still living in England and gathered family stories. He lives in London and has shared my name with numerous other cousins. This has been most helpful. One doesn't know David Walsh long to realize that he has a brilliant photographic memory and has endless energy.

Hanna, who also lives in London, has been working and sharing information with David on the Haine family. This has led to finding many new sources. In 2006, Hanna and I flew to Salt Lake City to spend a week researching the archives from 9:00 AM to 9:00 PM daily at the Mormon Family History Library. This was Hanna's third visit to Salt Lake City from London. She found that the parish records on film were much easier to research than trying to go to each village, church, or record office in England. In addition to researching the Haine family, she has continued with numerous marital lines.

While in Salt Lake City, I had to smile when the taxi driver taking us to the airport asked what we were doing in town. Our reply was that we were researching family history. He said with a Western cowboy drawl, "Most people know more about the pedigree of their horse than they do their own family."

On various visits to London, I found that Hanna kindly shared with us the sights of Kew Gardens and Windsor Castle. She also joined us for weekends in Somerset at various B&Bs such as The Hurling Pot, Lydford, and at Batcombe Farm. We have taken in more ancient churches, graveyards, and numerous curving countryside hedgerows than one could count. Additionally, we took a nighttime tour of Hornblotten, Somerset, down a one-way road in the dark of night. She is such a fun fellow traveler!

Richard Welsh, a third cousin from Gloucestershire and descendant of Job Hawkins, once shared, "Folklore says that if you were 'landed gentry' the first or oldest son would inherit the land, the second son would become an army officer and the third would become a parson . . . not sure what the rest were supposed to do!"

So if the second son happened to be no good at soldiering, you'd lose an empire, and if the third thought being a parson was just a matter of writing eloquent sermons, your country would go down the drain morally.

"A fellow who was rector or vicar of two churches, that were as far apart as five miles, one could not have pastored in both places. He would probably have taken the income and then hired a curate to stand in for him in one or both places. If he was conscientious, he would have taken only one church. The Evangelical Revival changed this, and it was partly sparked by the Methodist success in the 18th Century."

But I feel proud to say that Rector Wykes Huntley appears to have been well educated at Oxford University and was active for thirty-seven years as rector, performing baptisms, marriages, and burials until his death in 1726.

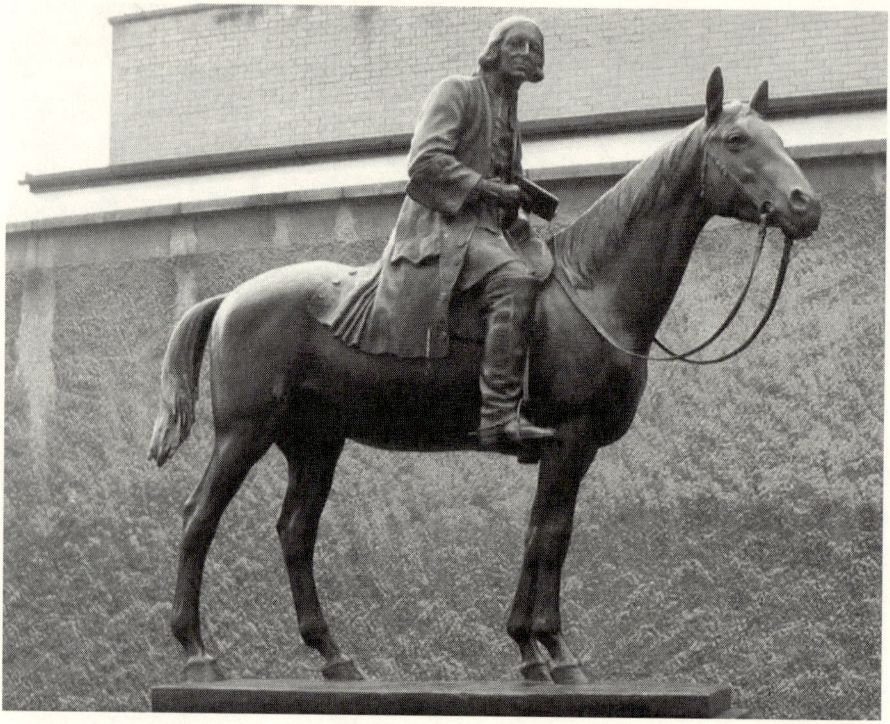

CHAPTER 21

John Wesley
Founder of the Methodist Church

DURING THE EARLY 1700s, John Wesley was born in the north of England, in Epworth, near Lincoln, along with his brother Charles Wesley, the songwriter. Charles wrote the words to over six thousand hymns. Their father, Samuel, was a rector of the church in Epworth, who attended Oxford University. John attended Christ Church, Oxford. Wesley and John helped to organize Christians throughout England, Scotland, Wales, and Ireland.

At this time, the Anglican Church was the Church of England. The early Methodists were largely drawn from the poorer classes, such as the tin miners of Cornwall and urban poor, whom the Church of England ignored. The established church, both Anglicans and aristocrats, treated the Methodist movement with deep suspicion. They were called Methodists for their emphasis of methodical study and devotion. Under Wesley's direction, the Methodist became leaders in many social injustices of the day, including prison reform and abolition movements. John Wesley was a keen abolitionist. He spoke out and wrote against the slave trade. He was a friend of John Newton, who was also influential in the abolition of slavery in Britain.

Throughout his life, Wesley remained within the Church of England and insisted that his movement was well within Anglican tradition. Church policy put him at odds with many within the Church of England, but he was widely respected toward the end of his life.

He was born in 1703, the fifteenth of twenty-five children. At the age of five, John was rescued from the burning rectory. This escape made a deep impression on his mind, and he felt set apart with a deep religious experience.

In his adult life, John Wesley never stopped preaching the importance of faith for salvation. John recognized the open-air services were successful in reaching men and women who would not otherwise enter most churches.

From that time, he took the opportunities to preach wherever an assembly would gather together. "The world was his parish." Wesley continued for fifty years, entering churches when he was invited and taking his stand in the fields, in halls, and chapels when the churches would not receive him.

The expansion of lay preachers was one of the keys of the growth of Methodism. Wesley traveled generally on horseback, preaching two or three times each day. It is noted that he rode two-hundred-fifty-thousand miles, gave away thirty thousand pounds, and preached more than forty-thousand sermons.

Wesley died on 2 March 1791 at eighty-seven years of age. He stated upon his death, "The best of all is that God is with us." He left 135,000 members and 541 itinerant preachers under the name Methodist.

The Methodist Chapel in Pilton dates back to 1794 with the present building opening in 1849. William Haine (1769-1853) was the founder and architect of the church. He was the brother of John Haine, a direct ancestor, and father of William Haine, who immigrated to Bloomfield, Ohio. William and Mary Haine in Ohio were faithful Methodists throughout their lives.

* * * * * * * * * * * *

Faith in the Family

When visiting the Pilton Methodist Chapel on a Sunday several years ago, we were drawn to the memorial tablets on the front wall of the church. It noted, "In memory of *William Haine* and *Betty Scott*." William was responsible for building this church in 1849 and two other churches in about 1850. He was born in 1769 in Pilton; he died in 1853. Betty (1778-1845) was from West Pennard, Somerset, England. "Both Lived and Died in the Faith." Both are buried in the churchyard. William Haine and Betty Scott are named on the flyleaf of a "Life of John Wesley" belonging to their descendants in Gloucestershire.

In memory of William Haine, born 1806 and died in the nineteenth of June 1898 at ninety-one years of age. And his wife *Eliza Cook* was born about 1815 and died on the fourth of January 1892 at eighty-one years. William is the son of William and Betty Scott.

An inscription was placed up high on the wall at the Pilton Chapel for William and Eliza: "Lord, I have loved the habitation of thy house, and the place where thine honour dwelleth."

Rarely did he miss a church service. He was helping in the hayfield just before he died at eighty-one years. "What a sermon! I would not have missed it for a sovereign."

During eighty years connection with the Wesleyan Society, he had filled all its offices and was, for many years, superintendent of the local Wesleyan School. They were buried in the churchyard.

* * * * * * * * * * *

Of the Haine and Hawkins families in England, many became Methodist ministers and traveled to different parts of the world.

Benjamin Hawkins, son of Peter and Nancy Hawkins, was committed to the faith at the Wesleyan Methodist Church in Glastonbury. Stained glass windows in the church continue in his memory and that of his son Henry Hawkins, who was mayor and alderman in Glastonbury. Benjamin was a trustee, superintendent of the Wesleyan Sunday school, and builder of many churches, chapels, and public halls. These were built in Somerset and will continue to be monuments to his sound workmanship.

Rev. Cuthbert Haine, from Pittsburgh, served in the Methodist church throughout the Pennsylvania area. He was born on 1910 and lived until 2003. Cuthbert was the grandson of John Haine, born in Tintinhull, Somerset, in 1844.

Rev. James Goddard Hawkins, born in Street, Somerset, and immigrated in 1850, went into the ministry, preaching in various churches in Ohio and Pennsylvania.

Family names reflecting the Methodist background are John Wesley Haine, Susanna Wesley Hawkins, and Emma Hawkins, Methodist deaconess, plus Wykes Huntley who was a rector for thirty-seven years in Boxwell, Gloucester.

A Final Word

Life is just a series of journeys, traveling from one place to another and full of adventures. Hopefully, future generations will find this journey more than just a list of names and dates. Instead, I hope that it will bring a sense of history, family and self. When sharing our history and stories it allows us to know who we are. It is with pride that our ancestors were able to learn, make decisions, take risks and love one another. Our respect for their hardships, losses, and perseverance, while building a life for their family, has brought us to where we are today.

Research is always an ongoing project. Descendant charts for the Hawkins and Haine family genealogy are included.

Villages in the Mendip Hill of Somerset.

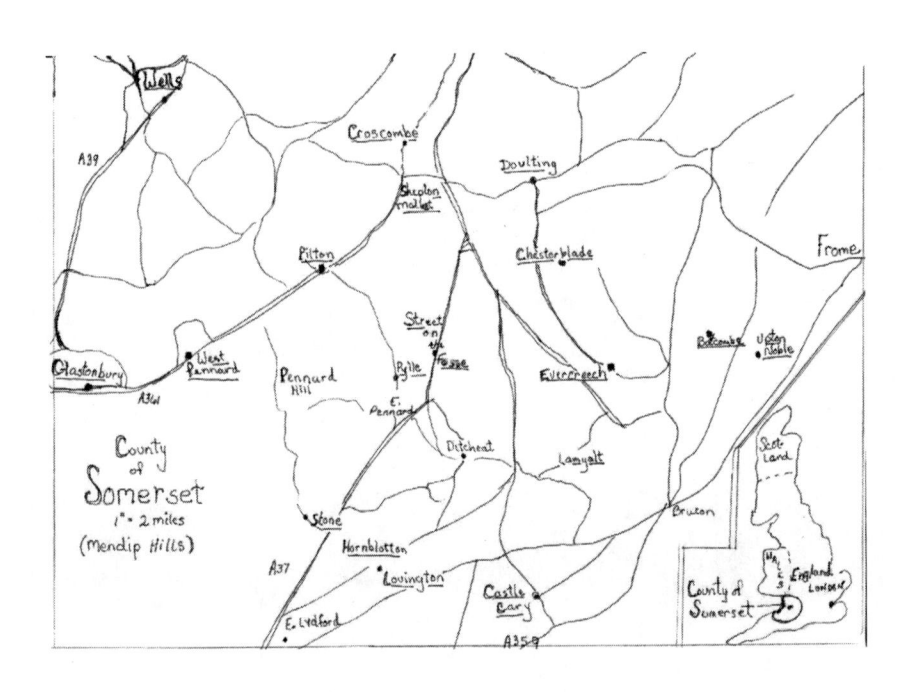

Hawkins-Huntley Linage Chart

Hawkins-Huntley Lineage Chart Page 1

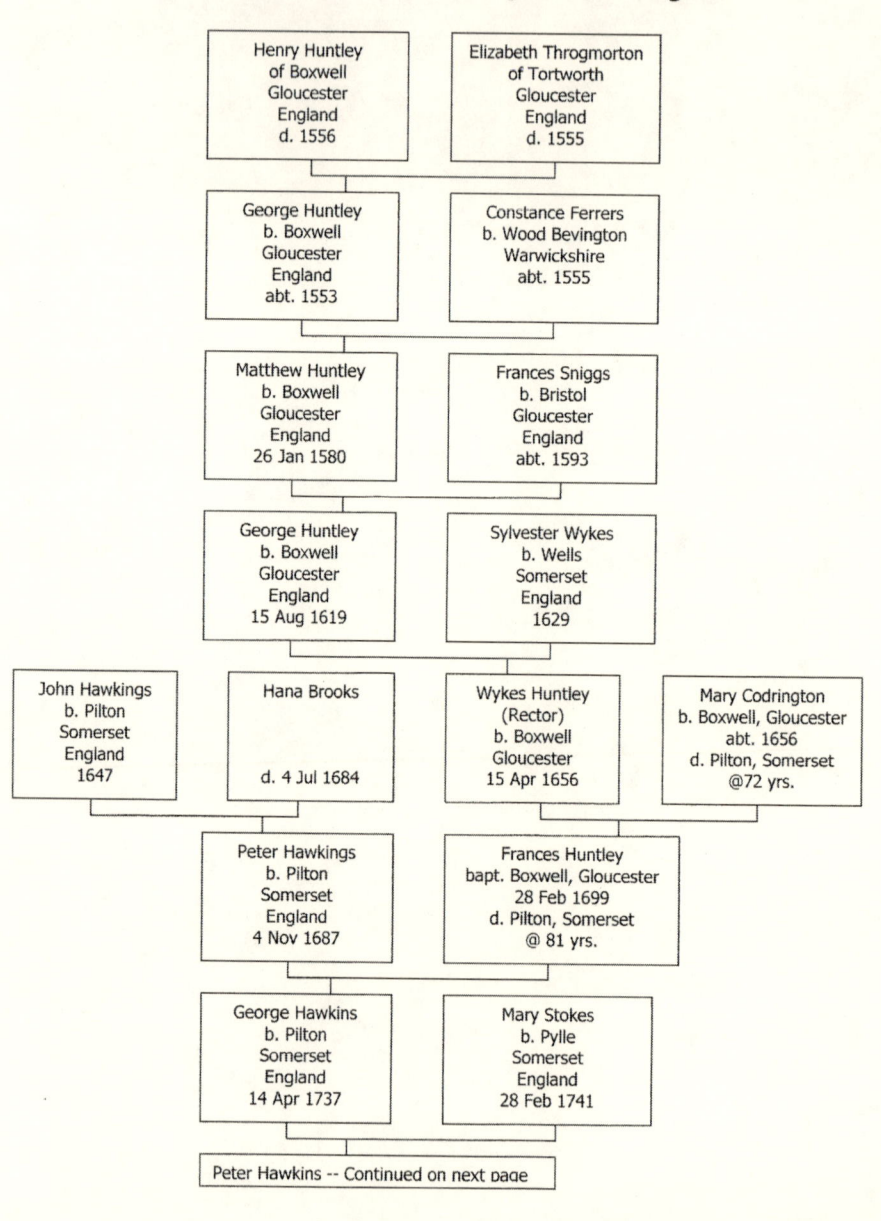

- Henry Huntley
  of Boxwell
  Gloucester
  England
  d. 1556

- Elizabeth Throgmorton
  of Tortworth
  Gloucester
  England
  d. 1555

- George Huntley
  b. Boxwell
  Gloucester
  England
  abt. 1553

- Constance Ferrers
  b. Wood Bevington
  Warwickshire
  abt. 1555

- Matthew Huntley
  b. Boxwell
  Gloucester
  England
  26 Jan 1580

- Frances Sniggs
  b. Bristol
  Gloucester
  England
  abt. 1593

- George Huntley
  b. Boxwell
  Gloucester
  England
  15 Aug 1619

- Sylvester Wykes
  b. Wells
  Somerset
  England
  1629

- John Hawkings
  b. Pilton
  Somerset
  England
  1647

- Hana Brooks
  d. 4 Jul 1684

- Wykes Huntley
  (Rector)
  b. Boxwell
  Gloucester
  15 Apr 1656

- Mary Codrington
  b. Boxwell, Gloucester
  abt. 1656
  d. Pilton, Somerset
  @72 yrs.

- Peter Hawkings
  b. Pilton
  Somerset
  England
  4 Nov 1687

- Frances Huntley
  bapt. Boxwell, Gloucester
  28 Feb 1699
  d. Pilton, Somerset
  @ 81 yrs.

- George Hawkins
  b. Pilton
  Somerset
  England
  14 Apr 1737

- Mary Stokes
  b. Pylle
  Somerset
  England
  28 Feb 1741

Peter Hawkins -- Continued on next page

Hawkins-Huntley Lineage Chart Page 2

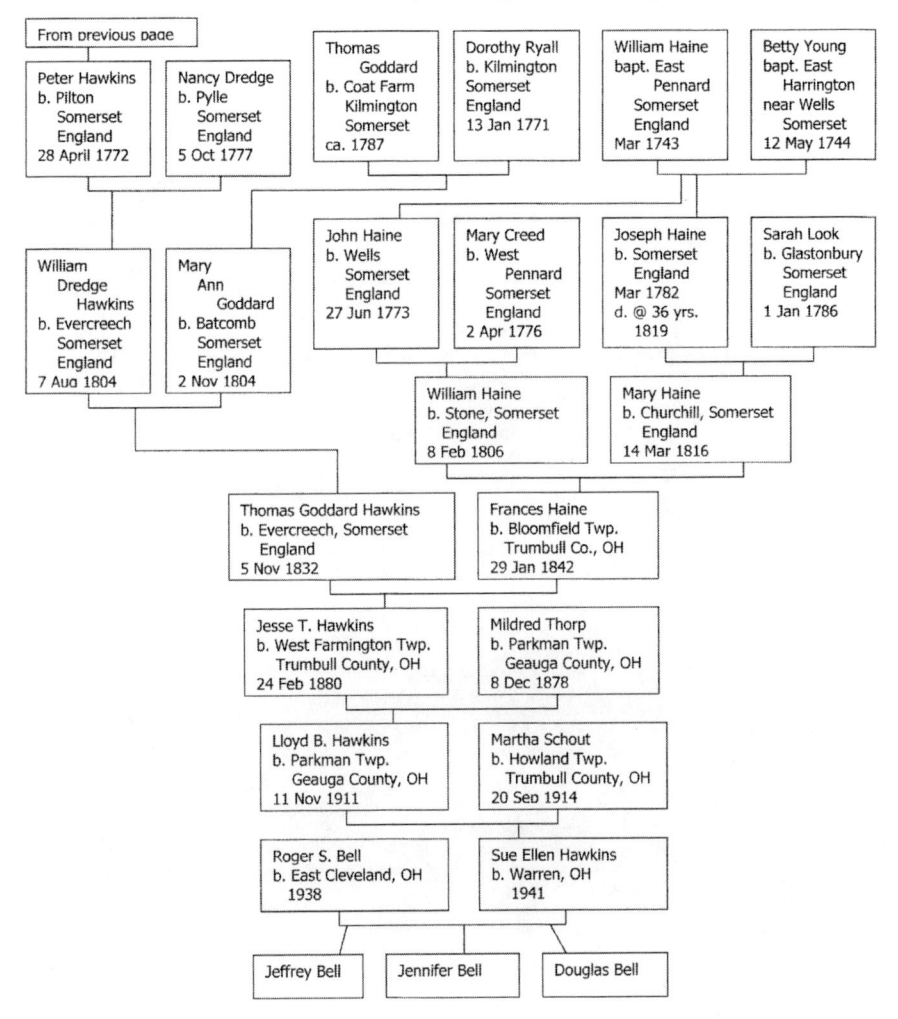

From previous page

- **Peter Hawkins**
  b. Pilton
  Somerset
  England
  28 April 1772

- **Nancy Dredge**
  b. Pylle
  Somerset
  England
  5 Oct 1777

- **Thomas Goddard**
  b. Coat Farm
  Kilmington
  Somerset
  ca. 1787

- **Dorothy Ryall**
  b. Kilmington
  Somerset
  England
  13 Jan 1771

- **William Haine**
  bapt. East
  Pennard
  Somerset
  England
  Mar 1743

- **Betty Young**
  bapt. East
  Harrington
  near Wells
  Somerset
  12 May 1744

- **William Dredge Hawkins**
  b. Evercreech
  Somerset
  England
  7 Aug 1804

- **Mary Ann Goddard**
  b. Batcomb
  Somerset
  England
  2 Nov 1804

- **John Haine**
  b. Wells
  Somerset
  England
  27 Jun 1773

- **Mary Creed**
  b. West Pennard
  Somerset
  England
  2 Apr 1776

- **Joseph Haine**
  b. Somerset
  England
  Mar 1782
  d. @ 36 yrs.
  1819

- **Sarah Look**
  b. Glastonbury
  Somerset
  England
  1 Jan 1786

- **William Haine**
  b. Stone, Somerset
  England
  8 Feb 1806

- **Mary Haine**
  b. Churchill, Somerset
  England
  14 Mar 1816

- **Thomas Goddard Hawkins**
  b. Evercreech, Somerset
  England
  5 Nov 1832

- **Frances Haine**
  b. Bloomfield Twp.
  Trumbull Co., OH
  29 Jan 1842

- **Jesse T. Hawkins**
  b. West Farmington Twp.
  Trumbull County, OH
  24 Feb 1880

- **Mildred Thorp**
  b. Parkman Twp.
  Geauga County, OH
  8 Dec 1878

- **Lloyd B. Hawkins**
  b. Parkman Twp.
  Geauga County, OH
  11 Nov 1911

- **Martha Schout**
  b. Howland Twp.
  Trumbull County, OH
  20 Sep 1914

- **Roger S. Bell**
  b. East Cleveland, OH
  1938

- **Sue Ellen Hawkins**
  b. Warren, OH
  1941

- Jeffrey Bell
- Jennifer Bell
- Douglas Bell

Ten Generations of Hawkins Family

Descendants of John Hawkings, Sr.

1 [1] John Hawkings, Sr. b: Abt. 1647 in Pilton,Som.,Eng. d: 14 Nov 1728 in Pilton, Som. at 81 yrs.
.... +Hanna Brooks m: Bef. 1671 in Pilton, Somerset, England d: 04 Jul 1684 in Pilton, Somerset
...... 2 Ann Hawkings b: 02 Jan 1671
...... 2 James Hawkings b: Jul 1673
...... 2 Elizabeth Hawkings b: 18 Dec 1675
...... 2 Mary Hawkings b: 01 Apr 1677
...... 2 Martha Hawkings b: 21 Apr 1679 in Pilton, Som.
...... 2 John Hawkings b: 01 Oct 1682 in Pilton, Som.
...... 2 Hana Hawkings b: 04 Jul 1684 in Pilton, Som. d: 11 Jul 1684 in Pilton, Somerset
*2nd Wife of [1] John Hawkings, Sr.:
.... +Hana Brooks m: Abt. 1684 in Pilton, Somerset, England d: 04 Jul 1684 in Pilton , Somerset
...... 2 George Hawkings b: 07 Feb 1685 in Pilton, Som. d: 27 Feb 1732
...... 2 PETER HAWKINGS b: 04 Nov 1687 in Pilton,Som.,Eng. d: 26 Apr 1758 in Pilton Church of England, at 71 yrs. Burial: Plaque on wall of Pilton Anglican Church
.... +FRANCES HUNTLEY b: 28 Feb 1699 in Bapt. Boxwell, Glos. England m: Bef. 1722 in Memorial on wall of Pilton Anglican Church d: 08 May 1781 in Pilton, Som. (at 81 yrs.) Burial: Heiress of Edward Wykes, Recorder of Wells 1644 of Shiplate, Som.
.... 3 [2] John (Sexton) Hawkins b: 01 Jul 1722 in Boxwell, Gloucester, England d: 12 Aug 1778 in Pilton, Somerset, England
.... +Mary???
.... 4 [3] Samuel Hawkins b: 17 Mar 1756 in Pilton, Somerset, England
.... 4 [4] Sarah Hawkins b: 06 Jun 1760 in Pilton, Somerset, England
.... 4 [5] John Hawkins b: 29 Jul 1762 in Pilton, Somerset, England
.... +[6] Mary ???
.... 5 [7] George Hawkins b: 28 May 1783 in Pilton, Somerset, England
.... 4 [8] George Hawkins b: 07 May 1765 in Pilton, Somerset, England
.... 4 [9] Sarah Hawkins b: 20 Jun 1767 in Pilton, Somerset, England
.... *2nd Wife of [2] John (Sexton) Hawkins:
.... +Martha (sec. wife m: Bef. 1765
.... 4 [3] Samuel Hawkins b: 17 Mar 1756 in Pilton, Somerset, England
.... 4 Eleanor Hawkins b: 08 Apr 1758 in Pilton, Somerset, England
.... 4 [4] Sarah Hawkins b: 06 Jun 1760 in Pilton, Somerset, England
.... 4 [5] John Hawkins b: 29 Jul 1762 in Pilton, Somerset, England
.... +[6] Mary ???
.... 5 [7] George Hawkins b: 28 May 1783 in Pilton, Somerset, England
.... 4 [8] George Hawkins b: 07 May 1765 in Pilton, Somerset, England
.... 4 [9] Sarah Hawkins b: 20 Jun 1767 in Pilton, Somerset, England
.... 3 Richard Hawkins b: 07 Feb 1725 in Pilton, Somerset, England
.... 3 Robert Hawkins b: 11 Oct 1727 in Pilton, Somerset, England
.... 3 [10] William Hawkins b: 08 Dec 1731 in Pilton, Somerset, England
.... +Ann ? (widow) m: 1754
.... *2nd Wife of [10] William Hawkins:
.... +Mary Reeves (widow) b: Abt. 1730 m: 14 Jul 1755 d: 14 Sep 1783
.... 4 Fanny Hawkins b: 06 Sep 1761 in Pilton,Som.,Eng.
.... 4 James Hawkins b: 03 Dec 1765 in Pilton,Som.,Eng. d: 06 Jan 1766 in Pilton, Somerset, England
.... 3 Mary Hawkins b: 23 Jun 1734 in Pilton, Somerset, England
.... +William Dunkerton m: 10 May 1767 in Pilton, Somerset, England
.... 3 GEORGE HAWKINS b: 14 Apr 1737 in Pilton, Somerset, England d: 19 Dec 1801 in Pilton, Somerset, England Burial: 19 Dec 1801 Pilton, Somerset, England, St. John the Baptist
.... +Mary Stokes b: 28 Feb 1741 in Of Pylle, Christened at Cossington, Som m: 26 Feb 1759 in By lic.. Pylle, Som. Eng. d: 1803 in Pilton,Som.,Eng.
.... 4 Robert Hawkins b: 27 Feb 1765 in Pilton, Somerset, England
.... +Mary Sheppard b: Abt. 1770 m: 30 Nov 1788 in Wells, Somerset, Eng.
.... 5 Harriet Hawkins b: 15 May 1788 in Pilton, Somerset, England
.... 5 Honour Hawkins b: 24 Apr 1793 in Pilton, Somerset, England
.... 5 Henrieta Hawkins b: 13 May 1798 in Pilton, Somerset, England
.... 5 Henry Hawkins b: 22 May 1804 in Pilton, Somerset, England
.... 5 Hester Hawkins b: 18 Sep 1805 in Pilton, Somerset29-11-1800

.... 4 Sarah Hawkins b: 25 Jan 1767 in Pilton, Somerset, England
.... +Robert Griffin m: 20 Oct 1795
.... 4 George Hawkins b: 13 Aug 1769 in Pilton, Somerset, England d: in (resided in Frome, Som)
.... +Mary Loxton m: 02 Apr 1799
.... 5 Samuel Hawkins b: 10 Jul 1799 in Pilton
.... 5 Hennery Hawkins b: 23 Jul 1801 in Pilton.
.... 5 Peter Hawkins b: 29 Jul 1804 in (Glazier) d: in Resided in Frome, Somerset
.... 5 Frances Hawkins b: 24 Nov 1805 in B. 23 Oct 1805
.... 5 James Hawkins b: 30 May 1808 in Born 5 Mar 1808 in Pilton
.... 5 Mary Hawkins b: 08 Mar 1812 in Born 8 Feb. 1812 at Pilton
.... 4 PETER HAWKINS b: 28 Apr 1772 in Pilton,Somerset ,England d: 26 Apr 1822 in Westbrook Cottage, Evercreech, Som., Eng.
.... +Nancy (Ann) Dredge b: 05 Oct 1777 in Pylle, Somerset, Eng. m: 01 Mar 1797 in Pylle,Somerset,England d: 06 Sep 1846 in Westbrook, Evercreech, Somerset,Eng. Fact 1: 1797 Marriage witnesses: Thom.Ivey, and Fact 2: John Dredge. Burial: 06 Sep 1846 At 67 yrs.
.... 5 Thomas Hawkins b: 04 Apr 1798 in Pilton, Somerset ,21-12-1797 d: 20 Nov 1880 in Westbrook House, Evercreech, Somerset,England Fact 1: 1798 Stone leaning on side of church. Burial: St. Peter's Church, Evercreech (stone present) Occupation: 200 acres- farmer
.... +Sarah Haine b: Abt. 1799 in Pilton, Somerset m: 05 Apr 1823 in Pilton , England -0- children d: 08 May 1867 in Westbrook Cottage, Evercreech, Somerset @68 yrs Burial: 13 May 1867 Evercreech, Somersetshire,England
.... 5 [11] George Hawkins b: 15 Sep 1799 in Pilton, Somerset, England (bapt.) d: 30 Jul 1863 in Midsomer Norton, Som(bur. Evercreech).
.... +/// Coliford
.... *2nd Wife of [11] George Hawkins:
.... +Ann Creighton b: 1802 in Evercreech, Somerset, Eng. m: 07 Feb 1828 in Evercreech, Somerset, England (Banns) d: 16 Dec 1852 in Evercreech, Somerset, Eng.(burial).
.... 6 Sarah Hawkins b: 17 Jul 1828 in Bapt. Evercreech, +9 Nov 1828
.... +Richard Ashman m: 1858 in Evercreech, Somerset, England
.... 5 John Hawkins b: 12 Apr 1801 in Evercreech, Somerset d: 1851 in 1841 Census-carpenter in Doulting Par.
.... +Ann Parfitt b: 1806 m: 10 Oct 1830 in Midsomer Norton, Som/
.... 6 Matilda Hawkins b: 17 Aug 1828 in Doulting, Somerset, England
.... +Edward Griffin m: 09 Feb 1850
.... 5 Jane Carey Hawkins b: 10 Sep 1803 in Evercreech, Somersetshire,England d: in Somersetshire,England Burial: 16 Sep 1803 Evercreech, Somerset
.... 5 WILLIAM Dredge HAWKINS b: 07 Aug 1804 in Chesterblade Hill, Evercreech,Som.,Eng. d: 11 Oct 1895 in Bloomfield Twp,Trumbull Co.,OH. -Wheelwright and farmer Burial: Brownwood Cemetery, Bloomfield, OH
.... +Mary Ann GODDARD b: 02 Nov 1804 in Pugh's Bottom,Batcombe,Somerset,England m: 10 Nov 1831 in Batcombe,Somersetshire,England,Anglican Church d: 13 Mar 1888 in Bloomfield Twp,Trumbull Co.,OH. Burial: Brownwood Cemetery, Bloomfield, OH
.... 6 Thomas Goddard HAWKINS b: 05 Nov 1832 in Evercreech,Somerset Co.,England d: 03 Aug 1903 in W. Farmington, Trumbull Co.OH Burial: Brownwood Cemetery, Bloomfield, OH
.... +FRANCES HARRIET HAINE b: 29 Jan 1842 in Bloomfield Twp, Trumbull Co.OH m: 01 Mar 1863 in Trumbull Co.OH d: 31 May 1911 in Forest Depot,VA, Bur:Bloomfield OH. Burial: Brownwood Cemetery, Bloomfield, OH
.... 7 Emma Hawkins b: 13 Feb 1864 in Bloomfield, Trumbull Co.OH d: 07 Mar 1893 in San Francisco,Ca, at 29 yrs. as deaconess -Meth.Church Burial: Died of smallpox, bur. San Francisco
.... 7 George William Hawkins b: 08 Feb 1865 in Bloomfield Twp,Trum. Co,OH d: 06 Oct 1868 in Cooperstown, PA Burial: "died from eatting too many grapes", perhaps dehydration
.... 7 Pliny Haine Hawkins b: 28 Oct 1869 in Bloomfield Twp,Trumbull Co.,OH. d: 15 Sep 1940 in Long Beach , CA
.... +Grace Alice Milner b: 20 Oct 1869 in BeetownTownship, Grant County, Wisconsin m: 01 Jan 1900 in Salt Lake City, Utah d: 16 Nov 1944 in Palos Verdes Estates, California
.... 8 [15] Milner Haine Hawkins b: 19 Oct 1901 in Columbus, Montana d: 02 Nov 1951 in Poughkeepsie, NY
.... +Vivian Carolyn Lansworth b: 07 Jul 1902 in Brule, Wisconsin m: 16 Dec 1925 in Iron Mountain, Michiagan d: 17 Dec 1997 in Ellensburg, WA
.... 9 [12] Milner James Hawkins b: 1927 in Caspian, Michigan
.... +Joan Young m: 28 Jan 1952 in Longview, Washington

```
                                        *2nd Wife of [12] Milner James Hawkins:
                                        +Carmen Masip Echazarreta  b: 1927 in Spain  m: 10 Dec 1955 in Mexico, D.F, Mexico  d: in
                                          res. Mexico
                                          10  Paulina Hawkins
                                     9  [13] Charles Haine Hawkins  b: 1929 in Columbus, Montana
                                        +Jacqueline Roberta Dorrington  b: 1928
                                        *2nd Wife of [13] Charles Haine Hawkins:
                                        +Ruth Maass  b: 20 Jan 1931 in Portland, OR  m: 02 Sep 1950  d: 23 Feb 1968
                                          10  Christoffer Haine Hawkins  b: 1951
                                          10  Charles Mead Hawkins  b: 1955
                                        *3rd Wife of [13] Charles Haine Hawkins:
                                        +Ida Edene Buckingham  b: 1945 in Pasco, WA  m:          1970
                                          10  Glacier Irene Hawkins  b: 1972 in Ellensburg, WA
                                        +Steven Kingsford-Smith  b: 1960 in Loveland, CO  m: 14 Oct 1995 in Port
                                          Gamble, WA
                                     9  [14] Robert Pearson Hawkins  b: 1931 in Silver City, NM  Fact 1: Dr. Of Psychology at
                                        West Virginia State  Fact 2: University.
                                        +Jane Nelson  b: 1931 in Portland, OR  m: 08 Jun 1958 in Portland, OR
                                          10  Larry Pearson Hawkins  b: 1953 in Portland, OR
                                          10  Jeffrey Milner Hawkins  b: 1954 in Portland, OR
                                            +Patty
                                        *2nd Wife of [14] Robert Pearson Hawkins:
                                        +Kathyn Kay Kott  b: 1940 in Kalamazoo, MI  m: 1970 :
                                          10  Anne Kathryn Hawkins  b: 1972
                                            +Thomas Young
                                        *2nd Wife of [15] Milner Haine Hawkins:
                                        +Wilberta Twogood Johnson  b: 1912  m: 23 Mar 1946 in Lansdowne, PA
                                     9  Angela Holbeach Hawkins  b: 1936 in Newburg, NY
                                        +Robert Fichter  b: 1923
                                          10  James Robert Fichter  b: 1979 in Scotland, CT.
                                 8  [16] Frances Milner Hawkins  b: 01 Jan 1909 in Bozeman, Montana  d: Nov 1982 in Absarokee,
                                    Montana
                                    +Carleton Wilder
                                    *2nd Husband of [16] Frances Milner Hawkins:
                                    +Joseph Walter Meek  m: 16 Aug 1933 in Absarokee, Montana  d: 1955
                                     9  Mary Milner Meek  b: 1936 in Tucson, AZ
                                        +Lawrence Locke
                                          10  Jonathan Locke  b: 1967
                                          10  Jason Locke  b: 1970
                                     9  Frances Luann Meek  b: 1939 in Glendale, CA
                                        +Yale Coombs  d: in res. CA.
                                          10  Stacy Coombs  b: 1963
                                          10  Wendy Coombs  b: 1966
                             7  Mary Alberta Hawkins  b: 03 Sep 1872 in Farmington Township, Trumbull Co.OH  d: 26 Oct 1958 in
                                Meadville,PA  Fact 1: 1911 Resided in Forest Depot,VA. at time of  Fact 2: Mothers death. Frances
                                Hawkins died  Burial: Brownwood Cemetery, Bloomfield, OH
                                +George W. Walker  b: 29 Apr 1871 in Virginia  m: 29 Apr 1896 in West Farmington, OH -0- children  d: 08
                                Aug 1960 in Meadville,Pa at 89 yrs.  Burial: Brownwood Cemetery, Bloomfield, OH
                             7  Charlotte Hawkins  b: 10 Feb 1875 in Farmington Township, Trumbull Co., OH  d: 08 Sep 1953 in
                                Warren,OH  Fact 1: Also called "Lottie"
                                +J. Ward Wolcott  m: 13 Mar 1894
                                 8  Clyde Wolcott  b: 1896  d: 1915 in Died in motorcycle accident
                                 8  Frances Wolcott  b: 07 Apr 1907 in Trumbull Co., OH  d: 31 Aug 1980 in Mayfield Hts. OH
                                    +Paul B. Rogers  m: 29 Aug 1931 in two daughters  d: in Mayfield Hts.,OH
                                     9  Carol Ann Rogers  b: 1934 in Warren, Ohio
                                        +David L. Beers  m: in Westfield, NJ
                                          10  David Rogers Beers  b: 1963
```

```
      9  Jean Rogers  b: 1939 in Warren, Ohio
         +Errol Kwait  b: in Cleveland Hts.,OH  m: Aug 1962 in 2 children
         10  Steven Paul Kwait  b: 1967
         10  Laura Ellen Kwait  b: 1969
   7  Angie Hawkins  b: 10 Nov 1876 in Farmington Township, Trumbull Co., OH  d: 25 Jan 1877 in Farmington
      Township, Trumbull
   7  Jerry Hawkins  b: 24 Feb 1880 in Farmington Township, Trumbull Co. OH  d: 24 Feb 1880 in Farmington
      Township, Trumbull Co.OH  Fact 1: 1880 Twin of Jeese, Died at birth.
   7  Jesse Thomas Hawkins  b: 24 Feb 1880 in Farmington Twp.,Trumbull Co., OH  d: 26 Oct 1957 in Warren,
      Trumbull Co. OH  Fact 1: Bur: Brownwood Cem. in Bloomfield,OH  Fact 2: Occupation:Farmer,real estate,
      Republic  Burial: 29 Oct 1957 Brownwood Cemetery, No. Bloomfield, Trum. Co., OH
      +Mildred Phoebe Thorp  b: 08 Dec 1878 in W. Farmington Twp.,Trumbull Co., OH  m: 22 Jun 1904 in
      Trumbull Co. ,OH  d: 05 Apr 1958 in Warren, Trumbull Co. OH  Burial: 07 Apr 1958 Brownwood Cemetery,
      No. Bloomfield, Trum. Co., OH
      8  Charles T. Hawkins  b: 20 Mar 1910 in Parkman, Geauga Co.,OH  d: 18 Dec 1999 in Penny Farms,
         Florida  Fact 1: Ohio State University  Fact 2: Occupation: Employed at Packard Electric- office.
         +Nancy Buckingham  b: 20 Mar 1910 in Urichsville, OH  m: 18 Jun 1938 in Warren, Trum.Co.OH  d:
         24 Apr 1987 in Penny Farms, Florida
         9  Thomas Frank Hawkins  b: 1941 in Warren, OH
            +Janet Sue Breystpraak  b: in Middleton, Ohio  m: 10 Jun 1967   no children
         9  Robert C. Hawkins  b: 1944 in Warren, Trumbull Co. OH
            +Mary Kay Branfield  b: in Warren, Trumbull Co. OH  m: Jun 1966 in Warren, Trumbull Co. OH
            10  Katherine Hawkins  b: 1968 in Michigan
               +Kevin Boardman  m: in New Wilmington, Delaware
            10  Robert Hawkins  b: 1971
               +Teresa Coppola  b: in Florida  m: 12 Jun 1997 in Boca Raton, Florida
      8  Lloyd B. Hawkins  b: 11 Nov 1911 in Parkman, Geauga Co.,OH  d: 01 Aug 1982 in Warren, Trumbull
         Co. OH  Fact 1: Occupation: Steel Mill -3 yrs, Warren City Fireman 35 yrs.  Fact 2: until retirement.
         Home construction and remodeling-  Burial: Brownwood Cemetery, No. Bloomfield, Trum. Co., OH
         +Martha Arlene Schout  b: 20 Sep 1914 in Howland Twp.,Trumbull Co. OH  m: 08 Jan 1938 in
         Howland Twp.,Trumbull Co. OH  d: 07 Feb 2007 in Warren, OH  Fact 2: General Electric on assembly
         line - 1-2 yrs.
         9  Ernest Eugene Hawkins  b: 11 Sep 1939 in Warren, Trumbull Co. OH  d: 09 Jan 1996 in
            Warren, Trumbull Co. OH  Fact 1: Occu: Wiring harness for autos at Packard Electric  Burial:
            Brownwood Cemetery, Bloomfield, Trum. Co. OH
            +Patricia Sue Heiple  b: 1942 in Champion Twp.,Trumbull Co., OH  m: 04 May 1963 in
            Champion Twp. Trumbull Co. OH
            10  Roberta Sue Hawkins  b: 1965 in Warren, Trumbull Co. OH       : Occupation:
               Needlework and stitchery.
               +Thomas King  b: 1963 in Champion Twp.,Trumbull Co., OH  m: 01 Nov 1986 in
               Warren, Trumbull Co. OH  Occupation: Meterologist with U.S. Weather Bureau
         9  Sue Ellen Hawkins  b: 1941 in Warren, Trumbull Co., OH  Occupation: R. N. ,
            quilter and hobby-genealogy.
            +Roger Stewart Bell  b: 1938 in East Cleveland, OH  m: 03 Nov 1962 in Warren, OH
            10  Jeffrey Lloyd Bell  b: 1963 in Cleveland, OH
               +Najma Begum Bachelani  b: 1963 in Mbale, Uganda  m: 21 Feb 1998 in St.Paul,
               Minnesota
            10  [17] Jennifer Elizabeth Bell  b:1965 in Cleveland, OH
               +Anthony Guy  b: in London, England  m: 15 Jun 1991 in London, England       divorced
               1994
               *2nd Husband of [17] Jennifer Elizabeth Bell:
               +James Shipman  b: 1953 in resides in Pittsburgh, PA  m: 25 Sep 1999 in
               Pittsburgh, PA
            10  Douglas Alexander Bell  b: 1968 in Cleveland, OH       1995 Married Rebecca
               Ching,
               +Tisha Goss  b:1972 in Parma Heights, Ohio  m: 02 Feb 2008 in Middleburg Hts.
               Ohio
```

.... 9 Larry Lloyd Hawkins b: 1944 in Warren, Trumbull Co. OH Fact 1: Occupation: WCI Steel- purchasing.
.... +Carol Oravecz b: 1944 in Cleveland, OH m: 26 Aug 1967 in Warren, Trumbull Co. OH Fact 1: Occupation: Dr. degree., Dir.of Day Care at Hosp.
.... 10 Michele Lynette Hawkins b: 1971 in Warren, Trumbull Co. OH Occupation: Architect; enjoyes horseback riding.
.... +Jeremy Schwartz b: 1971 in Cleveland, OH m: 21 Sep 1996 in Cleveland, OH Advanced degree in Economics.
.... 10 Meredith Paula Hawkins b: 1974 in Warren, Trum.Co.OH : Graduate of American Univ.- Public Relations.
.... +Paul Helter Melnick b: 1965 in Arlington, VA m: 18 Apr 1998 in Arlington, Va Fact 1: Occupation: Attorney, legal practice with his father.
.... 9 Mildred Anne Hawkins b: 18 Dec 1950 in Warren, Trumbull Co. OH   Resides in Warren, OH. Fact 2: Graduate of Bowling Green U.
.... 7 Ernest Hawkins b: 28 Jan 1882 in W. Farmington, Trumbull Co.OH d: 25 Apr 1930 in Yellowstone Park, WY Fact 1: Occupation: Head Bellhop at Yellowstone Fact 2: National Park's Lodge. Burial: Never married, bell hop at Yellowsttone Nat. Park
.... 6 Sarah Goddard Hawkins b: 26 Jul 1834 in Westbrook,Evercreech, Somersetshire,Eng. d: 06 Aug 1867 in Bloomfield Twp,Trumbull Co.,OH.,died at 33yrs.
.... +William Joseph Haine b: 11 Jan 1837 in Bloomfield Twp,Trumbull Co.,OH. m: 11 Aug 1862 in Warren, Trumbull Co.,OH d: 18 May 1923 in Ashville, NC. 105 Regt. OVI Infantry
.... 7 Theodosia Haine b: 15 Dec 1863 in No. Bloomfield, OH d: 10 Aug 1930 in Warren,Oh Fact 1: Never married. Fact 2: Crippled and unable to walk from approx.
.... 6 [22] Mary Ann Hawkins b: 04 Mar 1839 in Westbrook,Evercreech, Somersetshire,Eng. d: 18 Oct 1916 in Bloomfield Twp,Trumbull Co.,OH. Fact 1: 1862 Graduate of Wesleyan Seminary Fact 2: 1862 Married first cousin. Fathers were bro.
.... +[21] James Goddard Hawkins b: 19 Oct 1834 in Evercreech, Somersetshire,Eng. m: 23 Nov 1862 in Bloomfield Twp,Trumbull Co.,OH. d: 17 Oct 1916 in Bloomfield Twp,Trumbull Co.,OH.
.... 7 [23] Mary Florilla (Flora) Hawkins b: 18 Feb 1865 in Bloomfield Twp., Trum. Co OH d: 11 Nov 1919 in Farmington Twp,Trum. Co,OH
.... +[24] George Henry Fuller b: 10 Jan 1859 m: 1892 in Bloomfield, Ohio d: 27 Mar 1938 in Warren, OH
.... 8 [19] James Paul Fuller b: 08 Jul 1894 in Farmington Twp,Trum. Co,OH d: 07 Jan 1970 in Warren, OH
.... +[25] Bessie Marie Baugher m: 15 Oct 1915 in Southington Twp, Trum.Co.,OH
.... 9 [18] James Paul Fuller, Jr. b: 1918 in Warren, OH
.... +[26] Carol Louise Heckathorn m: 07 Dec 1940 in Warren, OH
.... 10 [27] Diane Elizabeth Fuller b: 1948
.... 10 [28] Barbara Ann Fuller b: 1942
.... *2nd Wife of [18] James Paul Fuller, Jr.:
.... +[29] Betty Jean Brown m: 06 Aug 1955 in Gates Mills, OH
.... 10 [30] Taina Marie Fuller b: 1958
.... 9 [31] George Emory Fuller b: 1916
.... +[32] Helen Louise Buber m: 1937
.... 10 [33] Ross Allan Fuller b: 1937
.... 10 [34] James George Fuller b: 1939
.... 10 [35] Sharyn Ann Fuller b: 1945
.... 10 [36] Janet Louise Fuller b: 1952
.... 10 [37] Carol Jean Fuller b: 1954
.... 9 [38] Norma Jean Fuller b: 1930 in Warren, OH
.... +[39] David Whiting m: 14 Dec 1957 in New York City
.... 10 [40] Mark David Whiting b: 1959
.... 10 [41] Diane Whiting b: 1962
.... *2nd Wife of [19] James Paul Fuller:
.... +[42] Ethel Mary Moore m: 16 Feb 1924 d: 25 Mar 1956 in Warren, OH
.... *3rd Wife of [19] James Paul Fuller:
.... +[43] Elizabeth Jones m: 07 Nov 1959 in Warren, OH (Tod Ave. Methodist Church)
.... 8 [44] Helen Louise Fuller b: 11 Jul 1897 in Farmington Twp., Ohio d: in Warren, OH

.... +[45] George Franklin Housel m: 03 Nov 1926 in W. Farmington, OH, (Methodist Parsonage. d: 24 May 1954 in Farmington, OH
.... 7 [46] Baby Boy Hawkins b: 04 Mar 1867 in Delaware Grove, PA
.... 7 [20] Susanna Wesley Hawkins b: 08 Jan 1869 in Cooperstown, PA d: 05 Sep 1923 in Warren, OH -No Children
.... +[47] Douglas Hill b: 03 May 1861 m: 14 Mar 1915 in Warren, Ohio d: 12 Aug 1921 in Bloomfield Twp. OH
.... *2nd Husband of [20] Susanna Wesley Hawkins:
.... +[48] John Stephens m: 12 May 1923 in North Bloomfield, Ohio
.... 7 [49] William David Hawkins b: 25 Sep 1871 in Ellsworth twp. Mahoning Co. OH d: 10 Sep 1920 in at 49 yrs.and single
.... 7 [50] Baby Girl Hawkins b: 12 Mar 1874 in Mantua, Ohio
.... 7 [51] James Goddard Hawkins, Jr. b: 28 Feb 1877 d: 07 Sep 1900 in N. Bloomfield, OH at 23 yrs of thyphoid, single
.... 6 Martha Hawkins b: 17 Apr 1842 in Somersetshire,England d: 20 Oct 1844 in Montreal, Lower Canada,Canada
.... 5 Mary Hawkins b: 17 Aug 1806 in Evercreech,Somerset, England d: in England
.... +William Dredge b: Abt. 1803 in Somerset, England m: 05 Apr 1826 in Evercreech, Somerset, witnesses: Thomas and Sarah Goddard. d: in "Uncle William" sent letters to Wm. Hawkins in Ohio.
.... 5 James Hawkins b: 22 Aug 1808 in Evercreech,Somerset,England- bapt. d: 11 Dec 1840 in Street on Fosse, Somerset, Eng. at 32 years of age. Burial: 20 Dec 1840 Somerset Co. England
.... +Dorothy Goddard b: 31 Jul 1806 in Batcombe, Somerset, England m: 07 Apr 1831 in Res: Shepton Mallet,Somerset, England d: 10 May 1882 in Pleasant Mounds, Blue Earth, MN
.... 6 James Hawkins b: 1832 in Somerset, Eng. d: 1832 in In infancy
.... 6 [21] James Goddard Hawkins b: 19 Oct 1834 in Evercreech, Somersetshire,Eng. d: 17 Oct 1916 in Bloomfield Twp,Trumbull Co.,OH.
.... +[22] Mary Ann Hawkins b: 04 Mar 1839 in Westbrook,Evercreech, Somersetshire,Eng. m: 23 Nov 1862 in Bloomfield Twp,Trumbull Co.,OH. d: 18 Oct 1916 in Bloomfield Twp,Trumbull Co.,OH. Fact 1: 1862 Graduate of Wesleyan Seminary Fact 2: 1862 Married first cousin. Fathers were bro.
.... 7 [23] Mary Florilla (Flora) Hawkins b: 18 Feb 1865 in Bloomfield Twp., Trum. Co OH d: 11 Nov 1919 in Farmington Twp,Trum. Co,OH
.... +[24] George Henry Fuller b: 10 Jan 1859 m: 1892 in Bloomfield, Ohio d: 27 Mar 1938 in Warren, OH
.... 8 [19] James Paul Fuller b: 08 Jul 1894 in Farmington Twp,Trum. Co,OH d: 07 Jan 1970 in Warren, OH
.... +[25] Bessie Marie Baugher m: 15 Oct 1915 in Southington Twp, Trum.Co.,OH
.... 9 [18] James Paul Fuller, Jr. b: 1918 in Warren, OH
.... +[26] Carol Louise Heckathorn m: 07 Dec 1940 in Warren, OH
.... 10 [27] Diane Elizabeth Fuller b: 1948
.... 10 [28] Barbara Ann Fuller b: 1942
.... *2nd Wife of [18] James Paul Fuller, Jr.:
.... +[29] Betty Jean Brown m: 06 Aug 1955 in Gates Mills, OH
.... 10 [30] Taina Marie Fuller b: 1958
.... 9 [31] George Emory Fuller b: 1916
.... +[32] Helen Louise Buber m: 11 Feb 1937
.... 10 [33] Ross Allan Fuller b: 1937
.... 10 [34] James George Fuller b: 1939
.... 10 [35] Sharyn Ann Fuller b: 1945
.... 10 [36] Janet Louise Fuller b: 1952
.... 10 [37] Carol Jean Fuller b: 21 Nov 1954
.... 9 [38] Norma Jean Fuller b: 1930 in Warren, OH
.... +[39] David Whiting m: 14 Dec 1957 in New York City
.... 10 [40] Mark David Whiting b: 1959
.... 10 [41] Diane Whiting b: 1962
.... *2nd Wife of [19] James Paul Fuller:
.... +[42] Ethel Mary Moore m: 16 Feb 1924 d: 25 Mar 1956 in Warren, OH
.... *3rd Wife of [19] James Paul Fuller:
.... +[43] Elizabeth Jones m: 07 Nov 1959 in Warren, OH (Tod Ave. Methodist Church)
.... 8 [44] Helen Louise Fuller b: 11 Jul 1897 in Farmington Twp., Ohio d: in Warren, OH

  +[45] George Franklin Housel m: 03 Nov 1926 in W. Farmington, OH, (Methodist Parsonage. d: 24 May 1954 in Farmington, OH
 7 [46] Baby Boy Hawkins b: 04 Mar 1867 in Delaware Grove, PA
 7 [20] Susanna Wesley Hawkins b: 08 Jan 1869 in Cooperstown, PA d: 05 Sep 1923 in Warren, OH -No Children
  +[47] Douglas Hill b: 03 May 1861 m: 14 Mar 1915 in Warren, Ohio d: 12 Aug 1921 in Bloomfield Twp. OH
  *2nd Husband of [20] Susanna Wesley Hawkins:
  +[48] John Stephens m: 12 May 1923 in North Bloomfield, Ohio
 7 [49] William David Hawkins b: 25 Sep 1871 in Ellsworth twp. Mahoning Co. OH d: 10 Sep 1920 in at 49 yrs.and single
 7 [50] Baby Girl Hawkins b: 12 Mar 1874 in Mantua, Ohio
 7 [51] James Goddard Hawkins, Jr. b: 28 Feb 1877 d: 07 Sep 1900 in N. Bloomfield, OH at 23 yrs of thyphoid, single
 6 Thomas Ryall Hawkins b: 04 Nov 1836 in Shepton Mallet,Somerset, Eng. d: 08 Feb 1850 in died at 14 yrs.
 6 Sarah Ann Hawkins b: 30 Jul 1838 in Evercreech, Somersetshire,England d: 07 Feb 1931 in Mt. Lake, Cottonwood Co., Minn Burial: Willow Creek Cem., Blue Earth Co., Minn
  +Abel James Pattridge m: 17 Mar 1869 in Beaver Dam, Dodge Co., Wisconsin
5 [53] Benjamin Hawkins b: 16 May 1810 in Evercreech, Somerset,England d: 07 Jul 1873 in Glastonbury,Somerset,England Fact 1: Occupation: Builder.
  +Louisa Jane Millard b: Abt. 1814 in Thurloxton,Somersetshire,England m: 1837 d: 1858 in Somerset, Englland
 6 [52] Joseph Hawkins b: 1839 in Evercreech, Somersetshire,England d: 22 Oct 1917 in Bournemouth (died on a tram while visiting a friend) Burial: official in Shepton Mallet
  +Sarah Ann Jackson
  *2nd Wife of [52] Joseph Hawkins:
  +Emily Smart m: 1892 d: 09 Jan 1908 in Glastonbury, Somerset
 6 Henry Hawkins b: 14 Jul 1843 in Somerton, Somerset, Eng. d: 13 May 1902 in Glastonbury,Som. (builder)
  +Jane Branfield b: 12 Aug 1846 in North Petherton, Som. m: 19 Mar 1868 in St Michael's Church, No. Petherton, Som. d: 17 Feb 1912 in Wells Road Villas Glastonbury
 7 Thomas Henry Hawkins b: 24 Jan 1869 d: 02 Oct 1870
 7 Frank Hawkins b: 12 Mar 1870 d: 06 Oct 1870
 7 George Hawkins b: 25 Aug 1871 d: 27 Aug 1871
 6 Edwin Hawkins b: 1845 in Somerton, Somerset, Eng. d: 08 Oct 1871 in 26yrs.Magdalem St.,Glastonbury, Somerset
 6 Lena Hawkins b: Abt. 1847 in Somerton, Somerset, Eng.
 6 Sarah Hawkins b: 1849
  *2nd Wife of [53] Benjamin Hawkins:
  +Ann Cottle b: 1817 m: Abt. 1860 d: 20 Nov 1880 in Westbrook House,
 6 Thomas Alfred Hawkins b: 11 Apr 1860 d: 24 Sep 1883 in Glastonbury, Somerset
 6 Fredrick William Hawkins, Sr. b: 04 Mar 1863 in Glastonbury,Somerset,England d: 09 Mar 1932 in Teddington, Middlesex,England
  +Georgina Clark b: 1863 in Melbourne,Australlia m: 03 May 1881 d: 1938
 7 Fredrick William Hawkins, Jr. b: 26 Oct 1881 in Wick Rd., Teddington,Middlesex,England d: 1966
  +Ada Ann Turner
  8 [58] Winifred Ada Hawkins b: 1912 d: 2002
   +[65] John Allan Frederick Cottrell (Jack) b: in England
   9 [54] John Cottrell b: in England
    +[66] Audrey
    10 [55] Robert Cottrell
    10 [56] Ian Cottrell
   *2nd Wife of [54] John Cottrell:
    +[67] Sylvia
    10 [55] Robert Cottrell
    10 [56] Ian Cottrell
   9 [63] Diane Cottrell b: 1945 in England
    +[64] Terry Miller
   9 [57] Rodney Cottrell b: 1938 in England

```
............................................ +[59] Pamela
............................................          10 [60] Attette Cottrell
............................................          10 [61] Richard Cottrell
............................................    *2nd Wife of [57] Rodney Cottrell:
............................................       +[62] Graciella
............................................    *2nd Husband of [58] Winifred Ada Hawkins:
............................................       +John Fred. Allan Cottlrell (Jack)
............................................    9  [57] Rodney Cottrell  b: 1938 in England
............................................       +[59] Pamela
............................................          10 [60] Attette Cottrell
............................................          10 [61] Richard Cottrell
............................................    *2nd Wife of [57] Rodney Cottrell:
............................................       +[62] Graciella
............................................    9  [63] Diane Cottrell  b: 1945 in England
............................................       +[64] Terry Miller
............................................    9  [65] John Allan Frederick Cottrell (Jack)  b: in England
............................................       +[58] Winifred Ada Hawkins  b: 1912  d: 2002
............................................          10 [54] John Cottrell  b: in England
............................................             +[66] Audrey
............................................          *2nd Wife of [54] John Cottrell:
............................................             +[67] Sylvia
............................................          10 [63] Diane Cottrell  b: 1945 in England
............................................             +[64] Terry Miller
............................................          10 [57] Rodney Cottrell  b: 1938 in England
............................................             +[59] Pamela
............................................          *2nd Wife of [57] Rodney Cottrell:
............................................             +[62] Graciella
............................................       9  John Cottrell  b: in lives near Swindon, Eng.
............................................    8  Frederick James Hawkins  b: 1914
............................................       9  Tina Hawkins
............................................    8  Lena Hawkins  b: 1919  d: 2000
............................................       +Edwin John England  d: 1981
............................................       9  Judith England
............................................    8  Ethel Rose Hawkins  b: 19 Jul 1919  d: 09 Jul 1966
............................................       +Walter Ernest Williams
............................................       9  Sheila Williams  b: 1938
............................................          +Robert Grahame Savage
............................................             10 Jane Samantha Savage
............................................       9  James Michael Williams  b: 29 Jul 1940  d: 1992
............................................          +Lorna Woods
............................................             10 Neil Christopher Williams
............................................    8  Frederick George Hawkins
............................................       +Pen Foreman
............................................       9  Tina Hawkins
............................................    7  Alfred Henry Hawkins  b: 12 Mar 1883 in Wick Rd., Teddington,Middlesex,England  d: 28 May 1955
............................................       +Edith Mary Clements  d: 1949
............................................       8  Phoebe Hawkins
............................................       8  Rhoda Hawkins
............................................       8  Ruth Hawkins  d: 1924
............................................       8  Stephen Hawkins
............................................       8  Mary Hawkins
............................................    7  Ethel Ann Hawkins  b: 07 Feb 1884  d: 1959
............................................       +James Milne Townsend  b: 1880  d: 1950
............................................       8  Audrey Lena Townsend  b: 1914  d: 1989
............................................          +Clifford Philip Gibbs  d: 1990
............................................          9  Ann Gibbs
............................................             +Stewart Norton  d: 1976
```

.... 10 Rachel Norton b: 1976
.... 10 Helen Norton b: 1978
.... 8 Ann Townsend
.... +Stewart Norton
.... 8 Helen Rachel Townsend
.... 7 Thomas Percival Hawkins b: 28 Feb 1886 d: Jun 1954
.... +Frances Louise Elkins d: 1984
.... 8 Thomas Frederick Hawkins b: 1909
.... 8 Doris Louise Hawkins b: 1913 d: in Australia
.... 8 Mabel Hawkins b: 1915 d: in Australia
.... 8 Harold Ronald Hawkins b: in Res New Zealand d: in Had 2 daughters
.... +Patricia Plater
.... 9 Phillippa Jane Hawkins
.... 9 Juliet Katrine Hawkins
.... 8 Ernest Charles Hawkins
.... 7 [68] Joseph Edwin Hawkins b: 18 Nov 1888 d: 09 Jul 1970
.... +Eleanor May Clements d: 1936
.... *2nd Wife of [68] Joseph Edwin Hawkins:
.... +Alice Louise Clements d: 1971
.... 7 Ernest Morley Hawkins b: 21 Jun 1890 d: 01 Jul 1916 in died single in WW I
.... 7 Arthur Hawkins b: 14 Jul 1892 d: Feb 1971
.... +Vera Alice Hawkins b: in Berkshire (not related)
.... 8 Beryl Hawkins b: Abt. 1925
.... +??? Barr
.... 9 Felicity Barr
.... 10 Joseph Barr
.... 10 Luke Barr
.... 8 Kenneth Arthur Hawkins b: 1927
.... 9 Christopher Hawkins
.... 9 Braeme Hawkins
.... 10 Stephen Hawkins
.... 8 Brian Fredrick Hawkins b: 1932
.... 8 Pamela Joan Hawkins b: 1936 in res. Feltham Bognor, West Sussex
.... +??? Glendenning
.... 9 Brenda May Glendenning
.... 9 Rosemary June Glendenning
.... 7 Dorothy Evelyn Hawkins b: 19 Oct 1895 d: 10 Jul 1980 in Had no family
.... +Joseph Goodfellow d: 1962
.... 7 Mabel Laura Hawkins b: May 1896 d: 1899
.... 7 Leslie Hawkins b: 23 Feb 1898 d: 13 Dec 1963
.... +Elsie Mary Matthews d: 1965
.... 8 Lily Evelyn Hawkins
.... 7 Herbert Hawkins b: 22 Aug 1898 d: 1899
.... 7 Edith Millicent Hawkins b: 1900 d: 1949
.... 7 Ada Winifred Hawkins b: 1902 d: 1903
.... 5 Elizabeth Hawkins b: 12 Aug 1813 in Bapt. East Lydford, Somerset, England d: 28 Dec 1891 in Vernon Twp, Trum. Co, OH
.... +THOMAS BIGGIN b: 21 Jun 1806 in Pylle, Somerset, England m: 23 Oct 1832 in Evercreech, Somerset, England d: 16 Mar 1890 in Vernon Twp, Trum. Co, OH
.... 6 William Hawkins Biggin b: 21 Jul 1834 in Somerset, England d: 09 Apr 1918 in Warren, Trum. Co, OH
.... +Emily Bolston b: 16 Sep 1837 m: 15 Oct 1856 in NY, Met on voyage over to America
.... 7 Albert William Biggin b: 30 Jun 1858 in Orwell, Ashtabula Co., OH d: 21 Sep 1938 in Vienna, OH
.... 7 Robert Lewis Biggin b: 16 Jun 1861 in Orwell, Ashtabula Co., OH
.... 7 Anna Biggin b: 1864 in Grimsby, Ontario, Canada
.... 7 Sarah (Sade) Biggin b: 10 Sep 1865 in Grimsby, Ontario, Canada
.... 7 George Stanley Biggin b: 06 May 1868 in Grimsby, Ontario, Canada
.... 6 Thomas Biggin b: 29 Sep 1836 in Somerset, England d: 22 Jan 1925 in Burg Hill, Trumbull City, OH

```
............................ +Harriet Martin  b: Abt. 1838 in England  m: 28 Sep 1870
............................    7  Philo Henry Biggin  b: Abt. 1856 in Bloomfield Twp. Trum. Co. OH  d: 10 Jul 1877 in Howwland
............................    7  Frederick Biggin  b: 1859
............................    7  Mina Elizabeth Biggin  b: 1861
............................    7  Clara Biggin  b: 1864
............................    7  Mary Biggin  b: 1866
............................    6  [69] Sarah Biggin  b: Apr 1838 in Somerset, England  d: 10 Apr 1910 in Youngstown, Mahoning Co. OH
............................       +James W. Biggin  m: in Warren, OH  -34 yrs.
............................       *2nd Husband of [69] Sarah Biggin:
............................       +John H. Woodford  m: 23 Sep 1884
............................    6  Martha Biggin  b: 19 Feb 1840 in Somerset, England  d: 07 Nov 1916 in Youngstown, Mahoning Co. OH
............................       +Lorenzo Swagger  m: 08 Jan 1863 in Fowler Twp. Trum. Co. OH
............................    6  Job D. Biggin  b: 27 Nov 1842 in Somerset, England  d: 10 Mar 1912 in Sharon, PA
............................       +Sarah E. Brown  b: 1847 in Pa.  m: in West Salem, PA
............................       7  Luella Maude Biggin
............................       7  Ruby Emma Biggin
............................       7  James Delbert Biggin
............................       7  Wilber Clyde Biggin
............................       7  Elsworth Biggin  b: 23 Apr 1873
............................       7  William Hurbert Biggin  b: 14 Jul 1875
............................       7  Orlo Lucius Biggin  b: 02 Feb 1877
............................    6  James H. Biggin  b: 29 Sep 1844 in Somerset, England  d: 05 Mar 1916 in Vernon Twp., Trumbull Co. OH
............................    6  Andrew Biggin  b: 20 Jul 1846 in Somerset, England  d: 16 Mar 1931 in Warren, Trumbull Co. OH
............................       +Anna Storier  m: 11 Jun 1883 in Trumbull Co. OH
............................       7  Arthur Biggin  b: 11 Jun 1883 in Trum. Co. OH  d: 23 Jul 1897 in Vernon Twp, Trum. Co, OH
............................       7  Willie Biggin  b: 01 Jun 1880 in Trum. Co. OH
............................    6  Henry Biggin  b: Jun 1848 in Somerset, England  d: 10 May 1918 in Redlands, CA
............................       +Lizzie Cochran
............................       7  Charlie Biggin  b: 07 Jun 1878 in Trum. Co. OH
............................       7  Jane E. Biggin  b: 14 Sep 1880
............................    6  George H. Biggin  b: May 1849 in Somerset, England  d: 18 Oct 1933 in Redlands, CA
............................    6  Elizabeth Ann Biggin  b: 29 Mar 1852 in Somerset, England  d: 23 Apr 1943 in Warren, OH 91 yrs.
............................       +John Moon  m: 29 Apr 1887 in Vernon Twp. Trum. Co. OH
............................       7  Alice Moon  b: in Cleveland in 1943
............................       7  L.C. Moon  b: in Warren, OH
............................          +??? Mitchel
............................       7  Joe A. Moon  b: in Of Chicago
............................       7  Henry Moon  b: in Of Warren, OH.
............................    6  Ellen Biggin  b: 17 Jul 1854 in Somerset, England  d: 18 Sep 1933 in Orangeville, Trum. Co. OH
............................       +John E. Langley  m: 08 Dec 1875 in Of Vernon, OH
............................  5  Daniel Hawkins  b: Abt. 1815 in "Nancy's boys in Ann Dredge's Will
............................  5  Job Hawkins  b: Abt. 1818 in Ditcheat, Som., Eng. Res. Moore Farm Holcombe, Som  d: 1894 in Midsomer Norton,
           Somerset, England
............................     +Eliza Pike  b: Abt. 1832 in W. Pennard, Somerset, Eng.  m: 25 Feb 1862 in 1881 Census, Holcombe, Som.  d: Sep
           1910 in W. Pennard, Somerset, Eng.
............................    6  Sarah Annie Hawkins  b: 1865 in Holcombe, Som.
............................       +Ernest Charles Bissex  b: Abt. 1860 in Holcombe, Som.  m: 14 Feb 1888 in Holcombe, Somerset
............................       7  William Henry Bissex  b: Abt. 1893 in Holcombe, Som.
............................          +??? Talbot  m: 22 May 1918 in Moors Farm Holcombe
............................       7  Harold Bissex  b: Abt. 1894 in Holcombe, Som.
............................       7  Agnes Bissex  b: Abt. 1898 in Holcombe, Som.
............................       7  Stanley Bissex  b: Abt. 1900 in Holcombe, Som.
............................    6  Eliza Ellen Hawkins  b: 1866 in Holcombe, Som.  d: 15 Apr 1904 in Bur: Midsomer Norton
............................       +George Henry Beachim  b: Abt. 1857 in Vobster (near Frome)  m: 02 Jun 1886 in Seven children 1887- 1903 d:
           10 May 1935
............................    6  Mary Elizabeth (Polly) Hawkins  b: 1869 in Holcombe, Som.  d: Bet. 1893 - 1901
............................       +F. J. Tucker  m: 1892 in Midsomer Norton, Som, England
```

.... 6 Emily Ada Hawkins b: 1870 in Holcombe, Som. d: 18 Aug 1944 in Bur. Midsomer Norton, Som.
.... +Ernest Herbert Galledge Welch m: 08 Sep 1897 in Wesleyan Chapel, Guildford
.... 7 Richard Welch
.... +Carole '
.... 8 David Welch
.... +Pam'
.... 8 John Welch
.... 8 Rachel Welch
.... 5 Andrew Hawkins b: Abt. 1819 in Somerset, England d: 15 Jan 1898 in Ste-Armand West, Que.,Canada
.... +Hannah Elizabeth Merick b: 1823 in Quebec, Canada m: 26 Jun 1844 in Ste-Armand West, Quebec, Canada
.... 6 Sarah Elizabeth Hawkins b: 1850 in Ste-Armand West, Que.,Canada
.... +Hiram Alonzo Fleming b: in Stanbridge, Mississiquoi County, Que, Can. m: 27 Apr 1875 in Ste-Armand West, Quebec, Canada
.... 6 Hobert B. Hawkins b: 1852 in Ste-Armand West, Que.,Canada
.... 6 "Kate" Hawkins b: 1854 in Ste-Armand West, Que.,Canada
.... 6 Mary L. Hawkins b: 1856 in Ste-Armand West, Que.,Canada
.... 4 John Hawkins b: 11 Nov 1774 in Pilton, Somerset, England
.... +Sarah ???
.... 5 Elizabeth Hawkins b: 31 Mar 1799 in Pilton.
.... 5 Sarah Hawkins b: 13 Jul 1800 in Pilton.
.... 5 Mathilda Hawkins b: 10 Jan 1804 in Pilton.
.... 4 Thomas Hawkins b: 30 May 1779 in Pilton, Somerset, England
.... 5 Robert Hawkins
.... 4 Elizabeth Hawkins b: 15 Jul 1781 in Pilton, Somerset, England d: in Burial rec. Pilton, Som.
...... 2 William Hawkings b: 03 Mar 1689 in Pilton, Somerset
...... 2 Hana Hawkings b: 25 Sep 1691 in Pilton, Somerset
...... 2 Gertrude Hawkings b: 1693 in Pilton, Somerset

Ten Generations of Haine Family

Descendants of William Haine

1 William Haine
.... +Mary Rogers m: 26 Sep 1736 in East Pennard, Somerset, England
...... 2 William Haine b: Mar 1743 in Baptized in East Pennard, Somerset, England d: 22 Apr 1809 in Pilton, Somerset, England Burial: Pilton Churchyard Occupation: Farming in Coxley, Stone, E. Pennard
.... +Betty (Elizabeth) Young b: 12 May 1744 in Bapt. E. Horrington, (near Wells) Somerset, Eng. m: 09 Apr 1768 in St. Cuthbert's, Wells, Somersetshire,England d: Bef. 1809
.... 3 William Haine b: 27 Oct 1769 in Of Westholme Farm, Pilton d: 27 Dec 1853 in Pilton, (Methodist for many years) at 84 yrs. Burial: Pilton Methodist Church, Pilton, Somerset(Built Church)
.... +Betty Scott b: 1778 in W. Pennard, Somerset, England m: 29 Mar 1796 in West Pennard, Somerset, Eng. d: 28 Sep 1845 in Pilton, Somerset at 67yrs. Burial: Pilton Methodist Church, Pilton, Somerset
.... 4 Martha Haine b: 1802 d: 02 Jan 1891 in North Brewham, at 88 yrs.
.... +Peter Padfield b: in Of Stoke, La m: in 2 children d: 28 Feb 1867 in killed by a cow at 28 yrs. Burial: Pilton Methodist Church, Pilton, Somerset
.... 5 Elizabeth Haine b: 1837 d: 1888
.... +Exton Treasure m: in 5 children d: 1888 in Farmer Burial: N. Bruham
.... 4 [53] Mary Ann Haine b: Abt. 1820 d: 30 May 1864 in Baltonsborough, Somerset, Eng.
.... +[52] John Haine b: 22 Jul 1810 in E. Pennard, Som. m: 1843 in Shepton Mallet, Somerset. (2 children, no issue d: 29 Aug 1860 in accident, of W. Bradley
.... 4 William Haine b: 1802 d: 19 Jun 1898 in Of Westholme Farm, Pilton, Somerset, England age 91 Burial: Pilton Methodist Church, Pilton, Somerset
.... +Eliza Cook b: 1811 d: 04 Jan 1892 in at 81 yrs. Burial: Pilton Methodist Church, Pilton, Somerset
.... 4 Susanna Haine b: 1812 d: 1899
.... +Benjamin Padfield b: in Manor Farm Holcombe d: in (younger brother of Peter)
.... 5 Edwin Haine Padfield b: 1840 d: 26 Jan 1922 in took on Westholme Farm-1898, road surveyor Burial: Pilton Methodist Church, Pilton, Somerset at 82yrs
.... +Arundel Creed b: 1841 in of Westholm, Pilton, Somerset m: in 8 children-none to continue d: 01 Jun 1917 in Pilton Methodist Church, Pilton, Somerset Burial: Pilton Methodist Church, Pilton, Somerset at 76 yrs.
.... 5 Jane Padfield
.... +John Bryant d: in Fosse Farm, Stratton on the Fosse, Somerset, Eng.
.... 5 Joseph Padfield b: in Of Birtsmorton Ct., Tewkesbury, Wores.
.... 5 James Padfield b: 1844 d: 1934 in "the singing preacher", farmer
.... +Ellen Creed m: in 8 children
.... 5 ANNIE PADFIELD d: 1909 in West Pennard, Somerset,
.... +William Creed b: Abt. 1835 in W. Pennard, Somerset, England d: in dairyman Burial: 1887 At 42 yrs.
.... 6 Egbert Creed
.... 6 Bessie Creed
.... 6 Edwin Creed
.... 6 Leonard Creed
.... 6 Ethel Creed
.... 6 ALBERT CREED
.... +Gladys Lowry
.... 7 Lowry Creed b: 1909 d: 1987
.... +Joyce ? m: in 3 children
.... 7 Irene Creed
.... 7 Mary Creed b: 1921
.... +Bill Francis b: in Shaftsbury
.... 8 Katherine ANN Francis
.... +D. P. WALSH
.... 9 DAVID WALSH b: 1977
.... 9 Jo Walsh
.... 9 Belinda Walsh
.... 8 Rose Francis
.... 8 Dot Francis d: in W. Yorkshire
.... 8 Joan Francis
.... 6 Gussie Creed
.... 6 May Creed b: 1887 d: 1972

```
................................ +Alan Green
................................ 5   Sarah Padfield  b: 1848  d: 1870
................................ +Frank Haddinott  m: in One daughter- unmarried
................................ 5   [1] William Padfield  b: in Of Manor Farm
................................ +Bessie Hernage
................................ *2nd Wife of [1] William Padfield:
................................ +Ada Bolton
.................. 4   [55] Jane Haine  b: 25 Nov 1814 in Pilton, Somerset, Eng.  d: 08 Oct 1883 in Of Stone, E. Pennard, Somerset, Eng.
.................. +[54] George Haine  b: 10 Feb 1815 in East Pennard, Somerset, Eng.  m: 21 Apr 1835 in Pilton, Somerset, (Cousins)  d: 19
                     Dec 1872 in Of Stone, Somerset, England
.................. 5   [56] John Haine  b: Dec 1839  d: 27 Sep 1902 in Went to PA, USA
.................. +[57] Elizabeth Gough  b: 22 Jan 1846 in Rodley, Westbury on Severn, W. Glo'ster, England  d: 26 Jan 1897 in orwell,
                     Oh
.................. 6   [58] John Howard Haine  b: 1872  d: 1958  Burial: Windsor, OH
.................. +[59] Harriette Cummins  b: 1875  d: 1947  Burial: Windsor, OH
.................. 7   [60] Cuthbert Elroy Haine  b: 17 Jun 1910  d: 06 Aug 2003 in Hershey, PA  Burial: Rochester, NY
.................. +[61] Amelia Carothers  b: 13 Jul 1911 in Beaver Falls, PA
.................. 8   [62] David Arthur Haine  b: 1940  d: 1946 in Rochester, NY
.................. 8   [63] James L. Haine
.................. 8   [64] Debra K. Haine
.................. +[65] ? Wentz
.................. 7   [66] James Howard Haine  b: 28 Sep 1913  d: 06 Jan 2003 in Hershey, PA
.................. 8   [67] Dean Haine
.................. +[68] Susie ??
.................. 9   [69] Oneson Haine
.................. 9   [70] Twoson Haine
.......... 4   [3] Ann Haine  b: 04 Jan 1803 in East Pennard, Somerset, Eng.  d: 22 Feb 1824 in E. Pennard, Somerset, Eng.
.......... 4   [2] Elizabeth Haine  b: 14 Dec 1804 in Somerset, England  d: 18 Sep 1886 in Bloomfield Twp,Trumbull Co.,OH.  Burial:
                Brownwood Cem. Bloomfield, OH
.......... +[4] Richard Dunkerton  b: 18 Jun 1796 in Pilton, Somerset, England  m: 15 Apr 1824  d: 12 Apr 1878 in Bloomfield
                Twp,Trumbull Co.,OH.  Burial: Brownwood Cemetery, Bloomfield, OH
.......... 5   [5] John Dunkerton  b: 06 May 1826  d: in Dunkerton, Iowa
.......... 5   [6] James Dunkerton  b: 18 Jul 1827  d: in Dunkerton, Iowa
.......... 5   [7] Mary Dunkerton  b: 20 Dec 1828
.......... 5   [8] Richard Dunkerton  b: 08 Mar 1830
.......... 5   [9] Samuel Dunkerton  b: 08 Mar 1832
.......... 5   [10] Elinor Dunkerton  b: 19 Jan 1834
.......... 5   [11] W.C. Dunkerton  b: 21 Feb 1836  d: in infant death
.......... 5   [12] Sarah Dunkerton  b: 27 Mar 1838
.......... 5   [13] George Dunkerton  b: Abt. 1842  d: 08 Nov 1897 in 55 yrs.Ohio
.......... +[14] Eliza Ann Green  d: in oh
.......... 6   [15] Ernest Dunkerton  b: 29 Jan 1868  d: 06 Oct 1892
.......... 5   [16] Susan Dunkerton  b: 01 Jan 1844
.......... 5   [17] George Dunkerton  b: 03 Mar 1846
.......... 5   [18] William Dunkerton  b: 07 Jan 1848
.......... 5   [19] Julia Dunkerton  b: 03 May 1850  d: Aug 1850
.......... *2nd Husband of [2] Elizabeth Haine:
.......... +[20] James Edney  m: 1828
.......... 4   Sarah Haine  b: Abt. 1799 in Pilton, Somerset  d: 08 May 1867 in Westbrook Cottage, Evercreech, Somerset @68 yrs
                Burial: 13 May 1867 Evercreech, Somersetshire,England
.......... +Thomas Hawkins  b: 04 Apr 1798 in Pilton, Somerset ,21-12-1797  m: 05 Apr 1823 in Pilton , England -0- children  d: 20
                Nov 1880 in Westbrook House, Evercreech, Somerset,England  Fact 1: 1798 Stone leaning on side of church.  Burial: St.
                Peter's Church, Evercreech (stone present)  Occupation: 200 acres- farmer
...... 3   Mary Haine  b: 05 Jul 1771 in Coxley, Wells, Somerset, England  d: Jul 1837 in Edgarly, Somerset, Eng.
...... +Thomas Millear  b: Abt. 1775 in England  m: 26 Mar 1799 in East Pennard, Somerset, England
...... 3   JOHN HAINE  b: 27 Jun 1773 in Wells, Somerset,Eng. Farmed at Stone, in fam. since 1600's  d: 01 Jul 1824 in E. Pennard,
                Somerset ,England  Burial: 04 Jul 1824 East Pennard, Somerset, Eng. -will1824
```

+[483] MARY CREED b: 12 May 1776 in W. Pennard, Somerset, England m: 01 Apr 1802 in W. Pennard ,Somerset, Eng. d: 13 Nov 1830 in E. Pennard, Somerset ,England
4 [3] Ann Haine b: 04 Jan 1803 in East Pennard, Somerset, Eng. d: 22 Feb 1824 in E. Pennard, Somerset, Eng.
4 [2] Elizabeth Haine b: 14 Dec 1804 in Somerset, England d: 18 Sep 1886 in Bloomfield Twp,Trumbull Co.,OH. Burial: Brownwood Cem. Bloomfield, OH
  +[4] Richard Dunkerton b: 18 Jun 1796 in Pilton, Somerset, England m: 15 Apr 1824 d: 12 Apr 1878 in Bloomfield Twp,Trumbull Co.,OH. Burial: Brownwood Cemetery, Bloomfield, OH
    5 [5] John Dunkerton b: 06 May 1826 d: in Dunkerton, Iowa
    5 [6] James Dunkerton b: 18 Jul 1827 d: in Dunkerton, Iowa
    5 [7] Mary Dunkerton b: 20 Dec 1828
    5 [8] Richard Dunkerton b: 08 Mar 1830
    5 [9] Samuel Dunkerton b: 08 Mar 1832
    5 [10] Elinor Dunkerton b: 19 Jan 1834
    5 [11] W.C. Dunkerton b: 21 Feb 1836 d: in infant death
    5 [12] Sarah Dunkerton b: 27 Mar 1838
    5 [13] George Dunkerton b: Abt. 1842 d: 08 Nov 1897 in 55 yrs.Ohio
      +[14] Eliza Ann Green d: in oh
        6 [15] Ernest Dunkerton b: 29 Jan 1868 d: 06 Oct 1892
    5 [16] Susan Dunkerton b: 01 Jan 1844
    5 [17] George Dunkerton b: 03 Mar 1846
    5 [18] William Dunkerton b: 07 Jan 1848
    5 [19] Julia Dunkerton b: 03 May 1850 d: Aug 1850
  *2nd Husband of [2] Elizabeth Haine:
  +[20] James Edney m: 1828
4 [76] WILLIAM HAINE b: 08 Feb 1806 in Stone, E. Pennard,Somersetshire,England d: 14 Sep 1895 in Bloomfield Twp,Trumbull Co.,OH. Fact 1: 11 Apr 1835 sailed and landed at Prince Edward Is. Fact 2: Soon went to Pictou, Nova Scotia. Burial: Brownwood Cemetery, No. Bloomfield, Trum. Co., OH
  +[75] MARY HAINE b: 14 Mar 1816 in Church Hill,Somersetshire,England m: 11 Apr 1836 in Lovington Church,Somerset,Eng. d: 31 Jul 1890 in Bloomfield Twp,Trumbull Co.,OH. Fact 1: Mary is one of nine children. Burial: Brownwood Cemetery, No. Bloomfield, Trum. Co., OH
    5 [21] William Joseph Haine b: 11 Jan 1837 in Bloomfield Twp,Trumbull Co.,OH. d: 18 May 1923 in Ashville, NC. 105 Regt. OVI Infantry
      +[77] Sarah Goddard Hawkins b: 26 Jul 1834 in Westbrook,Evercreech, Somersetshire,Eng. m: 11 Aug 1862 in Warren, Trumbull Co.,OH d: 06 Aug 1867 in Bloomfield Twp,Trumbull Co.,OH.,died at 33yrs.
        6 [78] Theodosia Haine b: 15 Dec 1863 in No. Bloomfield, OH d: 10 Aug 1930 in Warren,Oh Fact 1: Never married. Fact 2: Crippled and unable to walk from approx.
      *2nd Wife of [21] William Joseph Haine:
      +[79] Cornelia Wolcott b: 20 Oct 1848 in West Farmington, Ohio m: 05 Jun 1872 in West Farmington, Trumbull Co., OH d: 19 Feb 1923 in West Farmington, Ohio
        6 [80] Mary Jane Haine b: 16 Jan 1874 d: 18 Nov 1931 in divorced
          +[81] Dr. Kelly m: 26 Apr 1898
        6 [82] Emma Grace Haine b: 03 Sep 1876 d: 12 Aug 1946 in Never married, lived at home and cared for Theodosia.
        6 [83] George Austin Haine b: 28 May 1878
          +[84] Eva Marie Thompson m: 06 Feb 1919
            7 [85] Marie Cornelia Haine d: in unmarried and lived in Cleveland
        6 [86] William Jay Haine b: 12 May 1880 d: 01 Jan 1936 in No children
          +[87] Jesse B. Little m: 13 Jun 1923 d: 13 Jun 1923
        6 [88] Clarence Haine b: 13 Nov 1882 d: 21 Dec 1957 in Never married, died in rest home, Had a bicycle shop.
        6 [89] Mabel Haine b: 29 Nov 1884 d: Mar 1916 in Ashville, NC, No children
          +[90] Elmer Hughes d: 07 Oct 1914
        6 [91] Theodore Haine b: 1888 d: 1889 in died in infancy.
    5 [92] Mary Sarah Haine b: 08 Sep 1838 in Bloomfield Twp,Trumbull Co.,OH. d: 11 Jan 1910 in Bloomfield Twp,Trumbull Co.,OH.(lived and died at Clover Hill)
    5 [93] George E. Haine b: 28 Feb 1840 in Bloomfield Twp,Trumbull Co.,OH. d: 06 Feb 1920 in No children 105 Regt. Union Infantry OVI

3

+[94] Sarah Creed b: 24 Jul 1841 m: 14 Mar 1870 in Bristolville, Trumbull Co. OH-no children d: 12 Oct 1920 in Bloomfield Twp,Trumbull Co.,OH
5 [95] FRANCES HARRIET HAINE b: 29 Jan 1842 in Bloomfield Twp, Trumbull Co.OH d: 31 May 1911 in Forest Depot,VA, Bur:Bloomfield OH. Burial: Brownwood Cemetery, Bloomfield, OH
+[96] Thomas Goddard HAWKINS b: 05 Nov 1832 in Evercreech,Somerset Co.,England m: 01 Mar 1863 in Trumbull Co.OH d: 03 Aug 1903 in W. Farmington, Trumbull Co.OH Burial: Brownwood Cemetery, Bloomfield, OH
6 [97] Emma Hawkins b: 13 Feb 1864 in Bloomfield, Trumbull Co.OH d: 07 Mar 1893 in San Francisco,Ca, at 29 yrs. as deaconess -Meth.Church Burial: Died of smallpox, bur. San Francisco
6 [98] George William Hawkins b: 08 Feb 1865 in Bloomfield Twp,Trum. Co,OH d: 06 Oct 1868 in Cooperstown, PA Burial: "died from eatting too many grapes", perhaps dehydration
6 [99] Pliny Haine Hawkins b: 28 Oct 1869 in Bloomfield Twp,Trumbull Co.,OH. d: 15 Sep 1940 in Long Beach , CA
+[100] Grace Alice Milner b: 20 Oct 1869 in BeetownTownship, Grant County, Wisconsin m: 01 Jan 1900 in Salt Lake City, Utah d: 16 Nov 1944 in Palos Verdes Estates, California
7 [25] Milner Haine Hawkins b: 19 Oct 1901 in Columbus, Montana d: 02 Nov 1951 in Poughkeepsie, NY
+[101] Vivian Carolyn Lansworth b: 07 Jul 1902 in Brule, Wisconsin m: 16 Dec 1925 in Iron Mountain, Michiagan d: 17 Dec 1997 in Ellensburg, WA
8 [22] Milner James Hawkins b: 10 Apr 1927 in Caspian, Michigan
+[102] Joan Young m: 1952 in Longview, Washington
*2nd Wife of [22] Milner James Hawkins:
+[103] Carmen Masip Echazarreta b: 1927 in Spain m: 10 Dec 1955 in Mexico, D.F, Mexico d: in res. Mexico
9 [104] Paulina Hawkins
8 [23] Charles Haine Hawkins b: 1929 in Columbus, Montana
+[105] Jacqueline Roberta Dorrington b: 1928
*2nd Wife of [23] Charles Haine Hawkins:
+[106] Ruth Maass b: 20 Jan 1931 in Portland, OR m: 02 Sep 1950 d: 23 Feb 1968
9 [107] Christoffer Haine Hawkins b: 1951
10 [108] Natasha Laura Hawkins b: 1985 in Seattle, WA
9 [109] Charles Mead Hawkins b: 1955
10 [110] Lucas Christopher Hawkins b: 1979 in Seattle, WA
10 [111] Tyler Matthew Hawkins b: 1981 in Seattle, WA
*3rd Wife of [23] Charles Haine Hawkins:
+[112] Ida Edene Buckingham b: 1945 in Pasco, WA m: Abt. 1970
9 [113] Glacier Irene Hawkins b: 1972 in Ellensburg, WA
+[114] Steven Kingsford-Smith b: 1960 in Loveland, CO m: 14 Oct 1995 in Port Gamble, WA
10 [115] Genevive Kingsford-Smith b: 2007
8 [24] Robert Pearson Hawkins b: 1931 in Silver City, NM Fact 1: Dr. Of Psychology at West Virginia State Fact 2: University.
+[116] Jane Nelson b: 1931 in Portland, OR m: 08 Jun 1958 in Portland, OR
9 [117] Larry Pearson Hawkins b: 1953 in Portland, OR
9 [118] Jeffrey Milner Hawkins b: 1954 in Portland, OR
+[119] Patty
*2nd Wife of [24] Robert Pearson Hawkins:
+[120] Kathyn Kay Kott b:1940 in Kalamazoo, MI m: 1970
9 [121] Anne Kathryn Hawkins b: 1972
+[122] Thomas Young
10 [123] Alanna Zoe Young b: 1994 in Morgantown, WV
10 [124] Eli Thomas Young b: 1998 in Morgantown, WV
*2nd Wife of [25] Milner Haine Hawkins:
+[125] Wilberta Twogood Johnson b:1912 m: 23 Mar 1946 in Lansdowne, PA
8 [126] Angela Holbeach Hawkins b: 1936 in Newburg, NY
+[127] Robert Fichter b: 1923
9 [128] James Robert Fichter b: 1979 in Scotland, CT.
7 [26] Frances Milner Hawkins b: 01 Jan 1909 in Bozeman, Montana d: Nov 1982 in Absarokee, Montana
+[129] Carleton Wilder

*2nd Husband of [26] Frances Milner Hawkins:
+[130] Joseph Walter Meek m: 16 Aug 1933 in Absarokee, Montana d: 1955
8 [131] Mary Milner Meek b: 1936 in Tucson, AZ
+[132] Lawrence Locke
9 [133] Jonathan Locke b: 1967
9 [134] Jason Locke b: 1970
8 [135] Frances Luann Meek b: 1939 in Glendale, CA
+[136] Yale Coombs d: in res. CA.
9 [137] Stacy Coombs b: 1963
9 [138] Wendy Coombs b: 1966
6 [139] Mary Alberta Hawkins b: 03 Sep 1872 in Farmington Township, Trumbull Co.OH d: 26 Oct 1958 in Meadville,PA Fact 1: 1911 Resided in Forest Depot,VA. at time of Fact 2: Mothers death. Frances Hawkins died Burial: Brownwood Cemetery, Bloomfield, OH
+[140] George W. Walker b: 29 Apr 1871 in Virginia m: 29 Apr 1896 in West Farmington, OH -0- children d: 08 Aug 1960 in Meadville,Pa at 89 yrs. Burial: Brownwood Cemetery, Bloomfield, OH
6 [141] Charlotte Hawkins b: 10 Feb 1875 in Farmington Township, Trumbull Co., OH d: 08 Sep 1953 in Warren,OH Fact 1: Also called "Lottie"
+[142] J. Ward Wolcott m: 13 Mar 1894
7 [143] Clyde Wolcott b: 1896 d: 1915 in Died in motorcycle accident
7 [144] Frances Wolcott b: 07 Apr 1907 in Trumbull Co., OH d: 31 Aug 1980 in Mayfield Hts. OH
+[145] Paul B. Rogers m: 29 Aug 1931 in two daughters d: in Mayfield Hts.,OH
8 [146] Carol Ann Rogers b: 1934 in Warren, Ohio
+[147] David L. Beers m: in Westfield, NJ
9 [148] David Rogers Beers b: 1963
8 [149] Jean Rogers b: 1939 in Warren, Ohio
+[150] Errol Kwait b: in Cleveland Hts.,OH m: Aug 1962 in 2 children
9 [151] Steven Paul Kwait b: 1967
9 [152] Laura Ellen Kwait b: 1969
6 [153] Angie Hawkins b: 10 Nov 1876 in Farmington Township, Trumbull Co., OH d: 25 Jan 1877 in Farmington Township, Trumbull
6 [154] Jerry Hawkins b: 24 Feb 1880 in Farmington Township, Trumbull Co. OH d: 24 Feb 1880 in Farmington Township, Trumbull Co.OH Fact 1: 1880 Twin of Jeese, Died at birth.
6 [155] Jesse Thomas Hawkins b: 24 Feb 1880 in Farmington Township, Trumbull Co., OH d: 26 Oct 1957 in Warren, Trumbull Co. OH Fact 1: Bur: Brownwood Cem. in Bloomfield,OH Fact 2: Occupation:Farmer,real estate, Republic Burial: 29 Oct 1957 Brownwood Cemetery, No. Bloomfield, Trum. Co., OH
+[156] Mildred Phoebe Thorp b: 08 Dec 1878 in W. Farmington Twp.,Trumbull Co., OH m: 22 Jun 1904 in Trumbull Co. ,OH d: 05 Apr 1958 in Warren, Trumbull Co. OH Burial: 07 Apr 1958 Brownwood Cemetery, No. Bloomfield, Trum. Co., OH
7 [157] Charles T. Hawkins b: 20 Mar 1910 in Parkman, Geauga Co.,OH d: 18 Dec 1999 in Penny Farms, Florida Fact 1: Ohio State University Fact 2: Occupation: Employed at Packard Electric- office.
+[158] Nancy Buckingham b: 20 Mar 1910 in Urichsville, OH m: 18 Jun 1938 in Warren, Trum.Co.OH d: 24 Apr 1987 in Penny Farms, Florida
8 [159] Thomas Frank Hawkins b: 1941 in Warren, OH
+[160] Janet Sue Breystpraak b: in Middleton, Ohio m: 10 Jun 1967 in no children
8 [161] Robert C. Hawkins b: 1944 in Warren, Trumbull Co. OH
+[162] Mary Kay Branfield b: in Warren, Trumbull Co. OH m: Jun 1966 in Warren, Trumbull Co. OH
9 [163] Katherine Hawkins b: 1968 in Michigan
+[164] Kevin Boardman m: in New Wilmington, Delaware
10 [165] Meredith Boardman b: 1997
10 [166] Chase Ivan Boardman b: 1999
9 [167] Robert Hawkins b: 1971
+[168] Teresa Coppola b: in Florida m: 12 Jun 1997 in Boca Raton, Florida
7 [169] Lloyd B. Hawkins b: 11 Nov 1911 in Parkman, Geauga Co.,OH d: 01 Aug 1982 in Warren, Trumbull Co. OH Fact 1: Occupation: Steel Mill -3 yrs, Warren City Fireman 35 yrs. Fact 2: until retirement. Home construction and remodeling- Burial: Brownwood Cemetery, No. Bloomfield, Trum. Co., OH

................+[170] Martha Arlene Schout b: 20 Sep 1914 in Howland Twp.,Trumbull Co. OH m: 08 Jan 1938 in Howland Twp.,Trumbull Co. OH d: 07 Feb 2007 in Warren, OH Fact 2: General Electric on assembly line - 1-2 yrs.
....   8   [171] Ernest Eugene Hawkins b: 11 Sep 1939 in Warren, Trumbull Co. OH d: 09 Jan 1996 in Warren, Trumbull Co. OH Fact 1: Occu: Wiring harness for autos at Packard Electric Burial: Brownwood Cemetery, Bloomfield, Trum. Co. OH
....   +[172] Patricia Sue Heiple b:1942 in Champion Twp.,Trumbull Co., OH m: 04 May 1963 in 1963 in Champion Twp. Trumbull Co. OH
....   9   [173] Roberta Sue Hawkins b: 1965 in Warren, Trumbull Co. OH Fact 1: Occupation: Needlework and stitchery.
....   +[174] Thomas King b: 1963 in Champion Twp.,Trumbull Co., OH m: 01 Nov 1986 in Warren, Trumbull Co. OH Fact 1: Occupation: Meterologist with U.S. Weather Bureau
....   10 [175] Adrienne King b: 1988
....   10 [176] Jonathan King b: 1991 in Alabama
....   8   [177] Sue Ellen Hawkins b: 1941 in Warren, Trumbull Co., OH Fact 1: Occupation: R. N. , quilter and hobby-genealogy.
....   +[178] Roger Stewart Bell b: 1938 in East Cleveland, OH m: 03 Nov 1962 in Warren, OH
....   9   [179] Jeffrey Lloyd Bell b: 1963 in Cleveland, OH
....   +[180] Najma Begum Bachelani b: 1963 in Mbale, Uganda m: 21 Feb 1998 in St.Paul, ᵓaul, Minnesota
....   10 [181] Sara Soheila Bell b:1999 in Ann Arbor, Michigan
....   10 [182] Siraj Alexander Bell b: 2001 in Mountain View, California
....   9   [27] Jennifer Elizabeth Bell b: 1965 in Cleveland, OH
....   +[183] Anthony Guy b: in London, England m: 15 Jun 1991 in London, England   divorced 1994
....   *2nd Husband of [27] Jennifer Elizabeth Bell:
....   +[184] James Shipman b:1953 in resides in Pittsburgh, PA m: 25 Sep 1999 in Pittsburgh, PA
....   10 [185] Elizabeth Bell Shipman b: 2004 in Pittsburgh, PA
....   9   [186] Douglas Alexander Bell b: ʻ1968 in Cleveland, OH Fact 2: 1995 Married Rebecca Ching,
....   +[187] Tisha Goss b: 1972 in Parma Heights, Ohio m: 02 Feb 2008 in Middleburg Hts. Ohio
....   10 [188] Lleyton Alexander Bell b: 2009 in Middleburg Hts. Ohio
....   8   [189] Larry Lloyd Hawkins b: 03 Jul 1944 in Warren, Trumbull Co. OH Fact 1: Occupation: WCI Steel- purchasing.
....   +[190] Carol Oravecz b: 1944 in Cleveland, OH m: 26 Aug 1967 in Warren, Trumbull Co. OH Fact 1: Occupation: Dr. degree., Dir.of Day Care at Hosp.
....   9   [191] Michele Lynette Hawkins b: 1971 in Warren, Trumbull Co. OH   ؛ Occupation: Architect; enjoyes horseback riding.
....   +[192] Jeremy Schwartz b: 1971 in Cleveland, OH m: 21 Sep 1996 in Cleveland, OH Fact 1: Advanced degree in Economics.
....   9   [193] Meredith Paula Hawkins b: 1974 in Warren, Trum.Co.OH   Graduate of American Univ.- Public Relations.
....   +[194] Paul Helter Melnick b: 1965 in Arlington, VA m: 18 Apr 1998 in Arlington, Va Fact 1: Occupation: Attorney, legal practice with his father.
....   10 [195] Kelly Valentine Melnick b: 2002 in Arlington, VA
....   10 [196] Theodore Nathaniel Melnick b: 2005 in Arlington, VA
....   8   [197] Mildred Anne Hawkins b: 1950 in Warren, Trumbull Co. OH Fact 1: Resides in Warren, OH. Fact 2: Graduate of Bowling Green U.
....   6   [198] Ernest Hawkins b: 28 Jan 1882 in W. Farmington, Trumbull Co.OH d: 25 Apr 1930 in Yellowstone Park, WY Fact 1: Occupation: Head Bellhop at Yellowstone Fact 2: National Park's Lodge. Burial: Never married, bell hop at Yellowsttone Nat. Park
....   5   [199] Charlotte E. Haine b: 25 Sep 1844 in Bloomfield Twp,Trumbull Co.,OH. d: 16 May 1917 in Iowa
....   +[200] Zwinglius Paley Lyman b: 28 Aug 1844 in Chicago, IL m: 03 Jun 1882 in Bloomfield Twp,Trumbull Co.,OH. d: 03 Jan 1903 in Iowa
....   6   [201] Ralph Lyman b: 26 Jul 1883 d: 15 Mar 1954

```
            +[202] Fannie McIntosh  b: 10 Dec 1883  m: 12 Apr 1907  d: 04 Nov 1958
          7  [203] Ernest McIntosh Lyman  b: 1909 in Germany (while father was studing music)
          7  [204] Clara Margaret Lyman  b: 1913        Had 3 children
          7  [205] David L. Lyman  b: 10 May 1917  d: Aug 1962      4 children
       6  [206] Will Lyman  b: 18 Mar 1885  d: 1970 in Des Moines, Iowa
         +[207] Eva McIntosh  m: 24 Aug 1915
          7  [208] Elizabeth Lyman  b: 1916
          7  [209] William Lyman  b: 1919
          7  [210] Ruth Lyman  b: 1921
          7  [211] Doris Lyman  b: 1923
          7  [212] Eleanor Lyman  b: 1925
          7  [213] Rae Lyman  b: 1930
       6  [214] Marry Lyman  b: 16 Apr 1886
         +[215] George M. Hansen  b: 03 Apr 1887  m: 16 Sep 1908  d: 19 Jul 1972 in Kansas City, MO
          7  [216] Lyman Hansen  b: 1909  d: 1915
          7  [217] Phyllis Hansen  b: 1910
            +[218] Robert Earl McDowell  b: 1908  m: 10 Jun 1921
          7  [219] George (Bob) Hansen  b: 01 Sep 1915  d: 04 Jul 2004 in Missouri
            +[220] Gloria Marie Gregg  m: Nov 1938
             8  [221] John Lyman Hansen  b: 1940
             8  [222] Robert Martin Hansen Hansen  b: 1945
          7  [223] Betty Jean Hansen  b: 1921
            +[224] Charles Robert Nuckolle
             8  [225] Carol Ann Nuckolle  b: 1943
             8  [226] Jr. Charles Robert Nuckolle  b: 1948
             8  [227] John Nuckolle  b: 1954
             8  [228] Phyllis Jean Nuckolle  b: 1955
             8  [229] Paul Thomas Nuckolle  b: 1951
          7  [230] Richard Hansen  b: 1923
            +[231] Louise Curtis  m: Nov 1948
             8  [232] Karen Marie Hansen  b: 1951
             8  [233] Richard Jons Hansen  b: 1954
    5  [234] Mercy Jane Haine  b: 18 Dec 1846 in Bloomfield Twp,Trumbull Co.,OH.  d: 18 Dec 1849 in Bloomfield
       Twp,Trumbull Co.,OH.  Burial: Drowned in the mill race at Clover Hill
    5  [235] Ellen S. Haine  b: 22 Sep 1848 in Bloomfield Twp,Trumbull Co.,OH.  d: 25 Mar 1866 in Bloomfield Twp,Trumbull
       Co.,OH.  Burial: Never married- d. of TB
    5  [236] John Wesley Haine  b: 04 Mar 1852 in Bloomfield Twp,Trumbull Co.,OH.  d: 17 Jan 1912 in CT
      +[237] Hattie C. Burt  b: 27 Apr 1858  m: 01 Jan 1877 in Mesopotamia Twp, Trumbull Co. OH  d: 14 Jan 1933
       6  [238] Harry B. Haine  b: 30 Jun 1878  d: 1945  Burial: No children
         +[239] Myrtle Elder  b: 03 Sep 1878  m: 14 Feb 1900 in (no children)
       6  [240] Eugene Wesley Haine  b: 15 Aug 1883
         +[241] Neola Galbraith  b: 28 Jun 1885  m: 25 Oct 1903  d: 21 Oct 1952
          7  [242] David Eugene Haine  b: 09 Apr 1909  d: 10 Sep 1975
            +[243] Geraldine Nash  b: 1911
             8  [244] Judith Marjory Haine  b: 1933  residing in Texas
               +[245] Ray Fergerson  m: 27 Jun 1953  in 2 children
                9  [246] Stephanie Fergerson  b: in Ohio
                10  [247] Desirae Fergerson
                9  [248] Jennifer Fergerson  b: in Ohio
          7  [249] John Haine  b: 29 Nov 1916  d: 11 Aug 1995
            +[250] Joan Carpenter  m: 08 Jul 1944 in Stamford CT
             8  [251] Joan Dorothy Haine(Jodi)  b: 1950 in Stamford, CT        (single)
             8  [252] Sue Haine  b: 1952 in Stamford, CT
               +[253] Dirk Stanley Roberts  b: 1951 in New York City, NY
                9  [254] Logan Galbraith Haine Roberts  b: 1984 in New York City, NY
                9  [255] Evan Wesley Haine Roberts  b: 1987 in New York City, NY
```

```
       8   [256] Robin Carpenter Haine b: 1954 in Stamford, CT d: in resides in Saratoga Springs, NY, ɔs. NY,
           unmarried
       8   [28] John Haine  b: 1957 in Stamford, CT     resides near Minneapolis, MN
          +[257] Roxanne
       9   [258] John Wesley Haine  b: 1983 in Los Angles, CA
       9   [259] Emily Haine  b: :1985 in Minneapolis, MN
       9   [260] William Haine  b: 1987 in Minneapolis, MN
          *2nd Wife of [28] John Haine:
          +[261] Patricia
       8   [262] Matthew David Haine  b: 1964 in Stamford, CT
     7     [263] Jean Haine  d: 1994 in resided in Atwater and Akron, OH
          +[264] Gunther Haiss  b: 05 Mar 1911  m: 29 Jun 1953  d: Jan 1986
       8   [265] Nola Haiss- resides in Atwater, OH
       8   [266] Hugo Haiss resides in Akron, OH, marr. 2 children
       8   [267] Heidi Haiss
   6       [268] J. Rollin Haine  b: 01 May 1888  d: 24 Dec 1939
          +[269] Dorothy Watson  b: 14 Jan 1890
     7     [270] John Rolin Haine  b: 1916           2 children
          +[271] Anne Josephine McCleary  m: 20 Mar 1941 in 2 children
 5         [272] Emma Jane Haine  b: 06 May 1853 in Bloomfield Twp,Trumbull Co.,OH.  d: 29 Dec 1901 in California
          +[273] B. Frank Beatty  b: 13 Oct 1848  m: 01 Aug 1876 in Bloomfield Twp,Trumbull Co.,OH.  d: 1902
       6   [274] Hazel Beatty  b: in Adopted  d: in Made home w/ Aunt Lottie p/ folks died.
       6   [275] Georgie Beatty  b: 30 Jul 1887
 5         [276] Clara Haine  b: 28 May 1855 in Bloomfield Twp,Trumbull Co.,OH.  d: 26 Jan 1940 in Bloomfield Twp,Trumbull
           Co.,OH.  Burial: Brownwood Cem. Bloomfield, OH
          +[277] Phillip John Cox  b: 1847 in Hornblotten, Somerset, Eng.  m: 12 Jul 1883 in Bloomfield Twp,Trumbull Co.,OH,
           Methodist Church  d: 1929 in Bloomfield Twp,Trumbull Co.,OH  Burial: Brownwood Cem. Bloomfield, OH
       6   [278] Elmer Haine Cox  b: 15 Jun 1884 in Clover Hill, No. Bloomfield, OH  d: 30 May 1966 in Charolette Nursing
           Home, Rock Creek, Ash. Co. OH  Burial: Brownwood Cem. Bloomfield, OH
          +[279] Pearl Abbey  b: 1888  m: 06 Sep 1911 in W.C.&Emma Brainard Home, Warren, OH  d: 1981  Burial:
           Brownwood Cem. Bloomfield, OH
     7     [36] Charles Philip Cox  b: 17 Aug 1912 in Clover Hill, No. Bloomfield, OH  d: 1996 in Bloomfield
           Twp,Trumbull Co.,OH.
          +[35] Hazel Fern Carlson  b: 1913 in Indiana  m: 18 Jun 1936 in Nol Bloomfield, Trumbull Co. OH  ɔ. OH
       8   [37] Carol Ann Cox  b: 1939
          +[38] Edward Sasey  b: 1936  m: 20 Jun 1971
       9   [39] Seth Edward Sasey  b: 1976
          +[40] Linda
       10  [41] Samantha Sasey  b: 1999
       9   [42] Charles Steven Sasey  b: 1976
          +[43] Rebecca
       10  [44] Blake Sasey  b: 2006
       10  [45] Corrine Sasey  b: 2010 in Mantua, Ohio
       8   [46] Carrie Jean Cox  b: 1941
     7     [280] Robert Lee Cox  b: 1916 in Clover Hill, No. Bloomfield, OH
          +[281] Esther Neimi Dowling  b: 1918  m: 03 May 1947
       8   [282] Roy Cox  b: 1948
          +[283] Regina M. Kopesko  m: 1979
       8   [284] Phillip Cox  b: 1949
          +[285] Susan Shulman  m: 1976
       9   [286] Rachel S. Cox  b: 1975
       8   [287] Daniel Cox  b: 1951
       8   [288] David Edwin Cox  b: 1953
       8   [289] Susan Cox  b: 1960
     7     [290] John Henry Cox  b: 13 Aug 1922 in Warren, OH  d: 20 Jun 2010 in Brownwood Cemetery
          +[291] Marian Irene Payne  b: 1922  m: 22 Jul 1950
       8   [292] Mary Ann Cox  b: 1952
```

+[293] H. Douglas Bear b: 1952 m: 26 Jun 1976
9 [294] Matthew Thomas Bear b: 1979
9 [295] Andrew Douglas Bear b: 1982
9 [296] Rachael Bear
8 [297] Rev. James Jay Cox b: 1955
+[298] Rev. Kate Maxfield b: 1959 m: 28 May 1982
8 [299] Alan Lee Cox b: 1964
7 [300] Emogene Valeria Cox b: 15 Jun 1924 in Warren, OH d: 25 Aug 1976 Burial: Brownwood Cem. Bloomfield, OH
+[301] Eugene Ruehle b: 03 Dec 1913 m: in Divorce unk.
8 [302] John Irvin Ruehle b: 1949
+[303] Catherine Harris b:1948 m: 19 Dec 1969
9 [304] Melaine Lynn Ruehle b: 1970
9 [305] Stephinie Ann Ruehle b: 1972
9 [306] Jeffrey Ruehle b: 1975
9 [307] Christa Leann Ruehle b:1979
8 [308] Caroline Valeria Ruehle b: 1958
+[309] Gregery Sparks m: 1976
9 [310] Rebecca Allicon Sparks b: 1977
9 [311] Mathew Addison Sparks b: 1978
6 [312] Bertha Grace Cox b: 28 Apr 1887 in Clover Hill, No. Bloomfield, OH d: 04 Nov 1984 in Warren, OH
+[313] Clyde Cleveland McMillan b: 1886 m: 24 Oct 1911 in Clover Hill, No Bloomfield, OH
7 [314] Eldon McMillan b: 1913
+[315] Maude King b: 1917 m: 16 Nov 1934   3 children
8 [29] Donald McMillan b: 1935
+[316] Hildah Hassink
*2nd Wife of [29] Donald McMillan:
+[317] Barbara Keller m: 24 Feb 1962   divorice unknown
8 [30] June Evelyn McMillan b: 1938
+[318] Stanley Johnson m: 12 Jul 1954
9 [319] Scott M. Johnson Johnson b: 1958
*2nd Husband of [30] June Evelyn McMillan:
+[320] Fred Darling m: 14 May 1957
9 [321] Mary Ellen Darling
9 [322] Maurine Suzanne Darling
9 [323] Jr. Fred Darling
8 [324] Kathleen McMillan b: 1941
+[325] William J. McGrinna m: 1964
9 [326] Connie McGrinna b: 1965
9 [327] Thomas McGrinna b: 1966
7 [31] Leila McMillan b: 1915
+[328] Alvin Grimm b: 20 Dec 1908 m: 15 Nov 1941 in 2 children   d: 09 Oct 1965
8 [329] James Arthur Grimm b: 1945
+[330] Fatnsh Gozsecen
9 [331] Bulant Grimm b: in Adopted
8 [332] Rev. Joan Phyllis Grimm b: 1949
+[333] Jr. Donald Ross Fraser m: 07 Jul 1979 in Kenyon College, Gamblier, OH
9 [334] Lee Authur Fraser b: Adoption
*2nd Husband of [31] Leila McMillan:
+[335] Calvin Huntley m: 06 Jan 1973
7 [336] Delbert McMillan b: 1915
+[337] Hope Weir b: 1918 m: 05 Aug 1959   4 children
8 [338] William Ray McMillan b: 1942 in Warren, OH
+[339] Sandra Bill m: 12 Sep 1970
9 [340] Mike Scott McMillan b: 1973
9 [341] Maya Dawn McMillan b: 1975
8 [342] Fred James McMillan b: 1943 in Warren, OH

.... +[343] Mary Lee Braden m: 16 Sep 1967
.... 9 [344] James Richard McMillan b: 1968
.... 9 [345] Richard D. McMillan b: 1971
.... 9 [346] John Fred McMillan b: 1977
.... 8 [347] Carl Richard McMillan b: 1946 in Warren, OH
.... +[348] Janet Pimberton m: 28 Jun 1970
.... 9 [349] Heather McMillan b: 1976
.... 9 [350] Byron Allen McMillan b: 1978
.... 8 [351] Leah Beth McMillan b: 1951
.... 7 [352] Ralph McMillan b: 30 Dec 1917 d: 02 Aug 1981
.... +[353] Jean Lytle b: 07 Jan 1921 m: 07 Jun 1940 8 children
.... 8 [354] Jr. Ralph Edward McMillan b: 1941
.... +[355] Phyllis Boles m: 1963
.... 9 [356] Jr. Ralph McMillan
.... 9 [357] Eric McMillan
.... 9 [358] Patrick McMillan
.... 8 [359] Daniel Earl McMillan b: 1943
.... +[360] Anna Speaker m: 18 May 1963
.... 9 [361] Jr. Daniel McMillan
.... 9 [362] Gregory McMillan
.... 8 [363] Jack Reray McMillan b: 1947
.... +[364] Sarah Thompson m: 16 Oct 1966
.... 9 [365] John Wayne McMillan
.... 8 [366] Jean Louise McMillan b: 1947
.... +[367] Ronald Ruse m: 1966
.... 9 [368] Elizabeth Ann Ruse
.... 9 [369] Jr. Ronald Ruse
.... 8 [370] Timothy Paul McMillan b: 1950
.... 8 [371] Terrance Lee McMillan b: 25 Jul 1954 d: 09 Mar 1955
.... 8 [372] Wanda Loren McMillan b: 1956
.... +[373] Robert Stankewich m: 31 Aug 1974
.... 8 [374] Larina Grace McMillan b: 20 Nov 1957 d: 21 Nov 1957
.... 7 [32] Helen McMillan b: 1919
.... +[375] James Hearn b: 17 Mar 1900 m: 21 Oct 1936 in 6 children d: 1963
.... 8 [376] Patricia Ann Hearn b: 1937
.... 8 [377] Deloris Irene Hearn b: 1938
.... 8 [378] Gerald Francis Hearn b: 1941
.... 8 [379] Daniel Clyde Hearn b: 1949
.... 8 [380] Rose Ellen Hearn b: 1949
.... 8 [381] Thomas John Hearn b: 1953
.... *2nd Husband of [32] Helen McMillan:
.... +[382] Mike Blazevic m: 04 May 1968
.... 8 [383] James Blazevic b: in Adopted
.... 8 [384] Mary Elaine Blazevic b: in Adopted
.... 7 [385] Ruth McMillan b: 17 Sep 1920 d: 23 Mar 1985
.... +[386] Louis Chuhay b: 1913 m: 23 Mar 1942 2 children
.... 8 [33] Noma L. Chuhay b: 1946
.... +[387] James Bonheimer m: 08 Apr 1968
.... 9 [388] Owen James Bonheimer b: 1974
.... 9 [389] Nathan Wade Bonheimer b: 1976
.... *2nd Husband of [33] Noma L. Chuhay:
.... +[390] James Bonheimer m: 08 Apr 1968
.... 9 [391] Owen James Bonheimer b: 1974
.... 8 [392] Laura C. Chuhay b: 1950
.... +[393] Dan Keller m: 08 Feb 1974
.... 9 [394] Jeffrey D. Keller Keller b: 1979
.... 7 [395] Vera McMillan b: 1924

```
            +[396] Ray Willson  b: 21 Aug 1920  m: 13 Dec 1943 in 3 children  d: 2002
         8  [397] Lynn Rae Willson  b: 1945
            +[398] Gregory Christman  b: 1943  m: 17 Sep 1966
          9   [399] Ellen Elizabeth Christman  b: 1970
          9   [400] Leif Benjamin Christman  b: 1972
         8  [401] Karen Willson  b: 1948       4 sons
            +[402] Rev. Peter DeBartolo  m: 16 May 1981
          9   [403] Peter John DeBartolo  b: 1983
         8  [404] Robert Ray Willson  b: 1951
            +[405] Sue Gettig  m: 24 Aug 1968
          9   [406] Michelle Susan Willson  b: 1969
          9   [407] Kimberly Rae Willson  b: 1971
         8  [408] Jr. Delmare Ray Willson  b:1961
         8  [409] Heather Elizabeth Willson  b: 1965
            +[410] Donald Lockney  m: 09 Jan 1982
         8  [411] Tamara Sue Willson  b: 1969
      7  [34] Dorothy McMillan  b:1928
         +[412] Don Cole  b: 19 Sep 1921  m: 04 Apr 1948 in 2 children  d: Feb 1973
         8  [413] Lawrence E. Cole  b: 1949
            +[414] Cynthia Melone  m: 19 May 1968
          9   [415] Heather Lee Cole  b: 1974
          9   [416] Jennifer Cole  b: 1969
          9   [417] Micheal Cole  b: 1970
         8  [418] Janice Lynn Cole  b: 1951
            +[419] Paul Bowman  m: 21 Aug 1970
          9   [420] David Robert Bowman  b: 1975
            *2nd Husband of [34] Dorothy McMillan:
            +[421] Marvin Gannaway  m: 24 Dec 1975
      7  [422] Clara Alice McMillan  b: 1933
         +[423] William Talbert  b: 1931 in West Virginia  m: 18 Mar 1956    9 children
         8  [424] Roger Eugene Talbert  b: 1956
         8  [425] Deboroah Lynn Talbert  b: 1958
         8  [426] Terri Ann Talbert  b: 1959
         8  [427] Richard Wayne Talbert  b: 1963
         8  [428] Jack Edward Talbert  b: 1962
         8  [429] Albert Glen Talbert  b: 1963
         8  [430] Robert Allen Talbert  b:1964
         8  [431] Cynthia Dian Talbert  b: 1965
         8  [432] Pamela June Talbert  b: 1966
   6  [433] Mabel Cox  b: 30 Aug 1888 in Clover Hill, No.Bloomfield,Trumbull Co.,OH  d: 28 Jul 1979 in Community
      Skilled Nursing Home, Warren, OH  Burial: (Hazel Cox's stepmother)Brownwood Cem.
      +[434] Charles Carlson  b: 11 Jul 1871 in Hollingsburg, Sweden  m: 22 May 1922 in No. Bloomfield, OH  d: 05 Jul
      1945 in Bloomfield Twp,Trum. Co,OH  Burial: Brownwood Cem. Bloomfield, OH
      7  [435] Alfred Carlson  b: 1894
      7  [436] Emery Carlson  b: 1896
      7  [437] Florence Carlson  b: 1898
      7  [438] Myrtle Carlson  b: 1900
      7  [439] Clyde Carlson  b: 1903
      7  [440] Edward Carlson  b: 1908
   7  [35] Hazel Fern Carlson  b: 1913 in Indiana
      +[36] Charles Philip Cox  b: 17 Aug 1912 in Clover Hill, No. Bloomfield, OH  m: 18 Jun 1936 in No
      Bloomfield, Trumbull Co. OH  d: 1996 in Bloomfield Twp,Trumbull Co.,OH.
         8  [37] Carol Ann Cox  b: 1939
            +[38] Edward Sasey  b: 1936  m: 20 Jun 1971
          9   [39] Seth Edward Sasey  b:1976
                +[40] Linda
              10  [41] Samantha Sasey  b: 1999
```

.... 9 [42] Charles Steven Sasey b: 1976
.... +[43] Rebecca
.... 10 [44] Blake Sasey b: 2006
.... 10 [45] Corrine Sasey b: 2010 in Mantua, Ohio
.... 8 [46] Carrie Jean Cox b: 1941
.... 6 [441] Estella Cox b: 11 Jun 1890 in Clover Hill, No. Bloomfield, OH d: 23 Aug 1983 in Gillette Nursing Home, Warren, OH(never married) Burial: Brownwood Cem. Bloomfield, OH
.... 6 [442] Ethel Mae Cox b: 03 May 1892 in Bloomfield Twp,Trum. Co,OH d: 10 Sep 1985 in Williamsfield, Ashtabula Co. OH Burial: Hayes Cemetery, Williamsfield, OH
.... +[443] Samuel William Jones b: 18 Dec 1890 in Williamsfield, (Wayne), Ashtabula Co. OH m: 14 Jan 1913 in No. Bloomfield, OH d: 17 Jan 1974 in Williamsfield, (Wayne), Ashtabula Co. OH
.... 7 [444] Neoma Belle Jones b: 01 Jun 1918 in Williamsfield (Wayne), Ashtabula Co. OH d: 09 Apr 1994 in Columbia, MO Burial: Callao, MO
.... +[445] Jr. Herbert Virgil Cook b: 01 May 1918 m: 27 Oct 1946 in Jones House, Williamsfield, OH d: 19 Jul 1982 in Callao, MO
.... 8 [446] Linda Marie Cook b: 25 Jun 1948 d: 14 Jul 1952
.... 8 [447] William Douglas Cook b: 1951
.... +[448] Susan Spencer m: 05 Aug 1979 in Divorced 15 Jan 1995
.... 9 [449] Jonathan David Cook b: 1983
.... 9 [450] Hether Jolinne Cook b: 1987
.... 8 [451] Robert Dean Cook b: 1956
.... 7 [452] Willard Philip Jones b: 1933 in Andover, Ashtabula Co. OH
.... +[453] Ruth Joan Khota b: 1938 m: 30 Aug 1958 in Wayne Congregational Church, Williamsfield,OH
.... 8 [454] Rhonda Ann Jones b: 1959
.... 8 [455] Douglas Samuel Jones b: 20 Sep 1961 d: 16 Apr 1978 in Norristown, PA Burial: Hayes Cemetery, Williamsfield, OH
.... 8 [456] Stanley Craig Jones b: 1964
.... 8 [457] Marvin Todd Jones b: 1966
.... 6 [458] Earl Philip Cox b: 30 Nov 1894 in Clover Hill, No. Bloomfield, OH d: 04 Mar 1982 in Lake Forest, IL Burial: IL
.... +[459] Myra Howey b: 25 Feb 1894 in Congress, OH m: 26 May 1920 in Congress, OH d: Unknown Burial: IL
.... 7 [460] Marjorie Cox b: 1925 three sons
.... +[461] Devere Halvie m: 08 May 1948 in Hilton Chapel, Chicago University
.... 8 [462] Scott Philip Halvie b: 1950
.... 8 [463] Mark Allen Halvie b: 1953
.... 8 [464] Kirk Halvie
.... 8 [465] Brett Halvie
.... 7 [466] Roger Cox b: 1929 Never married
.... 6 [467] William Edward Cox b: 24 Apr 1902 in Clover Hill, No. Bloomfield, OH d: 04 Mar 1990 in ? Burial: Moved to Graymont IL, Pontiac, IL area
.... +[468] Maurine Annabelle Carlson b: 1906 m: 21 Jul 1928 in Graymont, IL d: Unknown
.... 7 [469] Ronald Jerome Cox b: 1931 in Warren, OH
.... +[470] Winnifred Kennedy m: 24 Aug 1958 in first Lutheran Church Pontiac, IL
.... 8 [471] Lynda Sue Cox b: 1959
.... 8 [472] Marsha Kay Cox b: 1965
.... 7 [47] Claire Yvonne Cox b: 1937 in Warren, OH
.... +[473] Gordon Eichelberger
.... *2nd Husband of [47] Claire Yvonne Cox:
.... +[474] Donald L. DeVore m: 20 Oct 1957 in Divorced
.... 8 [48] Kevin Lee DeVore b: 1963 Adopted
.... +[49] Sherri Kraft m: 30 Jun 1984 in First Methodist Church, El Paco, IL
.... *3rd Husband of [47] Claire Yvonne Cox:
.... +[475] Gordon Eichelberger b: 1936 m: 30 Dec 1967
.... 8 [48] Kevin Lee DeVore b: 1963 Adopted
.... +[49] Sherri Kraft m: 30 Jun 1984 in First Methodist Church, El Paco, IL
.... 5 [476] Charles Robert Haine b: 09 May 1857 in Bloomfield Twp,Trumbull Co.,OH. d: 02 Jul 1926

.... +[477] Beckie Millikin m: 13 May 1885 in Bloomfield Twp,Trumbull Co.,OH. d: 29 Jul 1945
.... 6 [50] William Haine b: 06 Mar 1891 d: 12 Nov 1970 in Hartford, CT
.... +[478] Norma Allen b: 1895 m: 20 Jun 1920 d: 1952
.... *2nd Wife of [50] William Haine:
.... +[479] Helen Francis m: 14 May 1955
.... 6 [480] Harold Haine b: 22 Mar 1898 Burial: No children
.... +[481] Madeline H. Thornton m: 24 Sep 1947 in Warren, OH
.... 4 [51] Mary Haine b: 17 Jun 1807 in E. Pennard, Somerset, Eng. d: 10 Feb 1848
.... +Stephen Symes b: in Hornblotten, Somerset, England d: 1837 in to US in 1835, died in Bloomfield, OH
.... 5 Albert Symes
.... *2nd Husband of [51] Mary Haine:
.... +James Haine m: 11 Nov 1826 in had 5 children
.... 4 Rhoda Haine b: 28 Nov 1808 in Pilton, Somerset, Eng. d: 06 Mar 1827 in At age 18, E. Pennard, Somerset, Eng.
.... 4 [52] John Haine b: 22 Jul 1810 in E. Pennard, Som. d: 29 Aug 1860 in accident, of W. Bradley
.... +[53] Mary Ann Haine b: Abt. 1820 m: 1843 in Shepton Mallet, Somerset. (2 children, no issue d: 30 May 1864 in Baltonsborough, Somerset, Eng.
.... 4 Eleanor Haine b: 03 May 1813 in E. Pennard, Som, England d: 29 May 1835 in East Pennard, Somerset, Eng.
.... +John Day b: 1813 in of Hunham, m: 24 Apr 1834 in East Pennard, Somerset, England d: 17 Dec 1896 in East Pennard, Somerset, Eng.
.... 5 Son Day b: 1833 d: 1835
.... 4 [54] George Haine b: 10 Feb 1815 in East Pennard, Somerset, Eng. d: 19 Dec 1872 in Of Stone, Somerset, England
.... +[55] Jane Haine b: 25 Nov 1814 in Pilton, Somerset, Eng. m: 21 Apr 1835 in Pilton, Somerset, (Cousins) d: 08 Oct 1883 in Of Stone, E. Pennard, Somerset, Eng.
.... 5 [56] John Haine b: Dec 1839 d: 27 Sep 1902 in Went to PA, USA
.... +[57] Elizabeth Gough b: 22 Jan 1846 in Rodley, Westbury on Severn, W. Glo'ster, England d: 26 Jan 1897 in orwell, Oh
.... 6 [58] John Howard Haine b: 1872 d: 1958 Burial: Windsor, OH
.... +[59] Harriette Cummins b: 1875 d: 1947 Burial: Windsor, OH
.... 7 [60] Cuthbert Elroy Haine b: 17 Jun 1910 d: 06 Aug 2003 in Hershey, PA Burial: Rochester, NY
.... +[61] Amelia Carothers b: 1911 in Beaver Falls, PA
.... 8 [62] David Arthur Haine b: 1940 d: 1946 in Rochester, NY
.... 8 [63] James L. Haine
.... 8 [64] Debra K. Haine
.... +[65] ? Wentz
.... 7 [66] James Howard Haine b: 28 Sep 1913 d: 06 Jan 2003 in Hershey, PA
.... 8 [67] Dean Haine
.... +[68] Susie ??
.... 9 [69] Oneson Haine
.... 9 [70] Twoson Haine
.... 4 Mercy J. Haine b: 01 Jan 1817 in West Pennard, Somerset, England d: 18 Jan 1892 in Charlottetown, Prince Edward Island, Canada Burial: St. Peter's Cemetery, Charlottetown, PEI.
.... +George H. Coles b: Sep 1810 in Charlottetown, Prince Edward Island, Canada m: 15 Aug 1833 in East Pennard, Somerset, England (12 children) d: 21 Aug 1875 in Charlottetown, Royality, Prince Edward Island, Canada
.... 5 Ellen Sarah Coles b: 30 Dec 1834 in Charlottetown, PEI, Canada d: 1878
.... 5 Jane Haine Coles b: 09 Oct 1836 in Charlottetown, PEI, Canada d: 06 Aug 1868
.... 5 Eliza Anne Coles b: 26 Jan 1840 in Charlottetown, PEI, Canada d: 19 Jun 1914 in Toronto, Canada
.... +Arthur Swabey b: 1839 in England m: 14 Dec 1864 in Charlottetown, PEI, Canada d: 1869
.... 6 Charles Swabey
.... 6 Isal Swabey
.... +Andrew Ridout
.... 6 dau Swabey
.... 5 Georgiana Louise Coles b: 19 Feb 1842 in Charlottetown, PEI, Canada d: 1911 in PEI
.... +Alexander Brown d: 1891
.... 6 Ella Mercy Brown b: 1864 d: 1910
.... +David A Starr m: 1887
.... 7 Marjorie Starr
.... +Jack Morrison

```
............................................  7  Norah Starr
............................................  +? Good
............................................  5  Mercy Anne Coles b: 05 Feb 1838 in Charlottetown, PEI, Canada d: 1921
............................................  5  Louisa Coles b: 09 Jun 1844 in Charlottetown, PEI, Canada
............................................  5  Mary Jane Coles b: 04 Apr 1846 in Charlottetown, PEI, Canada
............................................  5  Mary Victoria Coles b: 28 Jun 1847 in Charlottetown, PEI, Canada
............................................  5  Alexandrina Octavia Coles b: 29 Mar 1853 in Charlottetown, PEI, Canada
............................................  5  George Bannerman Russel Coles b: 01 Mar 1855 in Charlottetown, PEI, Canada d: 09 Sep 1878 in Oakland, CA
............................................  5  William Haine Coles b: 01 Mar 1857 in Charlottetown, PEI, Canada d: 10 Oct 1857 in Charolottetown, PEI
............................................  5  Charles Haine Coles b: 1859 in PEI
....................  3  George Haine b: Bef. 1778 in North Wootton, Somerset, Eng. d: 18 Oct 1810 Burial: (bachelor)
....................  3  [71] Thomas Haine b: Abt. 1780 in North Wotton, Somerset, Eng. d: 03 Dec 1850 in Resided in Croscombe, Ditcheat, Somerset,
                         Eng.
..........................  +Anna Look b: Abt. 1787 m: in Ditcheat
....................  *2nd Wife of [71] Thomas Haine:
..........................  +Ann Look b: Abt. 1787 in Glastonbury, Somerset, Eng. m: 01 Dec 1821 in Ditcheat, Somerset, England d: Bef. 1880 in Of
                            Edgarley, Coxbridge and W. Pennard. Burial: (sister of Sarah)
....................  4  [73] Thomas Haine b: 1822 d: 1892
..........................  +Mary Ann Look d: 1892 Burial: (daughter of Uncle G. Look)
..........................  5  [72] Robert John Haine b: 1856 d: 1921 in Farmed near Stratton-on-Avon from 1890
..........................  +Sally Vaux d: 1906
..........................  *2nd Wife of [72] Robert John Haine:
..........................  +Marianne Horne d: 1965
....................  *2nd Wife of [73] Thomas Haine:
..........................  +Ann Haine b: in manor Farm, Yeovilton m: 1845 d: in (daughter of Uncle Wm. Haine)
..........................  5  Sarah Mary Roberta Haine
..........................  +/// Bullard
....................................  6  Eileen Patrica Bullard b: Abt. 1933 d: 21 Nov 2004 in Biringham, England
....................................  +/// Nicholas
....................................  7  Hanna Nicholas
....................  4  Ann Haine
..........................  +Elijah Jacob b: in Surrey, England
..........................  5  Theodora Jacob
..........................  5  Fanny Jacobs
..........................  5  Ellen Jacobs
....................  4  Jane Haine b: 1827 in Coxbridge d: 1910
..........................  +W. W. Look
..........................  5  son Look d: 1911 in Toronto, Canada
..........  3  Joseph Haine b: Mar 1782 in Somerset, Eng. d: May 1819 in Ditcheat, Somerset, England @ 36 yrs.
....................  +SARAH LOOK b: 01 Jan 1786 in Glastonbury, Somerset, England-bapt. St. John's m: 06 Mar 1810 in St. John Parish Church,
                       Glastonbury d: 10 Oct 1859 in Ditcheat, Somerset, Bur. Burial: 15 Oct 1859
....................  4  Joseph Haine b: 04 Apr 1811 d: 1882 in Resided at Whitehall Farm, Egham, Surrey in 1870
..........................  +Harriet Bond m: in 5 sons, 4 daug.
..........................  5  John B. Haine b: 1839 d: 1880 in Sold milk at Wimbledon
....................................  6  Mable Haine
....................................  6  Gussie Haine
....................................  6  Frank Haine d: 1937 Burial: 2 children, 1 granddaughter
..........................  5  Fredrick Haine d: in Of Pooley Lodge Egham
..........................  5  Joe Haine b: 1851 d: in Farmer at Egham
....................................  6  Harold Haine
....................................  6  Mervyn Haine b: 1883
....................................  +Mag Hill m: in 1 daughter
....................................  6  Claude Haine b: 1883 d: in dentist in Aberdeen, Scot.
....................................  +Evie Hill m: in 5 children
..........................  5  Ellen Haine
..........................  +J. Caddey
..........................  5  Ernest Haine d: 1936 in Electrician at Paddington
```

.... 4 [74] George Haine b: 1812 in Croscombe, Somerset, England d: 1895 in Over, Glos., from Tintinhull
.... +Frances Look b: 13 Dec 1819 m: 18 Dec 1838 in Lovington, Somerset, England d: 13 Feb 1887
.... 5 Annie Haine d: 1906
.... +Job Corry d: in grocer
.... 5 Edward Haine b: in Of Churchdown
.... +Jane Priday
.... 6 Sidney Haine b: in to New Zealand
.... 6 Leonard Haine
.... 6 Frank Haine b: in Of Vancouver
.... 6 William Haine b: in to So. Africa
.... 6 Charles Haine
.... 6 Jane Haine
.... 6 Philip Haine b: in Of Glouster d: in 6 children
.... +Kate
.... 6 George Haine b: in Of S. Africa
.... 6 Dora Haine
.... +Hugh Wellington
.... 5 Joesph William Haine b: 1836 d: 1893 in Farmer in Churchham, Glos.
.... +Carolyn Priday d: 1896 in 15 children
.... 6 Minnie Rose Haine b: 1864 d: 1940 in Canada
.... +F. C. Simpson b: in Of Dartmouth
.... 6 Harry Haine b: 1867
.... 6 Lucy Agnes Haine
.... +Harry Oliver m: in paddington d: in India, 3 children
.... 6 Arthur Haine d: in lived in Canada, West coast
.... +Molly
.... 6 Norah Haine
.... 6 Fred Priday Haine Burial: S. Africa, 2 daughters
.... 6 Muriel Haine
.... +Thomas Whitley Burial: 2 children,
.... 6 Ernest Victor Haine Burial: 4 children
.... 6 Ethel Haine
.... 6 Gladys Haine d: in lived at Vancouver Is.
.... 5 [56] John Haine b: Dec 1839 d: 27 Sep 1902 in Went to PA, USA
.... +[57] Elizabeth Gough b: 22 Jan 1846 in Rodley, Westbury on Severn, W. Glo'ster, England d: 26 Jan 1897 in orwell, Oh
.... 6 [58] John Howard Haine b: 1872 d: 1958 Burial: Windsor, OH
.... +[59] Harriette Cummins b: 1875 d: 1947 Burial: Windsor, OH
.... 7 [60] Cuthbert Elroy Haine b: 17 Jun 1910 d: 06 Aug 2003 in Hershey, PA Burial: Rochester, NY
.... +[61] Amelia Carothers b: 13 Jul 1911 in Beaver Falls, PA
.... 8 [62] David Arthur Haine b: 1940 d: 1946 in Rochester, NY
.... 8 [63] James L. Haine
.... 8 [64] Debra K. Haine
.... +[65] ? Wentz
.... 7 [66] James Howard Haine b: 28 Sep 1913 d: 06 Jan 2003 in Hershey, PA
.... 8 [67] Dean Haine
.... +[68] Susie ??
.... 9 [69] Oneson Haine
.... 9 [70] Twoson Haine
.... 5 Edmund Haine b: 1854 d: 1921 Burial: (brother of Frances and Sarah)
.... +Emma Look b: 1860 d: 1943 in Niagara, Ont. Canada
.... 6 Percy Haine
.... 7 Frances Haine
.... +John Dawson
.... 8 Leelah Dawson
.... 7 Olive Haine
.... +George Seibel

.... 8 Elizabeth Seibel
.... +James Grice
.... 7 Kathleen Haine
.... 5 Fredrick Haine b: 1856
.... 5 Ernest Augustus Haine b: 1857 in Over, Gloucester, England d: 1932 in Granville, NSW Burial: Waverley Cemetery, Waverley, Australia
.... +Mary M. Elland b: 06 May 1853 in Glebe, NSW, Aust. m: 19 Jan 1886 in Sydney, NSW, Australia d: 30 Jun 1905 in Waverley Cemetary, Australia Burial: Waverley Cemetery, Waverley, Australia
.... 6 Reginald Ernest Haine b: 1886 in Balmain, Australia d: Abt. 1956
.... +Gladys M. Sperrin b: 1886 in Balmain, Australia m: 1912 in Sydney, Australia
.... 7 Oliver George Haine b: 1912 in Waterloo d: 1982 in died on a cruise ship
.... +Phyllis Victoria Marshall m: 1940 in Sydney, Australia d: 1969
.... 8 Michael Marshall Haine b: 1941 in Longueville, NSW, Australia
.... +Cleo b: 1943 in NSW, Australia m: 1968 in NSW, Australia
.... 9 Marnie Victoria Haine b: 1970 in NSW, Australia
.... +James Rodney Richards b: in Maryborough, Victoria m: 1993 d: in (Australian Navy)
.... 10 Samuel James Richards b: 1994 in Australia
.... 10 Hannah Victoria Richards b: 1996 in Australia
.... 10 Emma Richards b: 2003 in Australia
.... 10 William Michael Richards b: 2006 in Australia
.... 9 Ashley Gibson Haine b: 1972 in NSW, Australia
.... +"Bec"
.... 9 Stephen Michael Haine b: 1975 in NSW, Australia
.... 7 Reginald James Haine b: 1917 in Redfern, Australia d: 2007 in New South Wales, Australia
.... +Olga Patricia Jones m: 1944 in Petersham, Australia
.... 8 Bruce Leslie Haine b:1961 in Stanmore, Sydney (of Guildford, NSW)
.... +Trudy
.... *2nd Wife of [74] George Haine:
.... +Frances Look b: 13 Dec 1819 m: 01 Apr 1834 d: 13 Feb 1887
.... 5 John Haine b: 04 Sep 1844 in Ledbury, Glous., England d: 27 Sep 1902 in Orwell, OH
.... +[57] Elizabeth Gough b: 22 Jan 1846 in Rodley, Westbury on Severn, W. Glo'ster, England d: 26 Jan 1897 in Orwell, OH
.... 6 John Howard Haine b: 21 Oct 1872 in Ledbury, Glous., England d: 22 May 1958 in Wilkinsburg, PA USA
.... +Harriette Cordelia Cummings b: 01 Jul 1875 in Hartsgrove, OH m: 15 Oct 1898 d: 09 Nov 1947 in Rochester, PA
.... 7 [60] Cuthbert Elroy Haine b: 17 Jun 1910 d: 06 Aug 2003 in Hershey, PA Burial: Rochester, NY
.... +[61] Amelia Carothers b: 1911 in Beaver Falls, PA
.... 8 [62] David Arthur Haine b: 1940 d: 1946 in Rochester, NY
.... 8 [63] James L. Haine
.... 8 [64] Debra K. Haine
.... +[65] ? Wentz
.... 7 James Haine
.... 4 Thomas Haine b: 25 Dec 1813
.... +Ava Barnes m: 1856
.... 4 [75] MARY HAINE b: 14 Mar 1816 in Church Hill,Somersetshire,England d: 31 Jul 1890 in Bloomfield Twp,Trumbull Co.,OH. Fact 1: Mary is one of nine children. Burial: Brownwood Cemetery, No. Bloomfield, Trum. Co., OH
.... +[76] WILLIAM HAINE b: 08 Feb 1806 in Stone, E. Pennard,Somersetshire,England m: 11 Apr 1836 in Lovington Church,Somerset,Eng. d: 14 Sep 1895 in Bloomfield Twp,Trumbull Co.,OH. Fact 1: 11 Apr 1835 sailed and landed at Prince Edward Is. Fact 2: Soon went to Pictou, Nova Scotia. Burial: Brownwood Cemetery, No. Bloomfield, Trum. Co., OH
.... 5 [21] William Joseph Haine b: 11 Jan 1837 in Bloomfield Twp,Trumbull Co.,OH. d: 18 May 1923 in Ashville, NC. 105 Regt. OVI Infantry
.... +[77] Sarah Goddard Hawkins b: 26 Jul 1834 in Westbrook,Evercreech, Somersetshire,Eng. m: 11 Aug 1862 in Warren, Trumbull Co.,OH d: 06 Aug 1867 in Bloomfield Twp,Trumbull Co.,OH.,died at 33yrs.
.... 6 [78] Theodosia Haine b: 15 Dec 1863 in No. Bloomfield, OH d: 10 Aug 1930 in Warren,Oh Fact 1: Never married. Fact 2: Crippled and unable to walk from approx.
.... *2nd Wife of [21] William Joseph Haine:

+[79] Cornelia Wolcott b: 20 Oct 1848 in West Farmington, Ohio m: 05 Jun 1872 in West Farmington, Trumbull Co., OH d: 19 Feb 1923 in West Farmington, Ohio
6 [80] Mary Jane Haine b: 16 Jan 1874 d: 18 Nov 1931 in divorced
+[81] Dr. Kelly m: 26 Apr 1898
6 [82] Emma Grace Haine b: 03 Sep 1876 d: 12 Aug 1946 in Never married, lived at home and cared for Theodosia.
6 [83] George Austin Haine b: 28 May 1878
+[84] Eva Marie Thompson m: 06 Feb 1919
7 [85] Marie Cornelia Haine unmarried and lived in Cleveland
6 [86] William Jay Haine b: 12 May 1880 d: 01 Jan 1936 in No children
+[87] Jesse B. Little m: 13 Jun 1923 d: 13 Jun 1923
6 [88] Clarence Haine b: 13 Nov 1882 d: 21 Dec 1957 in Never married, died in rest home, Had a bicycle shop.
6 [89] Mabel Haine b: 29 Nov 1884 d: Mar 1916 in Ashville, NC, No children
+[90] Elmer Hughes d: 07 Oct 1914
6 [91] Theodore Haine b: 1888 d: 1889 in died in infancy.
5 [92] Mary Sarah Haine b: 08 Sep 1838 in Bloomfield Twp,Trumbull Co.,OH. d: 11 Jan 1910 in Bloomfield Twp,Trumbull Co.,OH.(lived and died at Clover Hill)
5 [93] George E. Haine b: 28 Feb 1840 in Bloomfield Twp,Trumbull Co.,OH. d: 06 Feb 1920 in No children 105 Regt. Union Infantry OVI
+[94] Sarah Creed b: 24 Jul 1841 m: 14 Mar 1870 in Bristolville, Trumbull Co. OH-no children d: 12 Oct 1920 in Bloomfield Twp,Trumbull Co.,OH
5 [95] FRANCES HARRIET HAINE b: 29 Jan 1842 in Bloomfield Twp, Trumbull Co.OH d: 31 May 1911 in Forest Depot,VA, Bur:Bloomfield OH. Burial: Brownwood Cemetery, Bloomfield, OH
+[96] Thomas Goddard HAWKINS b: 05 Nov 1832 in Evercreech,Somerset Co.,England m: 01 Mar 1863 in Trumbull Co.OH d: 03 Aug 1903 in W. Farmington, Trumbull Co.OH Burial: Brownwood Cemetery, Bloomfield, OH
6 [97] Emma Hawkins b: 13 Feb 1864 in Bloomfield, Trumbull Co.OH d: 07 Mar 1893 in San Francisco,Ca, at 29 yrs. as deaconess -Meth.Church Burial: Died of smallpox, bur. San Francisco
6 [98] George William Hawkins b: 08 Feb 1865 in Bloomfield Twp,Trum. Co,OH d: 06 Oct 1868 in Cooperstown, PA Burial: "died from eatting too many grapes", perhaps dehydration
6 [99] Pliny Haine Hawkins b: 28 Oct 1869 in Bloomfield Twp,Trumbull Co.,OH. d: 15 Sep 1940 in Long Beach , CA
+[100] Grace Alice Milner b: 20 Oct 1869 in BeetownTownship, Grant County, Wisconsin m: 01 Jan 1900 in Sa Lake City, Utah d: 16 Nov 1944 in Palos Verdes Estates, California
7 [25] Milner Haine Hawkins b: 19 Oct 1901 in Columbus, Montana d: 02 Nov 1951 in Poughkeepsie, NY
+[101] Vivian Carolyn Lansworth b: 07 Jul 1902 in Brule, Wisconsin m: 16 Dec 1925 in Iron Mountain, Michigan d: 17 Dec 1997 in Ellensburg, WA
8 [22] Milner James Hawkins b: 1927 in Caspian, Michigan
+[102] Joan Young m: 28 Jan 1952 in Longview, Washington
*2nd Wife of [22] Milner James Hawkins:
+[103] Carmen Masip Echazarreta b: 1927 in Spain m: 10 Dec 1955 in Mexico, D.F, Mexico res. Mexico
9 [104] Paulina Hawkins
8 [23] Charles Haine Hawkins b: 1929 in Columbus, Montana
+[105] Jacqueline Roberta Dorrington b: 1928
*2nd Wife of [23] Charles Haine Hawkins:
+[106] Ruth Maass b: 20 Jan 1931 in Portland, OR m: 02 Sep 1950 d: 23 Feb 1968
9 [107] Christoffer Haine Hawkins b: 1951
10 [108] Natasha Laura Hawkins b: 25 Apr 1985 in Seattle, WA
9 [109] Charles Mead Hawkins b: 1955
10 [110] Lucas Christopher Hawkins b: 1979 in Seattle, WA
10 [111] Tyler Matthew Hawkins b: 1981 in Seattle, WA
*3rd Wife of [23] Charles Haine Hawkins:
+[112] Ida Edene Buckingham b: 1945 in Pasco, WA m: Abt. 1970
9 [113] Glacier Irene Hawkins b: 1972 in Ellensburg, WA
+[114] Steven Kingsford-Smith b: 1960 in Loveland, CO m: 14 Oct 1995 in Port ı Port Gamble, WA
10 [115] Genevive Kingsford-Smith b: 2007

.... 8 [24] Robert Pearson Hawkins b: 1931 in Silver City, NM Fact 1: Dr. Of Psychology at West
                               Virginia State University.
....   +[116] Jane Nelson b: 1931 in Portland, OR m: 08 Jun 1958 in Portland, OR
.... 9 [117] Larry Pearson Hawkins b: 1953 in Portland, OR
.... 9 [118] Jeffrey Milner Hawkins b:1954 in Portland, OR
....   +[119] Patty
....   *2nd Wife of [24] Robert Pearson Hawkins:
....   +[120] Kathyn Kay Kott b:1940 in Kalamazoo, MI m: 1970
.... 9 [121] Anne Kathryn Hawkins b: 1972
....   +[122] Thomas Young
....   10 [123] Alanna Zoe Young b:1994 in Morgantown, WV
....   10 [124] Eli Thomas Young b: 1998 in Morgantown, WV
....   *2nd Wife of [25] Milner Haine Hawkins:
....   +[125] Wilberta Twogood Johnson b: 1912 m: 23 Mar 1946 in Lansdowne, PA
.... 8 [126] Angela Holbeach Hawkins b: 1936 in Newburg, NY
....   +[127] Robert Fichter b: 1923
.... 9 [128] James Robert Fichter b: 1979 in Scotland, CT.
.... 7 [26] Frances Milner Hawkins b: 01 Jan 1909 in Bozeman, Montana d: Nov 1982 in Absarokee, Montana
....   +[129] Carleton Wilder
....   *2nd Husband of [26] Frances Milner Hawkins:
....   +[130] Joseph Walter Meek m: 16 Aug 1933 in Absarokee, Montana d: 1955
.... 8 [131] Mary Milner Meek b: 1936 in Tucson, AZ
....   +[132] Lawrence Locke
.... 9 [133] Jonathan Locke b: 1967
.... 9 [134] Jason Locke b: 1970
.... 8 [135] Frances Luann Meek b:1939 in Glendale, CA
....   +[136] Yale Coombs d: in res. CA.
.... 9 [137] Stacy Coombs b: 1963
.... 9 [138] Wendy Coombs b: 1966
.... 6 [139] Mary Alberta Hawkins b: 03 Sep 1872 in Farmington Township, Trumbull Co.OH d: 26 Oct 1958 in
                               Meadville,PA Fact 1: 1911 Resided in Forest Depot,VA. at time of Fact 2: Mothers death. Frances Hawkins died
                               Burial: Brownwood Cemetery, Bloomfield, OH
....   +[140] George W. Walker b: 29 Apr 1871 in Virginia m: 29 Apr 1896 in West Farmington, OH -0- children d: 08
                               Aug 1960 in Meadville,Pa at 89 yrs. Burial: Brownwood Cemetery, Bloomfield, OH
.... 6 [141] Charlotte Hawkins b: 10 Feb 1875 in Farmington Township, Trumbull Co., OH d: 08 Sep 1953 in
                               Warren,OH Fact 1: Also called "Lottie"
....   +[142] J. Ward Wolcott m: 13 Mar 1894
.... 7 [143] Clyde Wolcott b: 1896 d: 1915 in Died in motorcycle accident
.... 7 [144] Frances Wolcott b: 07 Apr 1907 in Trumbull Co., OH d: 31 Aug 1980 in Mayfield Hts. OH
....   +[145] Paul B. Rogers m: 29 Aug 1931 in two daughters d: in Mayfield Hts.,OH
.... 8 [146] Carol Ann Rogers b:1934 in Warren, Ohio
....   +[147] David L. Beers m: in Westfield, NJ
.... 9 [148] David Rogers Beers b: 1963
.... 8 [149] Jean Rogers b: 1939 in Warren, Ohio
....   +[150] Errol Kwait b: in Cleveland Hts.,OH m: Aug 1962 in 2 children
.... 9 [151] Steven Paul Kwait b: 1967
.... 9 [152] Laura Ellen Kwait b: 1969
.... 6 [153] Angie Hawkins b: 10 Nov 1876 in Farmington Township, Trumbull Co., OH d: 25 Jan 1877 in Farmington
                               Township, Trumbull
.... 6 [154] Jerry Hawkins b: 24 Feb 1880 in Farmington Township, Trumbull Co. OH d: 24 Feb 1880 in Farmington
                               Township, Trumbull Co.OH Fact 1: 1880 Twin of Jeese, Died at birth.
.... 6 [155] Jesse Thomas Hawkins b: 24 Feb 1880 in Farmington Twp.,Trumbull Co., OH d: 26 Oct 1957 in Warren,
                               Trumbull Co. OH Fact 1: Bur: Brownwood Cem. in Bloomfield,OH Fact 2: Occupation:Farmer,real estate,
                               Republic Burial: 29 Oct 1957 Brownwood Cemetery, No. Bloomfield, Trum. Co , OH
....   +[156] Mildred Phoebe Thorp b: 08 Dec 1878 in W. Farmington Twp.,Trumbull Co., OH m: 22 Jun 1904 in
                               Trumbull Co. ,OH d: 05 Apr 1958 in Warren, Trumbull Co. OH Burial: 07 Apr 1958 Brownwood Cemetery, No.
                               Bloomfield, Trum. Co., OH

18

7 [157] Charles T. Hawkins b: 20 Mar 1910 in Parkman, Geauga Co.,OH d: 18 Dec 1999 in Penny Farms, Florida Fact 1: Ohio State University Fact 2: Occupation: Employed at Packard Electric- office.
+[158] Nancy Buckingham b: 20 Mar 1910 in Urichsville, OH m: 18 Jun 1938 in Warren, Trum.Co.OH d: 24 Apr 1987 in Penny Farms, Florida
8 [159] Thomas Frank Hawkins b: 1941 in Warren, OH
+[160] Janet Sue Breystpraak b: in Middleton, Ohio m: 10 Jun 1967 no children
8 [161] Robert C. Hawkins b: 1944 in Warren, Trumbull Co. OH
+[162] Mary Kay Branfield b: in Warren, Trumbull Co. OH m: Jun 1966 in Warren, Trumbull Co. OH
9 [163] Katherine Hawkins b: 1968 in Michigan
+[164] Kevin Boardman m: in New Wilmington, Delaware
10 [165] Meredith Boardman b: 1997
10 [166] Chase Ivan Boardman b: 1999
9 [167] Robert Hawkins b: 1971
+[168] Teresa Coppola b: in Florida m: 12 Jun 1997 in Boca Raton, Florida
7 [169] Lloyd B. Hawkins b: 11 Nov 1911 in Parkman, Geauga Co.,OH d: 01 Aug 1982 in Warren, Trumbull Co. OH Fact 1: Occupation: Steel Mill -3 yrs, Warren City Fireman 35 yrs. Fact 2: until retirement. Home construction and remodeling- Burial: Brownwood Cemetery, No. Bloomfield, Trum. Co., OH
+[170] Martha Arlene Schout b: 20 Sep 1914 in Howland Twp.,Trumbull Co. OH m: 08 Jan 1938 in Howland Twp.,Trumbull Co. OH d: 07 Feb 2007 in Warren, OH Fact 2: General Electric on assembly line - 1-2 yrs.
8 [171] Ernest Eugene Hawkins b: 11 Sep 1939 in Warren, Trumbull Co. OH d: 09 Jan 1996 in Warren, Trumbull Co. OH Fact 1: Occu: Wiring harness for autos at Packard Electric Burial: Brownwood Cemetery, Bloomfield, Trum. Co. OH
+[172] Patricia Sue Heiple b: 1942 in Champion Twp.,Trumbull Co., OH m: 04 May 1963 in Champion Twp. Trumbull Co. OH
9 [173] Roberta Sue Hawkins b: 1965 in Warren, Trumbull Co. OH Fact 1: Occupation: Needlework and stitchery.
+[174] Thomas King b: 1963 in Champion Twp.,Trumbull Co., OH m: 01 Nov 1986 in Warren, Trumbull Co. OH Fact 1: Occupation: Meterologist with U.S. Weather Bureau
10 [175] Adrienne King b: 1988
10 [176] Jonathan King b: 1991 in Alabama
8 [177] Sue Ellen Hawkins b: 1941 in Warren, Trumbull Co., OH Fact 1: Occupation: R. N. , quilter and hobby-genealogy.
+[178] Roger Stewart Bell b: 1938 in East Cleveland, OH m: 03 Nov 1962 in Warren, OH
9 [179] Jeffrey Lloyd Bell b: 1963 in Cleveland, OH
+[180] Najma Begum Bachelani b: 1963 in Mbale, Uganda m: 21 Feb 1998 in St.Paul, Minnesota
10 [181] Sara Soheila Bell b: 1999 in Ann Arbor, Michigan
10 [182] Siraj Alexander Bell b: 2001 in Mountain View, California
9 [27] Jennifer Elizabeth Bell b: 1965 in Cleveland, OH
+[183] Anthony Guy b: in London, England m: 15 Jun 1991 in London, England divorced 1994
*2nd Husband of [27] Jennifer Elizabeth Bell:
+[184] James Shipman b: 1953 in resides in Pittsburgh, PA m: 25 Sep 1999 in Pittsburgh, PA
10 [185] Elizabeth Bell Shipman b: 2004 in Pittsburgh, PA
9 [186] Douglas Alexander Bell b: 1968 in Cleveland, OH 1995 Married Rebecca Ching,
+[187] Tisha Goss b: 1972 in Parma Heights, Ohio m: 02 Feb 2008 in Middleburg Hts. Ohio
10 [188] Lleyton Alexander Bell b: 2009 in Middleburg Hts. Ohio
8 [189] Larry Lloyd Hawkins b: 1944 in Warren, Trumbull Co. OH Fact 1: Occupation: WCI Steel- purchasing.
+[190] Carol Oravecz b: 1944 in Cleveland, OH m: 26 Aug 1967 in Warren, Trumbull Co. OH Fact 1: Occupation: Dr. degree., Dir.of Day Care at Hosp.
9 [191] Michele Lynette Hawkins b: 1971 in Warren, Trumbull Co. OH Occupation: Architect; enjoyes horseback riding.

```
............................................  +[192] Jeremy Schwartz  b: 12 Jun 1971 in Cleveland, OH  m:  1996 in Cleveland, OH
                                                       Fact 1: Advanced degree in Economics.
............................................      9  [193] Meredith Paula Hawkins  b:1974 in Warren, Trum.Co.OH  Fact 1: Graduate of
                                                       American Univ.- Public Relations.
............................................  +[194] Paul Helter Melnick  b: 1965 in Arlington, VA  m: 18 Apr 1998 in Arlington, Va
                                                       Fact 1: Occupation: Attorney, legal practice with his father.
............................................     10  [195] Kelly Valentine Melnick  b: 2002 in Arlington, VA
............................................     10  [196] Theodore Nathaniel Melnick  b:  2005 in Arlington, VA
............................................      8  [197] Mildred Anne Hawkins  b: 1950 in Warren, Trumbull Co. OH  Fact 1: Resides in
                                                       Warren, OH.  Fact 2: Graduate of Bowling Green U.
............................................      6  [198] Ernest Hawkins  b: 28 Jan 1882 in W. Farmington, Trumbull Co.OH  d: 25 Apr 1930 in Yellowstone Park,
                                                       WY  Fact 1: Occupation: Head Bellhop at Yellowstone  Fact 2: National Park's Lodge.  Burial: Never married, bell
                                                       hop at Yellowsttone Nat. Park
............................................      5  [199] Charlotte E. Haine  b: 25 Sep 1844 in Bloomfield Twp,Trumbull Co.,OH.  d: 16 Mar 1917 in Iowa
............................................  +[200] Zwinglius Paley Lyman  b: 28 Aug 1844 in Chicago, IL  m: 03 Jun 1882 in Bloomfield Twp,Trumbull Co.,OH.  d:
                                                       03 Jan 1903 in Iowa
............................................      6  [201] Ralph Lyman  b: 26 Jul 1883  d: 15 Mar 1954
............................................  +[202] Fannie McIntosh  b: 10 Dec 1883  m: 12 Apr 1907  d: 04 Nov 1958
............................................      7  [203] Ernest McIntosh Lyman  b: 1909 in Germany (while father was studing music)
............................................      7  [204] Clara Margaret Lyman  b: 1913  Had 3 children
............................................      7  [205] David L. Lyman  b: 10 May 1917  d: Aug 1962  Burial: 4 children
............................................      6  [206] Will Lyman  b: 18 Mar 1885  d: 1970 in Des Moines, Iowa
............................................  +[207] Eva McIntosh  m: 24 Aug 1915
............................................      7  [208] Elizabeth Lyman  b: 1916
............................................      7  [209] William Lyman  b: 1919
............................................      7  [210] Ruth Lyman  b: 1921
............................................      7  [211] Doris Lyman  b: 1923
............................................      7  [212] Eleanor Lyman  b: 1925
............................................      7  [213] Rae Lyman  b: 1930
............................................      6  [214] Marry Lyman  b: 16 Apr 1886
............................................  +[215] George M. Hansen  b: 03 Apr 1887  m: 16 Sep 1908  d: 19 Jul 1972 in Kansas City, MO
............................................      7  [216] Lyman Hansen  b: 1909  d: 1915
............................................      7  [217] Phyllis Hansen  b: 1910
............................................  +[218] Robert Earl McDowell  b:  1908  m: 10 Jun 1921
............................................      7  [219] George (Bob) Hansen  b: 01 Sep 1915  d: 04 Jul 2004 in Missouri
............................................  +[220] Gloria Marie Gregg  b: 22 Apr  m: Nov 1938
............................................      8  [221] John Lyman Hansen  b:1940
............................................      8  [222] Robert Martin Hansen  b: 1945
............................................      7  [223] Betty Jean Hansen  b:1921
............................................  +[224] Charles Robert Nuckolle
............................................      8  [225] Carol Ann Nuckolle  b: 1943
............................................      8  [226] Jr. Charles Robert Nuckolle  b: 1948
............................................      8  [227] John Nuckolle  b:  1954
............................................      8  [228] Phyllis Jean Nuckolle  b: 1955
............................................      8  [229] Paul Thomas Nuckolle  b: 1951
............................................      7  [230] Richard Hansen  b: 1923
............................................  +[231] Louise Curtis  m: Nov 1948
............................................      8  [232] Karen Marie Hansen  b: 1951
............................................      8  [233] Richard Jons Hansen  b:1954
............................................      5  [234] Mercy Jane Haine  b: 18 Dec 1846 in Bloomfield Twp,Trumbull Co.,OH.  d: 18 Dec 1849 in Bloomfield
                                                       Twp,Trumbull Co.,OH.  Burial: Drowned in the mill race at Clover Hill
............................................      5  [235] Ellen S. Haine  b: 22 Sep 1848 in Bloomfield Twp,Trumbull Co.,OH.  d: 25 Mar 1866 in Bloomfield Twp,Trumbull
                                                       Co.,OH.  Burial: Never married- d. of TB
............................................      5  [236] John Wesley Haine  b: 04 Mar 1852 in Bloomfield Twp,Trumbull Co.,OH.  d: 17 Jan 1912 in CT
............................................  +[237] Hattie C. Burt  b: 27 Apr 1858  m: 01 Jan 1877 in Mespotamia Twp, Trumbull Co. OH  d: 14 Jan 1933
............................................      6  [238] Harry B. Haine  b: 30 Jun 1878  d: 1945  Burial: No children
............................................  +[239] Myrtle Elder  b: 03 Sep 1878  m: 14 Feb 1900 in (no children)
```

```
      6  [240] Eugene Wesley Haine  b: 15 Aug 1883
        +[241] Neola Galbraith  b: 28 Jun 1885  m: 25 Oct 1903  d: 21 Oct 1952
      7  [242] David Eugene Haine  b: 09 Apr 1909  d: 10 Sep 1975
        +[243] Geraldine Nash  b: 1911
         8  [244] Judith Marjory Haine  b: 1933  residing in Texas
           +[245] Ray Fergerson  m: 27 Jun 1953 in 2 children
            9  [246] Stephanie Fergerson  b: in Ohio
               10 [247] Desirae Fergerson
            9  [248] Jennifer Fergerson  b: in Ohio
      7  [249] John Haine  b: 29 Nov 1916  d: 1995
        +[250] Joan Carpenter  m: 08 Jul 1944 in Stamford CT
         8  [251] Joan Dorothy Haine(Jodi)  b: 1950 in Stamford, CT
         8  [252] Sue Haine  b: 1952 in Stamford, CT
           +[253] Dirk Stanley Roberts  b: 1951 in New York City, NY
            9  [254] Logan Galbraith Haine Roberts  b: 1984 in New York City, NY
            9  [255] Evan Wesley Haine Roberts  b: 1987 in New York City, NY
         8  [256] Robin Carpenter Haine  b: 1954 in Stamford, CT  resides in Saratoga Springs, NY,
            unmarried
         8  [28] John Haine  b:1957 in Stamford, CT  resides near Minneapolis, MN
           +[257] Roxanne ?
            9  [258] John Wesley Haine  b: 1983 in Los Angles, CA
            9  [259] Emily Haine  b: 1985 in Minneapolis, MN
            9  [260] William Haine  b:1987 in Minneapolis, MN
           *2nd Wife of [28] John Haine:
           +[261] Patricia '
         8  [262] Matthew David Haine  b: 1964 in Stamford, CT
      7  [263] Jean Haine  d: 1994 in resided in Atwater and Akron, OH
        +[264] Gunther Haiss  b: 05 Mar 1911  m: 29 Jun 1953  d: Jan 1986
         8  [265] Nola Haiss- Graingerjm@aol.com  d: in resides in Atwater, OH
         8  [266] Hugo Haiss  d: in resides in Akron, OH, marr. 2 children
         8  [267] Heidi Haiss
   6  [268] J. Rollin Haine  b: 01 May 1888  d: 24 Dec 1939
     +[269] Dorothy Watson  b: 14 Jan 1890
      7  [270] John Rolin Haine  b: 1916  2 children
        +[271] Anne Josephine McCleary  m: 20 Mar 1941 in 2 children
5  [272] Emma Jane Haine  b: 06 May 1853 in Bloomfield Twp,Trumbull Co.,OH.  d: 29 Dec 1901 in California
  +[273] B. Frank Beatty  b: 13 Oct 1848  m: 01 Aug 1876 in Bloomfield Twp,Trumbull Co.,OH.  d: 1902
   6  [274] Hazel Beatty  b: in Adopted  d: in Made home w/ Aunt Lottie p/ folks died.
   6  [275] Georgie Beatty  b: 30 Jul 1887
5  [276] Clara Haine  b: 28 May 1855 in Bloomfield Twp,Trumbull Co.,OH.  d: 26 Jan 1940 in Bloomfield Twp,Trumbull
   Co.,OH.  Burial: Brownwood Cem. Bloomfield, OH
  +[277] Phillip John Cox  b: 1847 in Hornblotten, Somerset, Eng.  m: 12 Jul 1883 in Bloomfield Twp,Trumbull Co.,OH,
   Methodist Church  d: 1929 in Bloomfield Twp,Trumbull Co.,OH  Burial: Brownwood Cem. Bloomfield, OH
   6  [278] Elmer Haine Cox  b: 15 Jun 1884 in Clover Hill, No. Bloomfield, OH  d: 30 May 1966 in Charolette Nursing
      Home, Rock Creek, Ash. Co. OH  Burial: Brownwood Cem. Bloomfield, OH
     +[279] Pearl Abbey  b: 1888  m: 06 Sep 1911 in W.C.&Emma Brainard Home, Warren, OH  d: 1981  Burial:
      Brownwood Cem. Bloomfield, OH
      7  [36] Charles Philip Cox  b: 17 Aug 1912 in Clover Hill, No. Bloomfield, OH  d: 1996 in Bloomfield
         Twp,Trumbull Co.,OH.
        +[35] Hazel Fern Carlson  b: 1913 in Indiana  m: 18 Jun 1936 in Nol Bloomfield, Trumbull Co. OH
         8  [37] Carol Ann Cox  b: 1939
           +[38] Edward Sasey  b:1936  m: 20 Jun 1971
            9  [39] Seth Edward Sasey  b: 1976
              +[40] Linda
               10 [41] Samantha Sasey  b: 1999
            9  [42] Charles Steven Sasey  b: 1976
              +[43] Rebecca ///
```

```
                                    10  [44] Blake Sasey  b: 2006
                                    10  [45] Corrine Sasey  b: 2010 in Mantua, Ohio
                          8   [46] Carrie Jean Cox  b: 1941
                   7  [280] Robert Lee Cox  b: 1916 in Clover Hill, No. Bloomfield, OH
                      +[281] Esther Neimi Dowling  b: 1918  m: 03 May 1947
                          8   [282] Roy Cox  b: 1948
                              +[283] Regina M. Kopesko  m: 19 Sep 1979
                          8   [284] Phillip Cox  b:1949
                              +[285] Susan Shulman  m: 1976
                                  9  [286] Rachel S. Cox  b:  1975
                          8   [287] Daniel Cox  b: 1951
                          8   [288] David Edwin Cox  b: 1953
                          8   [289] Susan Cox  b: 1960
                   7  [290] John Henry Cox  b: 13 Aug 1922 in Warren, OH  d: 20 Jun 2010 in Brownwood Cemetery
                      +[291] Marian Irene Payne  b: 1922  m: 22 Jul 1950
                          8   [292] Mary Ann Cox  b: 1952
                              +[293] H. Douglas Bear  b: 1952  m: 26 Jun 1976
                                  9  [294] Matthew Thomas Bear  b: 1979
                                  9  [295] Andrew Douglas Bear  b: 1982
                                  9  [296] Rachael Bear
                          8   [297] Rev. James Jay Cox  b: 1955
                              +[298] Rev. Kate Maxfield  b: 1959  m: 28 May 1982
                          8   [299] Alan Lee Cox  b: 1964
                   7  [300] Emogene Valeria Cox  b: 15 Jun 1924 in Warren, OH  d: 25 Aug 1976  Burial: Brownwood Cem.
                      Bloomfield, OH
                      +[301] Eugene Ruehle  b: 1913  m: in Divorce unk.
                          8   [302] John Irvin Ruehle  b: 1949
                              +[303] Catherine Harris  b: 1948  m: 19 Dec 1969
                                  9  [304] Melaine Lynn Ruehle  b: 1970
                                  9  [305] Stephinie Ann Ruehle  b: 1972
                                  9  [306] Jeffrey Ruehle  b: 1975
                                  9  [307] Christa Leann Ruehle  b: 1979
                          8   [308] Caroline Valeria Ruehle  b:1958
                              +[309] Gregery Sparks  m: 1976
                                  9  [310] Rebecca Allicon Sparks  b: 1977
                                  9  [311] Mathew Addison Sparks  b: 24 Mar 1978
            6   [312] Bertha Grace Cox  b: 28 Apr 1887 in Clover Hill, No. Bloomfield, OH  d: 04 Nov 1984 in Warren, OH
               +[313] Clyde Cleveland McMillan  b: 1886  m: 24 Oct 1911 in Clover Hill, No Bloomfield, OH
                   7  [314] Eldon McMillan  b: 1913
                      +[315] Maude King  b: 1917  m: 16 Nov 1934 in 3 children
                          8   [29] Donald McMillan  b: 1935
                              +[316] Hildah Hassink
                              *2nd Wife of [29] Donald McMillan:
                              +[317] Barbara Keller  m: 24 Feb 1962 in divorice  unknown
                          8   [30] June Evelyn McMillan  b: 1938
                              +[318] Stanley Johnson  m: 1954
                                  9  [319] Scott M. Johnson Johnson  b: 1958
                              *2nd Husband of [30] June Evelyn McMillan:
                              +[320] Fred Darling  m: 1957
                                  9  [321] Mary Ellen Darling
                                  9  [322] Maurine Suzanne Darling
                                  9  [323] Jr. Fred Darling
                          8   [324] Kathleen McMillan  b: 1941
                              +[325] William J. McGrinna  m: 1964
                                  9  [326] Connie McGrinna  b: 1965
                                  9  [327] Thomas McGrinna  b: 1966
                   7  [31] Leila McMillan  b: 1915
```

+[328] Alvin Grimm b: 20 Dec 1908 m: 15 Nov 1941 in 2 children d: 09 Oct 1965
   8 [329] James Arthur Grimm b: 1945
     +[330] Fatnsh Gozsecen
      9 [331] Bulant Grimm b: in Adopted
   8 [332] Rev. Joan Phyllis Grimm b: 1949
     +[333] Jr. Donald Ross Fraser m: 07 Jul 1979 in Kenyon College, Gamblier, OH
      9 [334] Lee Authur Fraser b: 17 Sep in Adoption
*2nd Husband of [31] Leila McMillan:
    +[335] Calvin Huntley m: 06 Jan 1973
7 [336] Delbert McMillan b: 1915
   +[337] Hope Weir b: 1918 m: 05 Aug 1959 in 4 children
   8 [338] William Ray McMillan b: 1942 in Warren, OH
     +[339] Sandra Bill m: 12 Sep 1970
      9 [340] Mike Scott McMillan b: 1973
      9 [341] Maya Dawn McMillan b: 1975
   8 [342] Fred James McMillan b: 1943 in Warren, OH
     +[343] Mary Lee Braden m: 16 Sep 1967
      9 [344] James Richard McMillan b: 1968
      9 [345] Richard D. McMillan b: 1971
      9 [346] John Fred McMillan b: 1977
   8 [347] Carl Richard McMillan b: 1946 in Warren, OH
     +[348] Janet Pimberton m: 28 Jun 1970
      9 [349] Heather McMillan b: 1976
      9 [350] Byron Allen McMillan b: 1978
   8 [351] Leah Beth McMillan b: 1951
7 [352] Ralph McMillan b: 30 Dec 1917 d: 02 Aug 1981
   +[353] Jean Lytle b: 1921 m: 07 Jun 1940 in 8 children
   8 [354] Jr. Ralph Edward McMillan b: 1941
     +[355] Phyllis Boles m: 1963
      9 [356] Jr. Ralph McMillan
      9 [357] Eric McMillan
      9 [358] Patrick McMillan
   8 [359] Daniel Earl McMillan b: 1943
     +[360] Anna Speaker m: 18 May 1963
      9 [361] Jr. Daniel McMillan
      9 [362] Gregory McMillan
   8 [363] Jack Reray McMillan b: 1947
     +[364] Sarah Thompson m: 1966
      9 [365] John Wayne McMillan
   8 [366] Jean Louise McMillan b: 1947
     +[367] Ronald Ruse m: 1966
      9 [368] Elizabeth Ann Ruse
      9 [369] Jr. Ronald Ruse
   8 [370] Timothy Paul McMillan b: 1950
   8 [371] Terrance Lee McMillan b: 25 Jul 1954 d: 09 Mar 1955
   8 [372] Wanda Loren McMillan b: 1956
     +[373] Robert Stankewich m: 31 Aug 1974
   8 [374] Larina Grace McMillan b: 20 Nov 1957 d: 21 Nov 1957
7 [32] Helen McMillan b: 1919
   +[375] James Hearn b: 17 Mar 1900 m: 21 Oct 1936 in 6 children d: 1963
   8 [376] Patricia Ann Hearn b: 1937
   8 [377] Deloris Irene Hearn b: 1938
   8 [378] Gerald Francis Hearn b: 1941
   8 [379] Daniel Clyde Hearn b: 1949
   8 [380] Rose Ellen Hearn b: 1949
   8 [381] Thomas John Hearn b: 1953
*2nd Husband of [32] Helen McMillan:

.... +[382] Mike Blazevic m: 04 May 1968
.... 8 [383] James Blazevic b: in Adopted
.... 8 [384] Mary Elaine Blazevic b: in Adopted
.... 7 [385] Ruth McMillan b: 17 Sep 1920 d: 23 Mar 1985
.... +[386] Louis Chuhay b: 18 Jul 1913 m: 23 Mar 1942 in 2 children
.... 8 [33] Norna L. Chuhay b: 1946
.... +[387] James Bonheimer m: 08 Apr 1968
.... 9 [388] Owen James Bonheimer b: 1974
.... 9 [389] Nathan Wade Bonheimer b: 1976
.... *2nd Husband of [33] Norna L. Chuhay:
.... +[390] James Bonheimer m: 08 Apr 1968
.... 9 [391] Owen James Bonheimer b: 1974
.... 8 [392] Laura C. Chuhay b: 1950
.... +[393] Dan Keller m: 1974
.... 9 [394] Jeffrey D. Keller Keller b: 1979
.... 7 [395] Vera McMillan b: 1924
.... +[396] Ray Willson b: 21 Aug 1920 m: 13 Dec 1943 in 3 children d: 2002
.... 8 [397] Lynn Rae Willson b: 1945
.... +[398] Gregory Christman b: 1943 m: 17 Sep 1966
.... 9 [399] Ellen Elizabeth Christman b: 1970
.... 9 [400] Leif Benjamin Christman b: 1972
.... 8 [401] Karen Willson b: 1948
.... +[402] Rev. Peter DeBartolo m: 16 May 1981
.... 9 [403] Peter John DeBartolo b: 1983
.... 8 [404] Robert Ray Willson b: 1951
.... +[405] Sue Gettig m: 24 Aug 1968
.... 9 [406] Michelle Susan Willson b: 1969
.... 9 [407] Kimberly Rae Willson b: 1971
.... 8 [408] Jr. Delmare Ray Willson b: 1961
.... 8 [409] Heather Elizabeth Willson b: 1965
.... +[410] Donald Lockney m: 09 Jan 1982
.... 8 [411] Tamara Sue Willson b: 1969
.... 7 [34] Dorothy McMillan b: 1928
.... +[412] Don Cole b: 19 Sep 1921 m: 04 Apr 1948 in 2 children d: Feb 1973
.... 8 [413] Lawrence E. Cole b: 1949
.... +[414] Cynthia Melone m: 19 May 1968
.... 9 [415] Heather Lee Cole b: 1974
.... 9 [416] Jennifer Cole b:1969
.... 9 [417] Micheal Cole b:1970
.... 8 [418] Janice Lynn Cole b:1951
.... +[419] Paul Bowman m: 21 Aug 1970
.... 9 [420] David Robert Bowman b:1975
.... *2nd Husband of [34] Dorothy McMillan:
.... +[421] Marvin Gannaway m: 24 Dec 1975
.... 7 [422] Clara Alice McMillan b: 1933
.... +[423] William Talbert b: 1931 in West Virginia m: 18 Mar 1956 in 9 children
.... 8 [424] Roger Eugene Talbert b: 1956
.... 8 [425] Deboroah Lynn Talbert b: 1958
.... 8 [426] Terri Ann Talbert b: 1959
.... 8 [427] Richard Wayne Talbert b: 1963
.... 8 [428] Jack Edward Talbert b: 1962
.... 8 [429] Albert Glen Talbert b: 1963
.... 8 [430] Robert Allen Talbert b: 1964
.... 8 [431] Cynthia Dian Talbert b 1965
.... 8 [432] Pamela June Talbert b: 1966
.... 6 [433] Mabel Cox b: 30 Aug 1888 in Clover Hill, No.Bloomfield,Trumbull Co.,OH d: 28 Jul 1979 in Community Skilled Nursing Home, Warren, OH Burial: (Hazel Cox's stepmother)Brownwood Cem.

+[434] Charles Carlson b: 11 Jul 1871 in Hollingsburg, Sweden m: 22 May 1922 in No. Bloomfield, OH d: 05 Jul 1945 in Bloomfield Twp,Trum. Co,OH Burial: Brownwood Cem. Bloomfield, OH
   7 [435] Alfred Carlson b: 1894
   7 [436] Emery Carlson b: 1896
   7 [437] Florence Carlson b: 1898
   7 [438] Myrtle Carlson b: 1900
   7 [439] Clyde Carlson b: 1903
   7 [440] Edward Carlson b: 1908
   7 [35] Hazel Fern Carlson b: 15 Oct 1913 in Indiana
      +[36] Charles Philip Cox b: 17 Aug 1912 in Clover Hill, No. Bloomfield, OH m: 18 Jun 1936 in Nol Bloomfield, Trumbull Co. OH d: 1996 in Bloomfield Twp,Trumbull Co.,OH.
      8 [37] Carol Ann Cox b: 30 Jan 1939
         +[38] Edward Sasey b:1936 m: 20 Jun 1971
         9 [39] Seth Edward Sasey b:1976
            +[40] Linda
            10 [41] Samantha Sasey b: 1999
         9 [42] Charles Steven Sasey b: 1976
            +[43] Rebecca ///
            10 [44] Blake Sasey b: 2006
            10 [45] Corrine Sasey b: 2010 in Mantua, Ohio
      8 [46] Carrie Jean Cox b: 1941
  6 [441] Estella Cox b: 11 Jun 1890 in Clover Hill, No. Bloomfield, OH d: 23 Aug 1983 in Gillette Nursing Home, Warren, OH(never married) Burial: Brownwood Cem. Bloomfield, OH
  6 [442] Ethel Mae Cox b: 03 May 1892 in Bloomfield Twp,Trum. Co,OH d: 10 Sep 1985 in Williamsfield, Ashtabula Co. OH Burial: Hayes Cemetery, Williamsfield, OH
      +[443] Samuel William Jones b: 18 Dec 1890 in Williamsfield, (Wayne), Ashtabula Co. OH m: 14 Jan 1913 in No. Bloomfield, OH d: 17 Jan 1974 in Williamsfield, (Wayne), Ashtabula Co. OH
      7 [444] Neoma Belle Jones b: 01 Jun 1918 in Williamsfield (Wayne), Ashtabula Co. OH d: 09 Apr 1994 in Columbia, MO Burial: Callao, MO
         +[445] Jr. Herbert Virgil Cook b: 01 May 1918 m: 27 Oct 1946 in Jones House, Williamsfield, OH d: 19 Jul 1982 in Callao, MO
         8 [446] Linda Marie Cook b: 25 Jun 1948 d: 14 Jul 1952
         8 [447] William Douglas Cook b: 1951
            +[448] Susan Spencer m: 05 Aug 1979 in Divorced 15 Jan 1995
            9 [449] Jonathan David Cook b: 1983
            9 [450] Hether Jolinne Cook b: 1987
         8 [451] Robert Dean Cook b: 1956
      7 [452] Willard Philip Jones b:1933 in Andover, Ashtabula Co. OH
         +[453] Ruth Joan Khota b:1938 m: 30 Aug 1958 in Wayne Congregational Church,   ırch, Williamsfield,OH
         8 [454] Rhonda Ann Jones b:1959
         8 [455] Douglas Samuel Jones b: 20 Sep 1961 d: 16 Apr 1978 in Norristown, PA Burial: Hayes Cemetery, Williamsfield, OH
         8 [456] Stanley Craig Jones b: 1964
         8 [457] Marvin Todd Jones b: 1966
  6 [458] Earl Philip Cox b: 30 Nov 1894 in Clover Hill, No. Bloomfield, OH d: 04 Mar 1982 in Lake Forest, IL Burial: IL
      +[459] Myra Howey b: 25 Feb 1894 in Congress, OH m: 26 May 1920 in Congress, OH d: Unknown Burial: IL
      7 [460] Marjorie Cox b: 19 Jul 1925 Burial: three sons
         +[461] Devere Halvie m: 08 May 1948 in Hilton Chapel, Chicago University
         8 [462] Scott Philip Halvie b: 1950
         8 [463] Mark Allen Halvie b: 1953
         8 [464] Kirk Halvie
         8 [465] Brett Halvie
      7 [466] Roger Cox b: 27 Oct 1929 d: in Never married
  6 [467] William Edward Cox b: 24 Apr 1902 in Clover Hill, No. Bloomfield, OH d: 04 Mar 1990 in ? Burial: Moved to Graymont IL, Pontiac, IL area

.... +[468] Maurine Annabelle Carlson b: 27 Jan 1906 m: 21 Jul 1928 in Graymont, IL d: Unknown
.... 7 [469] Ronald Jerome Cox b: 1931 in Warren, OH
.... +[470] Winnifred Kennedy m: 24 Aug 1958 in first Lutheran Church Pontiac, IL
.... 8 [471] Lynda Sue Cox b: 1959
.... 8 [472] Marsha Kay Cox b: 1965
.... 7 [47] Claire Yvonne Cox b: 1937 in Warren, OH
.... +[473] Gordon Eichelberger
.... *2nd Husband of [47] Claire Yvonne Cox:
.... +[474] Donald L. DeVore m: 20 Oct 1957 in Divorced
.... 8 [48] Kevin Lee DeVore b: 1963 Adopted
.... +[49] Sherri Kraft m: 30 Jun 1984 in First Methodist Church, El Paco, IL
.... *3rd Husband of [47] Claire Yvonne Cox:
.... +[475] Gordon Eichelberger b:1936 m: 30 Dec 1967
.... 8 [48] Kevin Lee DeVore b: 1963 Adopted
.... +[49] Sherri Kraft m: 30 Jun 1984 in First Methodist Church, El Paco, IL
.... 5 [476] Charles Robert Haine b: 09 May 1857 in Bloomfield Twp,Trumbull Co.,OH. d: 02 Jul 1926
.... +[477] Beckie Millikin m: 13 May 1885 in Bloomfield Twp,Trumbull Co.,OH. d: 29 Jul 1945
.... 6 [50] William Haine b: 06 Mar 1891 d: 12 Nov 1970 in Hartford, CT
.... +[478] Norma Allen b: 1895 m: 20 Jun 1920 d: 1952
.... *2nd Wife of [50] William Haine:
.... +[479] Helen Francis m: 14 May 1955
.... 6 [480] Harold Haine b: 22 Mar 1898 Burial: No children
.... +[481] Madeline H. Thornton m: 24 Sep 1947 in Warren, OH
.... 4 [482] William Haine b: 08 May 1818 in Coscombe, Somerset, England d: 1906 in W. Camel
.... +Sarah Look
.... *2nd Wife of [482] William Haine:
.... +Sarah (mrs.) Parsons
.... 3 James Haine b: in Somersetshire,England d: Jul 1833
.... +[483] MARY CREED b: 12 May 1776 in W. Pennard, Somerset, England m: 11 Nov 1826 in somersetshire,England d: 13 Nov 1830 in E. Pennard, Somerset ,England

ENDNOTES AND BIBLIOGRAPHY

Bible information was taken from the Hawkins and the Haine Family Bibles, noting births, deaths and marriages. Haine family Bible is held at Clover Hill. Hawkins Family Bible, center pages are on file with Sue Bell.

U.S. Census, 1850 of the Haine and **Hawkins** families, available Ohio Census, Bloomfield, Trum. Co. OH, Roll M 432_733:pg. 264B, Image 331 Library Film. Thom.G.17, Sarah G. 16, Mary Ann Hawkins, 11yrs.

Haine Pg.264A, Image 332.(listing children: Wm. J.13, Sarah M.11, George E.10, Frances H. 5 Charlotte E. 5 ,Ellen S. age 1), Also the 1860, 1870 and the 1880 are present, located 1880,Census, Bloomfield, Trumbull Co, OH, roll 1070,Family Hist ,film 1255070:pg.18B, edu;184; Image 0039.

U.S. Census 1840—lists only Haine Family: Bloomfield, roll 429:Image:270, FHL Film 0020178 Family members and ages not listed.

U.S.Census-1860—Thomas Hawkins, age 27, b. abt 1833, Bloomfield, Trum. Co .OH. Wm Hawkins 55, Mary Hawkins 55, Thom Hawkins 27, Sarah Hawkins 25, Mary Ann Hawkins, 21, James Biggin: 15 yrs (cousin)? NARA microfilm, m653, Roll 1,438, Washington D.C.

U.S. Census-1870-Thomas G. Hawkins, resided Bloomfield, Trum. Co OH. Household: Wm. D. Hawkins, 65, Mary A. Hawkins 65, T.G.H. age 37, Frances 28, Emma 6 yrs. Pliny 6 Mos. Roll M 593_1271: Pg. 20A: Image:44, FHL 552770.

U.S.Census-1880—Thomas G. Hawkins, Farmington, Trum. Co. OH, b. Eng,. Occupation: Farmer-47, Spouse-Frances H. Hawkins: household: Emma L. Hawkins, 16yrs, Pliny H. Hawkins, 10 years; Alberta Hawkins. 7yrs; Lotta A. Hawkins, 5 yrs.; ____ Hawkins, 4 Mo. Roll1076, FHL Film 125502 ; pg. 95B, ED:189; image 0194.

U.S.Census-1900: Farmington, Trum. Co, OH.: Thomas G. Hawkins, age 67, b Eng., Nov. 1832,m.1863, yrs m.37. Wife: Frances Hawkins,59, son Jessie Hawkins, age 20, son Ernest Hawkins, age 18.(Roll T623_1325; Pg.12 B; ED:101.

1841 Census from Great Britain, Somerset Co., Evercreech, noting only Elizabeth Hawkins Biggin, living at Westbrook Farm, with her mother Ann Hawkins.. Elizabeth and family eventually emigrated to Trumbull Co., OH. in 1854. (Ancestry.com.).

1881 Census from Great Britain,: Job Hawkins, Moore Farm, Holcombe, b. abt. 1817 E. Pennard, Somerset, England. Spouse: Eliza. Occ: Farmer of 156 acres, employer of 5 men. (Class RG11;, Piece 2406; Folio:131; Pg. 2; GSU roll 1341579. Sarah Anne 16 yrs; Eliza Ellen 15 yrs; Mary Elizabeth 12 yrs.; Emily Ada, 11 yrs. (Jane Newport 23 yrs.). (Job Hawkins, brother of William Dredge Hawkins).

Cemetery: Brownwood Cemetery in No. Bloomfield, Ohio has tomb stones for William and Mary Ann Hawkins, and William and Mary Haine. Also it is the burial site of all their children who died in the area. Thomas and Frances Hawkins, Jesse T. and Mildred Hawkins and Lloyd and Martha Hawkins are all at Brownwood Cemetery, with clearly engraved birth and death dates.

Canadian Census, Quebec, 1851, at Missisquoi notes Andrew Hawkins, single, left UK in 1842 and Marriage Record in 1844 for 26 day of June at Methodist Church in St. Armand, Quebec, from Ancestry.com, to Hannah Elizabeth Merick.

Canadian Census for 1871, 1881 and 1891, noted that they had four children and a death record, states he died Jan 15th 1898 at 79 years of age, at Frelighsburg, Methodist Church Record. (1881 Census: Ste-Armand West, Missisquoi, Quebec, film 1375840 FHL Film, page 1).

A History of Somerset, by Robert Dunning, 2003,, Pg. 106. Emigration from the County during the years of Agricultural Depression. First published 1978,1987, and 2003.Halsgrove House, Lower Moor Way, Tiverton, Devon EX1 6SS. pg100, (Traveling in Somerset in 18C. and 19C.). Pg.. 100-1.

Beyond the Beeches, A Somerset Girlhood 1900-22, edited by Diana Hargreaves. An autobiography of Norah Cleacee. Published in Great Britain 2000 by ISIS Publishing, Ltd., 7 Centremead, Osney Mead, Oxford, OX2 OES. ISBN 0-7531-9661-1, Pg. 64, 65, 67. (Frances Goddard).

Republic Steel, Warren Plant 1937, Strike Scrapbook, Youngstown Historical Center of Industry and Labor. *yhcil@ohiohistory.org*. Youngstown, Ohio.

Warren Tribune Chronicle, June 1st and 15th, 1937. Steel Strike.

Riding the Rails—Teenagers on the Move, During the Great Depression, by Errol Lincoln Uys, pub. 2003, by Rouledge, Taylor & Francis Books, Inc. 29 W.35th St., NY, NY, 10001, pg. 104-105.(AHP-American History Project).

Interview of Journey to Montana, by Lloyd Hawkins in 1933, as told by Dr. Robert Hawkins, 1981.

Trumbull County, Ohio, Birth Records 1867-1908, editors: Rosemary Stroup Grayson, Roberta Graves Hyde and Barbara Houser Layfield., Archives of Trumbull County, Ohio. Copyright 2001.
Pliny Haine Hawkins, b. 28 Oct 1869, Bloomfield, son of Thomas Goddard and Frances H. Hawkins, Vol. 1/ pg.92. **Mary Alberta Hawkins, b. 3 Sept 1872** Farmington, daughter of Thom G. and Frances H. Hawkins, Vol. 1/ pg.252.
Jesse Thomas Hawkins (twin) Farmington, Vol. 2/pg.297, BC 1/pg229. James Goddard Hawkins, b. 28 Feb 1877 Bloomfield, son of James Goddard and Mary Ann Hawkins, Vol..2/pg 167. (died age 21 years of accident). **Angie Hawkins, b. 10 Nov 1876** Farmington, Vol.2/pg117, daughter of Thos. G. and Frances H. Hawkins, (unnamed).: 29 Jan 1882, Farmington, son Thos. G. Hawkins and Frances H. Hawkins(.Ernest Hawkins). **(Unnamed), Feb 10 1875**, Farmington, **daughter** of Thos. G. Hawkins and Frances H. Hawkins, Vo. 2/pg61. (named Charlotte).
No names listed for William and Mary Haine, but lists children of John, Charles and William J Haine.
Trumbull County Ohio, Marriage Book Index, 100 Years 1800-1900, Vol. I A-M index and Vol. II N-Z index. Mary Ann Hawkins marriage to James Goddard Hawkins 21 Nov 1862 <1858-66 p. 374>. Thomas G. Hawkins marriage to Frances H.Haine; 1 Feb 1863 by C.R.Patter MG <1858066 pg. 349>.Licence, Marriage, 1 Marcn 1862. Sarah Goddard Hawkins marriage to William J. Haine. 1st. 11August 1862 (1858-66, pg. 322). 2nd marriage Cornelia Wolcott of Farmington, 5 June 1872 (1871-76, pg. 114).
Trumbull Co. Death Records. Published 2004. Years 1867-1890. Mary Haine 31 July 1890, (at 75 years-heart disease) (3/425. William Haine, 14 Sept 1895. (90 years of age) 3/101. Mary A. Hawkins, 13 Mar 1888.at 83 yrs., "old age" , William D. Hawkins, died 11 Oct 1895 at 91 years. "old age". Angie F Hawkins, d. 25 Jan 1877, at 2 mo. Pneumonia, (2/87). George W. Hawkins, d. 3 years. (Brain disease).
History of Trumbull County Ohio, by Harriet Taylor Upton of Warren, Vol. II. Lewis Publishing Company, Chicago, **1909.** pg.449. "Western Reserve Seminary." Vol. I, pg. 316, Treatment of TB and, Medical practices in Trumbull Co.
History of Trumbull and Mahoning Counties, 1882, by H.Z. Williams, Vol. l, pg. 138. Civil War, 105 OVI, comp B. to Covington, KY. Vol. ll, pg.393, "Clover Hill Cheese Factory" and Grist Mill, owned by Wm. Haine. Page 396 names John Haine as Wm's father and Joseph and Sarah Haine as Mary Haines parents. Wm's birthdate as Feb. 8, 1806 and names ten of their children.

Maps: Trumbull County Ohio, Atlas, 1874 by L.H. Everts, Properties of William Hawkins, 100 acres in Bloomfield and William Haine 150 acres. In **1899 Atlas:** W.D. Hawkins 75 acres, plus 52.5 acre owned by Frances H Hawkins,..Thos. G.
Hawkins in Farmington: 60 acres, plus 20 and 13.85 acres. William Haine,—0—acres, Sarah Haine 25 acres, Charles Haine 47.5 acres. (As land was divided.)

Account Book, written by Thomas Goddard Hawkins, 1857-1875. Income and expenditures, noting the purchase of wedding ring, baby items, etc., owned by Sue Hawkins Bell.

Diary: Thomas Goddard Hawkins, 1860, owned by Charles Haine Hawkins. Noted dates when his parents married, his birthday, and date when they arrived in America, June 8, 1845 and left England April 8, 1844.

Diary: Frances Harriet Haine, January 1st, 1862, How Civil War affected the family.

Diary: Mary Haine, 1874-5. Noted the family's everyday life at Clover Hill.

Diary: News article written about **William Goddard's** voyage to America.

Diary: Emma Hawkins, described her trip to San Francisco, owned by Sue Bell.

Letter: Dosia Haine sent to her Uncle George Haine, concerning her father, Dr. Haine. Original letter owned by Carrie Jean Cox.

Letters, Seven letters, which were sent from Lloyd Hawkins to Martha, during the steel strike of June 1937. The shooting and unrest was followed by news articles in the Warren Tribune Newspaper, dated June 1st and 15th, 1937.

Bible: Marriage Record of Charles Hawkins and Nancy Buckingham on June 18, 1938 in Urichesville, Ohio.

Marriage Certificate: Lloyd Hawkins and Martha Schout married Jan 8, 1938 in Howland Township, Trumbull County, Ohio.
Canadian Archives,

Dictionary of Canadian biography, of George Coles by Robertson, Ian Ross, Toronto: University Press, 1972. Vol. 10, p. 182-188., First Premier of Prince Edward Island.

Family Records by Ashworth P. Burke, 1965, Heraldic Publishing Co.. NY,NY. Pgs 332-340. Of the Huntley Family

INDEX

A

abolitionists, 38
Amalgamated Association of Iron, Steel, and Tin Workers, 96
architectural and historical tidbits, 158

B

Beatty, B. Frank, 72, 75
Beatty, Emma (Haine), 46, 71, 73, 75-76
Beers, Carol Ann (Rogers), 70
Bell, Douglas, 70, 109
Bell, Jeffrey, 69
Bell, Najma (Bachelani), 69
Bell, Roger, xv, 69-70, 109, 116, 134, 163
Bell, Sara, 69
Bell, Sue Ellen (Hawkins), 18, 68, 70, 76, 105, 155, 163
Bell, Tisha (Goss), 109
Beyond the Beeches, a Somerset Girlhood 1900–1922 (Hargreaves), 125
Bible, 3-4
Biggin, Elizabeth (Hawkins), 122, 135-36
Biggin, Thomas, 122, 135-36
Bloomfield, Ohio, 8, 31
Boxwell, Gloucester, 144
  ancient history of, 159
  Manor. *See* Boxwell Court
Boxwell Court, 155, 157, 160
boxwood, 158
Bristol, England, 5-6, 11
British Steam Railway, 114
Brown, Ephrim, 26
Brownwood Cemetery, 67f, 76, 78, 83, 88
  visiting, 3, 67
Butcher of Evercreech. *See* Hawkins, William Dredge

C

California, xii, 73, 77
Central Pacific Railroad, 57, 77
cheddar cheese, 16-17
childbirth, 117
Church
  Methodist Episcopal, 39, 55f
  St. John the Baptist (Pilton), 145
  St. Mary's (Boxwell), 151-53f
  St. Peter's Anglican (Evercreech), 24, 127
Civil War soldiers, 36f-37
Clover Hill, 3, 44f, 53-54, 66
Clover Hill Farm, 53

Coles, George, 26-27, 216f
Coles, Mercy (Haine), 26-27f
Committee for Industrial Organization, 96
commutation, vi, 37-38
Cook, John, 35
Cottrell, Graci, 163-64
Cottrell, Rodney, 163-64
Cox, Carol Ann (Sassey), 66, 70
Cox, Carrie Jean, 47f, 66-68, 70f, 104f
Cox, Charles, 66, 68-69f, 104f
Cox, Clara (Haine), 46, 95
Cox, Hazel, 66f, 69-70, 104f
Cox, John, 70f
Cox, Marian, 70f
Cox, Phillip, 69f
Creed family, 28, 54
Creighton family, 35, 52, 121, 136
Cromwell, Thomas, 137

D

Dawson, Frances (Haine), 69f
diary
 of Emma Hawkins, 72-75
 of Frances (Haine) Hawkins, 33-37, 65
 of Mary Ann Haine, 54, 62
 of Thomas Goddard Hawkins, 8, 28-30, 65f, 124
 of William Goddard, 8-9, 13
Dickens, Charles, 114-15, 117
 Christmas Carol, A, 115
Dowding, Frances Goddard, 9, 17-18, 126
Dunkerton, Delores, 70
Dunkerton, Joseph, 70
Dunkerton, Richard, 28

E

education, 117
Elizabeth I (queen), 144, 158
emigration scheme, 18
Enrollment Act, 37
Erie Canal, 26
Evercreech, England, viii, 3-4, 42, 60, 121-22, 127, 129, 135-36, 158, 163, 214
 clock, 128
 St. Peter's Church, 24f, 127
 village cross, 103

F

family reunion
 of 1907, *38, 46, 89f, 90*
 of 1978, *66, 68*
 of 1979, 68
 of 2000, *69f*
 of 2005, *45*
 of 2008, *163*
Fichter, Angela (Hawkins), 68f, 70f
Fichter, Rev. Robert, 69-70f
Fitz, Elizabeth (Goddard), 8-9, 11, 15
Fitz, Stephen, 10
food preservation, 114-15
Forest Depot, Virginia, 78
Free Education Act of 1852, *27*
Fuller, George, 53

G

Glastonbury, Somerset, 60, 115, 122, 136, 171
Glastonbury Abbey, 124, 138, 164
Goddard, Dorothy (Ryall), 10, 123
Goddard, John Gibbons, 125

Goddard, William, 8-9, 11, 15, 124
Great Depression
  in America, 61, 93-94
  in England, 18
Great Western Railway, 114
gristmill
  Clover Hill Farm, 53, 63, 110f
  Eastcombe Farm, 10

H

Haine, Betty (Scott), 170
Haine, Charles, 46f, 88
Haine, Clarence, 87
Haine, Cleo, 164-65
Haine, Cornelia (Wolcott), 46, 84-85, 87f
Haine, Eliza (Cook), 170
Haine, Ellen, 32
Haine, Emma Grace, 87
Haine, George Austin, 87
Haine, George E., 46f
Haine, Harold, 78, 88
Haine, James, 106f, 108
Haine, John, 46f, 170-71
Haine, Joseph, 54
Haine, Mabel, 87
Haine, Mary, 25, 54f, 67f, 79, 89f, 170
  diary of, 54, 62, 64-65
  family name of, 28
  home of, 53
  marriage of, 26
  return to Prince Edward Island, 27
Haine, Mary Jane, 87
Haine, Mercy Jane, 32
Haine, Michael, 164
Haine, Rev. Cuthbert, 171
Haine, Sarah (Look), 54

Haine, Theodore, 87
Haine, Theodosia, 53, 84f-86, 88-89
Haine, William (1769), 170
Haine, William Jay, 87
Haine, William Joseph, 46f, 84
Hargreaves, Diana
  Beyond the Beeches, a Somerset Girlhood 1900–1922, 125, 214
Hawkins, Andrew, 122, 137
Hawkins, Angie, 77, 215
Hawkins, Benjamin, 122, 136, 171
Hawkins, Beryl, xv, 127, 131f, 163-64
Hawkins, Carol (Oravecz), xv, 69f-70f
Hawkins, Charles Haine, 61, 105f, 123
Hawkins, Daniel, 122, 136
Hawkins, Dorothy (Goddard), 15, 122, 136
Hawkins, Elizabeth, 139, 141
Hawkins, Emma J., 39, 55, 71-72, 75f, 171
Hawkins, Ernest (1882), 83
Hawkins, Ernest (1939), 129f
Hawkins, Frances (Huntley), 134, 140, 142, 145
Hawkins, Frances Harriet (Haine), 33, 39, 46, 65, 69
Hawkins, George, 134, 138
Hawkins, Gladys, 68
Hawkins, Grace (Milner), 44f, 57, 59f-61f, 95
  home in Palos Verdes, 62, 95
  marriage of, 58
  trip around the world, 59
Hawkins, Hannah Elizabeth (Merick), 122
Hawkins, James, 15, 122, 136
Hawkins, James Goddard, 30, 171f
Hawkins, Jan, 70, 110

Hawkins, Janet Sue (Jan) (Breystpraak), 103f
Hawkins, Jerry, 77-78
Hawkins, Jesse Thomas, 78, 80-81f
Hawkins, Job, 122, 136, 166
Hawkins, John, 121, 136
Hawkins, Larry Lloyd, 93-94, 96, 104, 165
Hawkins, Lloyd B., 105, 134
Hawkins, Martha (baby), 53
Hawkins, Martha (Schout), 96-97, 134
Hawkins, Mary (Stokes), 134, 138, 140
Hawkins, Mary Ann (Goddard), 4, 7f, 136
  birth of children, 23
  birthplace of, 10, 123
  immigration to Ohio, 8
  marriage of, 4, 15, 121, 134
Hawkins, Mary Kay (Branfield), 103
Hawkins, Mildred Ann (Millie), 80-82
Hawkins, Mildred Phoebe, 45, 80, 82
Hawkins, Millie, 66, 69-70, 105, 110
Hawkins, Milner (Haine), 44f, 58f-62
Hawkins, Nancy (Buckingham), 102, 216
Hawkins, Nancy Ann (Dredge), 23, 135, 138
Hawkins, Patricia (Heiple), 69f, 110
Hawkins, Peter Jr. (1772), 121, 134-35, 138
Hawkins, Peter Sr. (1687), 131, 135, 140, 142, 145-46, 155, 159
Hawkins, Pliny (Haine), 39, 44f-45f, 59f-60f
  death of, 62, 95
  educational history of, 57-58, 61
  home in Palos Verdes, 62, 94-95
  memories of grandparents, 51-53
  trip around the world, 59-60
  work history of, 57-58
Hawkins, Robert, 66, 69-70f, 95f
Hawkins, Robert (1765), 138
Hawkins, Sarah (Goddard), 4, 16, 30, 32, 84, 124
Hawkins, Sarah (Haine), 23, 46, 121, 136, 215-16
Hawkins, Thomas (1798), 23, 121, 136
Hawkins, Thomas Goddard, 8, 10, 15, 33, 38
  account book of, 30
  birth of, 4, 23
  diary of, 28-30, 65, 124
  marriage of, 134
Hawkins, Vivian (Lansworth), 61-63f
Hawkins, William Dredge, 7, 15f
  birth and marriage of, 4, 121, 134, 136
  start of Hawkins Farm, 28
Hawkins Farm, 28, 43, 53, 67
Henry VIII (king), 137, 158
Hobdy, Fanny, 51
Huntley, Constance (Ferrers), 154f-55, 159
Huntley, Elizabeth, 145
Huntley, Elizabeth (Adam), 153
Huntley, George (sheriff), 158
Huntley, Henry (esquire), 144, 155, 158-59
Huntley, John, 152-53, 156, 158
Huntley, Mary (Codrington), 145-46, 156, 159
Huntley, Matthew, 155, 159
Huntley, Rev. Wykes, 131, 142, 145-46, 156, 167

I

immigrant ship, 6

J

Jenkins, Janie, 65-66
Jones, Ruth, 70f
Jones, Willard, 70f
Judah, Theodore, 77

K

King, Adrienne, 69, 108f
King, Jonathan, 69f, 108
King, Roberta (Hawkins), 69-70f
King, Thomas, 70f
Kingsford-Smith, Glacier (Hawkins), 69f
Kwait, Jean (Rogers), 70f

L

Linton, William, 51
Liverpool, England, 5, 18
London, England, 113-14
Look, Cary, 28
Lower Eastcombe Farm, 9-10
Lyman, Charlotte (Haine), 46, 72

M

map
  Batcombe, v, 11f
  Evercreech, 130f
  Haine and Hawkins farm, 31f
marriage license, 39, 41f
McAdam, J. L., 113
McGarvie, Michael, 9

Meek, Frances (Hawkins), 62-63
Meek, Joe, 61
Melnick, Meredith (Hawkins), 70, 110
Melnick, Paul, 110f
Melnick, Theo, 103f
Methodist Church, 74, 76
  founder of, 169-70
  in Glastonbury, 122, 171
  Tod Avenue, 82, 96
  in Warren, 88
Methodist deaconess, 74-75f, 171
Miller, Marilyn, 108f
Miller, Ron, 108f
Montana, 57, 93-96
Montreal, Quebec, 4-5, 7-8, 53

N

Nicholas, Hanna, 46f, 110f, 165-66

O

Ohio
  center for cheese making, 16
  families in, 28, 59
  immigrating to, 8, 15
  life in, 23
  maple syrup in, 81
  Underground Railroad in, 38
Oregon, 62, 65-66, 68
Over, Gloucester, 164

P

Pacific Railway Act of 1862, 77
Pennsylvania Railroad, 97-98
Pilton, Somerset, 121, 127, 142, 146, 158

A JOURNEY FROM SOMERSET, ENGLAND TO OHIO

poverty, 117
Prince Edward Island, 26-28, 216
Pugh's Bottom Farm, 10

Q

Quebec, Canada, 5, 7, 137

R

Republic Steel, 82, 96-97, 214
Rogers, Frances (Wolcott), 45-46f, 63, 66

S

Salt Lake City, xv, 58, 137, 145, 148, 166
Savage, Sheila (Williams), 5
Sanson, Henry W., 28
Sassey, Samantha, 69f
Schwartz, Jeremy, 70f
Schwartz, Michele (Hawkins), 70f
Scott, Betty, 170
ship, *Casino*, 11
Shipman, Elizabeth (Bell), vii, 68f, 83
Shipman, Jennifer (Bell), 66, 70f, 105f
ships, 5
  Great Britain, 6
  steam-powered, 16, 114
  Suffolk, 11
  Superb, 11

small pox, 75
Somerset, history of, 5, 16, 23, 114-15, 123
Steel Strike of 1937, 96-101
Sunshine Corner. *See* Haine, Theodosia

T

Thorp Farm, 81-82
transcript, 65, 144, 148
transportation, 113
tuberculosis, 53

U

Underground Railroad, vi, 38
Union Pacific Railroad, 77

V

vegetable oysters, 56
voyage, 8, 11-13, 53

W

Walker, George, 45, 78-79, 95
Walker, Mary Alberta (Hawkins), 59, 72, 77-79, 95
Walsh, David, xv, 45, 70, 108, 165-66
Warren, Ohio, 8, 46, 95, 102, 165
Welsh, Carole, 163

Welsh, Richard, xv, 151, 155, 163-64, 166
Wesley, John, 170
Westbrook Cottage. *See* Westbrook Farm
Westbrook Farm, 23, 129-30, 164
West Country, 3, 123
Western Reserve Seminary, 33, 38, 57
West Farmington, Ohio, 29, 38-39, 85
West Pennard, Somerset, 16, 122, 170
Wolcott, Charlotte (Hawkins), 63, 80
Wolcott, Clyde, 45
Wolcott, J. Ward, 45, 59
Wykes, Edward, 159
Wykes, Sylvester, 155, 159

Y

Yellowstone National Park, 58, 61, 83
Youngstown Vindicator, 65

Names of those attending the 2005 Reunion, pg. 106
Alexander, Connie
Bonheimer, Nona
Cox, James (Rev.)
Dawson, Deirdre
Detweiler, Lynn, Dave and Lillyan
Haine, Dean and Sue
Haine, Susan
Haiss, Haidi
Jones, Will and Ruth
Keller, Laura
Manning, Evelyn
McMillan, Delbert
McMillan, Leah
Melnick, Theodore
Rogers, Carol Ann (Beers)
Rogers, Jean (Kwait)

Reunion 1979: page 68
Hawkins, Larry Pearson
Fichter, James

Reunion 1907: page 108
Haine, Mary Sarah (Sade)

Photo at their Wedding: pg. 119
Hawkins, Charles Thomas and Nancy Buckingham

Edwards Brothers,Inc!
Thorofare, NJ 08086
04 March, 2011
BA2011063